D1871812

ECONOMICS OF MICRO FINANCE

ECONOMICS OF MICRO FINANCE

TATA RAO DUMMU

KALPAZ

Economics of Micro Finance

Rs. 945

© Tata Rao Dummu

ISBN: 978-93-5128-029-3

All rights reserved. No part of this book may be reproduced in any manner without written permission.

Published in 2014 in India by
Kalpaz Publications
C-30, Satyawati Nagar,
Delhi-110052
E-mail: kalpaz@hotmail.com

Laser Typesetting: Rudra Computer Graphics, Delhi
Printed at: G. Print Process, Delhi

Contents

Foreword

This book, the Research Study on Tribal Life and State Policy is welcome edition to the literature on tribal development. This area can still be regarded as a virgin field for research. For, while tribal development is a high priority area in the development strategies of the Union and State Governments, it is only since a decade that research tended to focus its attention on these issues.

This volume affords a comprehensive analysis of the profiles of tribal communities in the State of Andhra Pradesh touching upon the ecological and cultural differences that exist between these communities. Thereafter, a systematic survey of the resources in the tribal areas is undertaken highlighting the depletion and degradation of these resources. Paradoxically enough, it is the process of development that seems to also contribute to the depletion phenomenon. Then, the diverse development strategies adopted by the State are taken up in the study with very commendable amount of statistical analysis of a wide data base. The particular credit of this study lies in the fact that the general criticism of the deleterious effects of some of the tribal development policies are supported by statistical evidences. Yet, another merit of this publication is that it affords a bird's-eye view of the context of tribal situation, the conceptual bases of development policies, the process of implementation of these and the consequences that flow from these.

The findings in the study indicate that which tribal development may not have yielded all the results targeted; there could be no denial that benefits do accrue to the tribal communities. However, the paradoxes of tribal development investment being siphoned off by interlopers and the increasing opportunities that this very development process affords to greedy sections of the plains people getting into the act of further exploitation still remain. In this context, the study focuses extensively on the extent and nature of tribal indebtedness.

I congratulate Dr. D. Tata Rao for undertaking this study and welcome the publication in the confidence that it will be well received by the public.

Prof. H. Lajapathi Rai
Dr. B.R. Ambedkar University,
Vice-Chancellor

Preface

Andhra Pradesh is the traditional home of nearly 33 tribal groups and most of them can be found inhabiting in the border areas of Andhra Pradesh in the North-and North-East. Among the 33 tribal groups, this study covers the Savaras and Jathapu of Seethampeta mandal of Srikakulam district of Costal Andhra.

Among many problems, indebtedness is considered as one of the major problems of the tribal people all over the country. The net result is that the subsistence economy of tribal is turned into deficit economy with the increased indebtedness and this chain reaction from poverty to indebtedness has led to land alienation and the consequent upsurge in some tribal areas from time to time. Indebtedness in India in reality a crystallized form of tribals' poverty, misery, penury, wretchedness and squalor and naked starvation of the deprived class. Once a tribal falls in the grip of indebtedness, he gets a life sentence of indebtedness in the prison and leads to a miserable life conditions.

I owe a deep sense of gratitude to Prof. H. Lajapathi Rai, Vice-Chancellor, Dr. B.R. Ambedkar University, Srikakulam for his encouragement, and Foreword for this book. We are dedicating this book to our beloved Teacher, Prof. R. Ramakrishna, Dept. of Economics, Andhra University. I was grateful to Prof. G. Ramachandrudu, Chairman, Board of Studies, Dept. of Economics, Andhra University and also Prof. R. Sudharshna Rao, Head, Dept. of Economics, Andhra University. I owe a great deal to Prof. P. Chiranjeevulu, Head, Dept. of Rural Development, Dr. B.R. Ambedkar University, Srikakulam and to Prof. M. Chandraiah, Coordinator, Examinations of Dr. B.R. Ambedkar University, Srikakulam for my success in this endeavour. I express my sincere thanks to all my teachers in the Dept. of Rural Development, Dr. B.R. Ambedkar Univerisity, Srikakulam for their cooperation, help and support extended during my research work.

I would like to express my sincere thanks to the staff members of Dr. V.S. Krishna Memorial Library, Andhra University and Dr. B.R. Ambedkar University Silver Jubilee Library, Srikakulam for providing me with all the necessary facilities. I am thankful to Mr. D.R.R. Prasad, Librarian, School of Economics, Andhra University, for readily supplying me any information required regarding my work. I am also thankful to the office staff of the Department of Economics for their help in the completion of my work. I am very much impressed by the generous help rendered by Mr. Sankar Reddy, Dr. Jayasheela Prakash and Dr. B. Padma Narayana for their cooperation in collecting the data and the help extended at various stages of my work. I am much obliged to Mr. K. Vijay Kumar for his efficiency in computerizing the material and carrying out the work.

I would be failing in my duty if I do not place on record my deep sense of gratitude to my mother Mrs. D. Appalamma and my wife Sneha Latha, brothers Lakshminarayana, Narayan Rao, Gurumurty and my sister B. Parvathi for their cooperation in completion of my research work.

TATA RAO DUMMU

List of Figures

List of Tables

List of Appendices

1

Introduction

1.1. The Problem

India ranks second in tribal population in the world next only to Africa. India holds unique position in the concentration of tribal communities. There are about 532 scheduled tribes in India. They speak about 100 languages and 255 subsidiary languages. Topographically the tribal areas are generally inaccessible due to hilly terrains, deep forests and lack of communications. Nearly 80 percent of the tribals live in rural areas and 93 per cent of them depend on agriculture and allied sectors. They are at different stages of culture and development, which vary from area to area in regard to the size of population, language and socioeconomic organization (Nayar, 1974). Tribal India depicts the persistence of a large number of problems. As the geographical configuration of tribal areas is mostly located at altitudes between 1000 to 3000ft. and the terrain is hilly with the consequent loss of fertility and soil erosion, agriculture as a source of their livelihood has been mostly unproductive (Das and Guglani, 1980). Due to prevalence of unemployment and underemployment, agriculture alone cannot sustain them throughout the year. So the tribals must rely on labour works and the forest produce which plays an important role in their daily life. Hence the tribal economy may rightly be called as "Agro forest based economy".

According to 2001 Census the tribal population is estimated to be 84.3 millions constituting 8.2 per cent of the total population of India. It is estimated that the predominant tribal areas comprise about 15 per cent of the total geographical area of the country. Andhra Pradesh is one of the states having large tracts of hilly and agency areas and sizeable scheduled tribe population. The total Scheduled Tribe (ST) Population in 1951 was 7.66 lakhs which increased to 56.76 lakhs in 2001, an eightfold, as a result the proportion in total population has increased from 2.46 per cent in 1951 to 6.59 per cent 2001, a three–fold increase (Appendix-1.1). The tribal economy, especially in the inaccessible tribal areas is non-monetised. Age-old social and cultural handicaps coupled with environmental factors have significantly contributed towards their low living conditions (Quraishi, 1974). The tribals are not materialists in the modern sense of the term. They are easily satisfied if their bare necessities of life are fulfilled. Their institutions are mostly informal, socio-cultural and enjoy un-questioned traditional loyalty and obedience (Mishra, 1974). Their indifference to material wealth invites criticisms like lack of effort, laziness, carefree life etc.

Tribals Before and After Independence

The tribal people living in the hills and forests for many centuries led a life of their own, generally un-influenced by the main currents of development outside. This helped them to preserve their social customs, tradition and beliefs to a large extent (Sinha, 1985). During the British period the "Policy of Isolation" was adopted. This isolation denied them certain advantages. The existing state of backwardness in tribal areas is due to continuous neglect over a long period and lack of appreciation of their special problems, in- adequate investments and non-integration of the tribal economy with the mainstream of the Indian society or the economy. The educational backwardness of the tribals is both the cause and effect of their economic backwardness. Large scale land alleviation, heavy indebtedness, lack of extension and infrastructural facilities are major deficiencies impeding the growth of tribals.

In the post-independent India, the Government is pursuing the policies of protection, integration and development (Ramaiah, 1981). The Constitution of India guaranteed certain safeguards to the tribal people under various matters of public interest, keeping in view of their long isolation and arrested growth. In pursuance of these, the Government has initiated several policy measures and programmes to ensure a better quality of life and to protect them from exploitation. A shift in the policy of isolation to integration of Indian tribes was indeed a very healthy trend and a major landmark in tribal development. Despite the positive impact of these measures on the well being of tribals, majority of them still derive their livelihood by cultivation, manual jobs, hunting and collection of minor forest produce (Jain and Das, 1981).

In the process of development, the hitherto inaccessible tribal areas are thrown open by modern means of communications resulting in the influx of several non-tribal traders-cum-money lenders and non-tribal farmers into the domain of the tribals. The immigrant non-tribes advance loans to the tribals at exorbitant rate of interest, which grow beyond the credit worthiness of the tribals. The tribal is ultimately forced to either mortgage or sell his land to the non-tribals to reduce his debt. Loss of land further weakens the economic position of the tribals making them permanent debtors. In the absence of diversification of occupation, land is the only valued possession of the tribals. Any shrinkage on this account naturally affects their economy which is already in a deplorable condition. Thus the money lenders cum traders and non-tribal landlords are chiefly responsible for the misery of the tribals over the years.

In the post-Independence era, a large number of Industrial projects have been located in the tribal areas, but tribals could not take full advantage of the employment opportunities thrown open by these projects. On the contrary, they have lost the land they have been ploughing for generations. They generally get employed in these projects at the time of construction but they are thrown out of employment once these projects are commissioned for want of education, technical skills etc. The tribals who are enjoying equal rights under constitution have not yet developed political consciousness like other weaker sections of the society (Jena, 1986).

The most important problems affecting and disturbing the tribal communities are land alienation, exploitation by money lenders, traders and contractors, lack of access to institutional marketing of their products. The tribal lands continue to be unsurveyed or partly surveyed. Although alienation of tribal lands and the resultant unrest has become a burning problem, there is very little authentic data on the nature and magnitude of the problem at the national and regional levels. The attention to the deteriorating land situation in the tribal areas was first pointed out by U.N. Dhebar Commission in 1961 and A.O.Shilo Committee in 1969.

Credit and Product/Labour Market Linkages

One of the most serious problems faced by the tribals is indebtedness. Tribal debts are perpetuated by various devices and it is often reported that "a tribal is born in debt, lives in debt and finally dies in debt". Generally speaking, the tribals appear to accept indebtedness as a normal almost inescapable aspect of their existence. The tribals whose income is below the subsistence level and who indulged in costly religious and social practices have to necessarily depend on the traditional sources of finance, viz., moneylenders or traders. The trader-cum-moneylenders aggravate the tribal debts through unscrupulous methods. Indebtedness and exploitation grew faster in an atmosphere of ignorance prevailing in tribal communities.

Most of the tribals do not transport the produce to the nearby urban centers to get better prices, because of the problems of transportation, sales tax etc. The traders besides being traditional money lenders also used to help them in disposing of agricultural produce and minor forest produce (MFP)* collected by the tribals. Usually, the money lender advances money to the needy tribals whenever they wanted it, but on the condition that the tribal should sell through them whatever they produced or collected from the forest. The entire crop is thus mortgaged in advance and very little remains for their self-consumption. This results in further borrowings not only in cash but grain too, from the same trader at exorbitant rates of interest, which varies from 50 to 100 per cent and sometimes even more. The burden of debt is thus passed on from one generation to another. Thus in the tribal areas, the interlinking of the credit and product markets has strengthened the trader-money lender hegemony over the tribals and their economy.

Indebtedness is a strong factor that begins the process of exploitation in the sense that no sooner a person incurs debt, other economic and social consequences undermining his status follow (Linga Murty and Siva Ramakrishna Rao, 1982). The Planning Commission, therefore, was right in concluding that "no Programme of economic development is likely to have any impact on the tribal economy unless vigorous measures are taken to rescue the tribals from the clutches of money lenders. Several surveys revealed that the indebtedness of tribals is mainly responsible for the Existence of the bonded labour system (Narayana Prasad Sharma, 1990). Tribal economy is characterized by low agricultural output on the one hand and highly exploitative credit and product market on the other. This forces the tribals into the debt trap from which he is unable to redeem himself. In the process the tribal is ultimately forced to either mortgage or sell his land to the non-tribal, to reduce his debt burden. As a result, the tribal people have been reduced to the status of landless agricultural labourers. The incidence of agricultural labourers among the scheduled tribes has registered an increase since 1961 (13th Report of the Commissioner for SCs and STs, 1963-64).

In spite of the heavy dependence of the informal sector for credit on informal sources in India, there are also institutional sources of credit. The impressive growth of the banking sector, in India in the last four and half decades and introduction of different poverty alleviation programmes

---

* The collection and sale of minor forest produce such as gum, beedi leaves and adda leaves, tamarind, nux vomica and a Host of other forest herbs constitute a most important Subsidiary occupation on which the tribals mainly depend for their livelihood.

like IRDP, Jawahar Rojgar Yojana, increased access of credit to weaker sections. However, the emphasis throughout has been on achieving certain quantitative targets, leading to loan defaults and virtual erosion of repayment ethics. The end result was the disturbing growth in overdues which has not only hampered the recycling of scarce resources of banks but also affected the profitability and viability of the financial institutions. This is so especially in the case of IRDP Programme.

It is worthwhile to produce the following observations made by the Agricultural Credit Review Committee (1993) in its report (Nair, 2000). "But these achievements in (IRDP) disbursements do not, however, reflect the quality of performance. Nor does it indicate that everything is moving well with IRDP. The targets are achieved mainly because the banks have been compelled to do so. In fact, considerable importance has been attached by government of India and other authorities to ensure that IRDP targets are achieved by banks without fail and this message has percolated to the field level. Several relaxations have been made by RBI in respect of eligibility criteria, procedure, the rate of interest, collateral security and guarantee for the loan, etc. In view of the special status accorded to IRDP loans these concessions have been extended despite the fact that viability of many of the loans is open to question and recovery performance has not been satisfactory. This excessive concern with target achievements has resulted in marginalizing the function of branch managers. They have been reduced to the position of mere instruments to carry out the instructions of governmental functionaries at local level... (p.117)".

The structural setup of the formal institutions as reflected by stringent collateral requirements, cumbersome and lengthy procedures for obtaining loans lack of knowledge on the part of the borrower, constrained the provision of credit to the informal sector. Further the small regular and urgent loan demands for consumption of the poor informal sector households are not addressed by financial institutions. But small loans for consumption were readily available from money lenders who also placed the poor on the track of increasing debt and bondage. At times, conventional banks either funded by soft international loans or national government as a social response have opened "windows" to offer low cost loans to small and micro-businesses and have been surprised at the failure of their efforts. The non monetary transaction costs go a long way in explaining lack of success. Two points need to be noted here: in the first place, borrowers view the funds they receive as aid and not as a commercial transaction and therefore may not feel obligated to repay. Secondly, the conventional bank is not organised to effectively handle the task of collection. It may be more cost effective for the institution to write off the loan than to seek recovery (Michael, 1995).

Given the non-suitability of the formal financial institutions for the credit needs of the rural and urban informal sectors specialized micro credit programme which can cater to the need of the informal sector participants has emerged in the last two decades in many developing countries of Asia, Africa and Latin America. Institutions offering financial services exclusively to the economically marginalized sections of the population have originated, proved their viability and come to stay in many of these countries. There is also a similar mechanism in some developing countries for providing credit to informal enterprises. This is through community organizations like self-help groups and NGOs. In India, for example, self help groups have been set up to take care of the credit needs of micro producers. The best example that can be mentioned here is SEWA. NGOs have also been involved in the provision of credit in the informal sectors. An NGO can act as an intermediary for expanding credit from formal institutions. Moreover, they act as loan guarantors and can extend their activities beyond credit to training and skill development. Informal entrepreneurs usually need funds in small amount and NGOs are most suited to satisfy such demand.

Micro-Credit Institutions evolved their own design features such as class, eligibility for membership in the group ranging from landless to minimum land holding; prior entrepreneurial experience to no experience; monthly repayments to weekly repayments; individual lending to group-based lending; requirement of collateral to no collateral and group lending contracts to no group lending contracts (Morduch Jonathan, 1999). The group formation under micro-credit institutions is based on a growing institutional concept in terms of resources and management skills of the women members to reduce the gender inequality and to increase their confidence to get involved in issues and programmes in the public and private spheres. The success of group lending is attributed to various factors such as the ability of the group to mitigate asymmetric information problems in the credit markets through active screening of members (Wenner, 1995); information advantage of the groups about the applicant's creditworthiness (Zeller, 1995 and Rajaram Dasgupta, 2005); social cohesion and heterogeneity of asset holdings (Zeller, 1998); assortative matching of members (Ghatak and Guinnone, 1999); social ties between borrowing group members (Floro and Yotopoulos, 1991); group pressure to repay the loans (Besely and Coate, 1995, Paxton, 2000 and Sampti Gupta and Gautam Gupta, 2005); and peer monitoring through intra group insurance (Wydick Bruce, 1999).

Micro finance revolution in recent times occupies a prime role on women's empowerment and poverty alleviation. Studies on micro finance indicate that adopting the method of group lending through SHGs could reduce the lending and supervision costs of public sector banks (Puhazhendi, 1995 and Madhura Swaminathan, 2007) and raise repayment rates (Karmakar, 1998 and Puhazhendhi, Satyasai, 2000) Khandkar Shahidur 1998; Ramakrishna 2001,2003,2004; Pallavi Chavan, Ramakumar 2002; Frances Sinha 2005; Priya Basu and Prdeep Srivastava 2005; Kabeer 2005; Satish, 2005; Shylendra, 2006; Vasimalai, and Narendar, 2007 In their studies have systematically analysed the various aspects of micro-finance. While answering the various aspects of micro finance, the borrower's viewpoint is frequently missing. The access of the poor to formal credit through SHGs and its cost efficiency in reducing the transaction costs for the borrower's needs have to be analysed in order to understand the benefits of group lending for the poor. However, the existing studies are limited in number. More field studies are required to pass any judgment on the outcome of the Micro Finance innovation.

1.2. Relevance of the Study

In India during the last five decades the strategy to increase in real per capita income had indicated increasing unemployment, poverty and income inequalities. The socioeconomic position of the poorest of the poor had worsened. Indebtedness has been considered as one of the most vicious causes of the exploitation of tribals in the country. In fact, the tribal economy is essentially non-monetary with little cash surplus being generated. Once debt has been incurred, it is very difficult to repay by the poor tribals, even over generations due to exorbitant interest rates and lack of knowledge of repayment terms etc.

The laws passed by the Government to check the problem of usury were totally inadequate and largely ineffective. The institutional credit agencies, however, have come to play a significant role in providing development credit to tribal communities for their economic upliftment. In fact, the supply of adequate and timely credit through institutional credit agencies is considered as a sine-qua non for balanced development of the tribal economy. An attempt is made in the present study to assess the levels of employment, income and expenditure, poverty and indebtedness of the tribal households, in the light of micro credit innovations.

1.3. Objectives

1. To bring together the available evidence on the magnitude of indebtedness among tribals, the purposes for which loans are contracted and sources of finance.
2. To review the credit policy for the poor and to assess the significance of Micro Finance.

3. To study the factors influencing borrowing and indebtedness among tribals.
4. To study the factors determining the access towards different sources of finance.
5. To assess the relative efficiency of alternative channels of credit in reducing transaction costs of loans.
6. To examine the effect of micro credit in enhancing loan repayment rates among borrowers.
7. To examine the impact of micro credit on the socioeconomic empowerment and nutritional development of borrowers.
8. To suggest policy for further improvement of Micro Finance mechanisms.

1.4. Methodology

The methodology, used in the study, has been presented under three heads viz., sampling design, database, and techniques of analysis.

1.4.1. Sampling Design

A Multi-stage sampling technique is used in this study for the selection of units. Out of the nine districts of Andhra Pradesh which have more tribal concentration Srikakulam District is selected due to the fact that the district has drawn worldwide attention through the tribal participation in the political upheaval of 1969-71. The second stage of sampling is the selection of Mandal. Out of the 38 mandals in the Srikakulam District, Seetampeta Mandal was selected for the study which had the maximum coverage of tribal poor households and also maximum coverage of Self-Help Groups (SHGs) households (Appendix-1.2). The third stage of sampling involves the selection of households. In all 300 households were selected for the study by using random sampling technique. While 150 of these households are members of newly formed SHGs (NMFB), the remaining 150 households are members of old SHGs (OMFB). New Micro Finance Borrowers are borrowers whose membership in SHGs is less than two years from the data of the Survey and Old Micro Finance Borrowers are those whose membership in SHGs is five years from the data of the survey. The reference period selected for the old SHGs is 2000-01 and for the new SHGs is 2003-04. These two groups of sample households have been chosen, keeping in view, that the old SHGs will fare better when compared to new SHGs in improving the living conditions of Tribal households in the study area.

1.4.2. Data Base

For the present study both primary and secondary data were collected and analysed. Secondary Data was collected from All India Debt and

Investment Survey (AIDIS), National Sample Survey 48th Round, NABARD etc. The primary data was collected through well-designed schedule. Detailed structured schedule was used to elicit information from the sample households. It covered the demographic details, occupational patterns, productive assets, income and expenditure particulars, indebtedness, agencies and forms of land transfer, land restoration process etc. Besides, personal interviews were held through formal and informal discussions with a cross section of the tribal people. A survey was conducted during the period from 1st December 2006 to 30th April 2007. In addition to the primary data, Supplementary information was collected from various Government offices, like ITDA, MRO, MDO, TCR & TI, Collectorate of Srikakulam and Census reports, etc.

4.3. Techniques of Analysis

In analyzing the data, different statistical techniques are used apart from tabular analysis. Tabular analysis with averages and percentages are used to explain the general profile of the sample tribal households.

Poverty Measures

To examine the poverty levels, the Head-Count Ratio (HCR) is used. Since all the sample households are poor, PGR and Sen's Index Poverty are used to measure shortfall and severity of poverty.

1. HCR = $\frac{q}{n}$

   Where

   'q' is the number of poor,

   'n' is the total population

2. PGR = $\frac{(z-m)}{Z}$ HCR

   Where

   'm' is mean per capita monthly expenditure of the poor,

   'z' is the poverty line expressed in the monetary terms.

3. Sen's Index of Poverty (p)

$$p = \frac{q\,\left|(z-m)(1-Gp)\right|}{zxm}$$

Where 'GP' is the Ginni Coefficient of the distribution of expenditure among poor and the other terms carry the same definitions.

Probit Analysis

The participation of the individuals in borrowings is analysed with the help of Probit Model. The following equation is used for estimating the probability of participation in borrowing.

Prob (BORROW) = F (IC, HC)

Where Prob (BORROW) is the probability of an individual borrowing and IC is vector of Individual Characteristics and HC is a vector of Household Characteristics.

Individual Characteristics

SEX = Sex of the individual
AGE = Age of the individual (18 years of age and above)
REL = Dummy variable, whether the individual is relationship of head of Household
EDU = Number of Years of Education of Individual
WP = Dummy variable, whether the individual is working participation.
IINC = Annual Earnings of the Individual

Household Characteristics

FINC = Annual family income of the household
FEXP = Annual food expenditure of household
NPEXP = Annual non-food expenditure of household

Tobit Analysis

Tobit model is used to assess the determinants of access to different sources of credit. The amount borrowed from a particular source is determined by different factors, which will have influence on amont demanded and borrowed. These factors are crucial in assessing the credit worthiness of the individual and other aspects, which limit his access to different sources of credit.

The following function is used for estimating the amount borrowed from different sources of credit.

AMT = f (SEX, AGE, REL, EDU, WP, IINC, FINC, FEXP, NFEXP)
SEX = Sex of the individual
AGE = Age of the individual (18 years of age and above)
REL = Dummay variable, whether the individual is relationship of head of household
EDU = Number of Years of Education of Individual
WP = Dummay variable, whether the individual is working status
IINC = Annual Earnings of the individual
FINC = Annual Income of the household family

FEXP = Annual food expenditure of household
NFEXP = Annual non-food expenditure of household.

Econometric Model

For estimating the effective cost of borrowing tribal loans from different sources, the following Econometric Model for calculating the effective rate of interest, is used.

$$E = (1+r)\ n\sqrt{L/(L-TC)-1}$$

Where

E = the effective rate of interest
r = Nominal rate of interest
L = Amount of loan borrowed
TC = Amount of Transaction Costs
n = Loan duration in years

Regression Analysis

To assess the factors responsible for repayment of debt, regression model is used. The amount of repayment from a particular source is determined by different factors. The following equation is used for estimating the probability of participation in repayment.

$$Y = a + x_1b_1 + x_2b_2 + x_3b_3 + x_4b_4 + x_5b_5 + x_6b_6 + x_7b_7 + x_8b_8 \ldots\ldots\ldots\ldots$$

AGE = Age of the respondent
Head = Dummy variable, whether the respondent is head of household
Education = Number of Years of Education of respondent
Work participation = Dummy variable, whether the respondent is working or not
Occupation = Dummy variable, whether the respondent is employee
Family size = Family size of the house
Assets = Value of the Assets owned by the household
Income = Annual income of the household
Expenditure = Expenditure of the household
Dependent ratio = Dependency ration of the household
Food expenditure = Food Expenditure of Household
Non-food Expenditure = Non-food Expenditure of the household.

1.5. Plan of the Study

The Study has been organised into eight chapters.

The introductory chapter highlights the tribal problems in general and indebtedness in particular. This chapter also covers the objectives, methodology and Plan of the study.

The Second chapter is organised into three sections. In the first section, an attempt is made to examine the credit policy for the poor and tribal development in India under five year plans. Second section attempts to examine the magnitude of indebtedness among tribals based on data from Debt and Investment Survey (NSSO 48th Round). The Genesis of micro credit system and its progress in India is presented in the third section.

The socioeconomic profile of the study area and sample respondents has been presented in the third chapter.

The fourth chapter presents the factors influencing the participation of the tribals in borrowing as well as the determinants of their access to different sources of credit.

The relative efficiency of alternative channels of credit with respect to the transaction costs of borrowing and its implications on the effective cost of borrowing for different sources of credit is presented in chapter-5.

In the sixth chapter the repayment performance of sample tribal households in respect of borrowings from different sources is examined.

The chapter seven explains the factors responsible for social mobilization and empowerment of tribal poor households in the study area.

The major conclusions of the study are highlighted in the final and concluding chapter.

References

1. Besely, t. and Coate S (1995): *"Group Lending, Repayment Incentives and Social Collateral"*, Journal of Development Economics, Vol. 46, No.1, pp. 1-18.
2. Das P.K., Guglani, P.L., (1980): *"Credit Needs of Tribal Farms of Singhbhum District Bihar"*, - Financing Agriculture, Oct-Dec, pp. 22.
3. Floro and Yotopoulos (1991): *"Informal Credit Markets and the New Institutional Economics: The Case of Philippine Agriculture"*, Westview Press, Boulder, Colorado, U.S.A.
4. Frances Sinha (2005): *"Access, Use and Contribution of Micro Finance In India-Finding from a National Study"*, *Economic and Political Weekly*, April 23.

5. Ghatak and Guinnone (1999): *"The Economics of Lending with Joint Liability: Theory and Practice"*, Journal of Development Economics, Vol. 60, No.1, October.

6. Jain H.C. and Das N (1981): *"A Study Into Aspects of Farm Credit Provided by SBI to Tribal Farmers of Jagadalpur Block of Bastar Dist"*, Financing Agriculture, Jan-Mar, pp.16-20.

7. Jena A.C. (1986): *"Forms of Exploitation in Tribal Areas and Their Consequences-Some Observations In Keonjhar Dist. Of Orissa"*, - Man and life,Vol.12, No.3-4, July-December, pp.173-179.

8. Karmakar, K.G (1998): *"Rural Credit and Self-Help Groups: Micro Finance Needs and Concepts in India"*, Sage Publications, New Delhi.

9. Khandker R. Shahidur (1998): *"Fighting Poverty with Micro Credit (Experience in Bangladesh)"*, Oxford University Press, Inc., p. 145.

10. Linga Murty N., Siva Ramakrishna Rao C (1982): *"Debt Bondage In Tribal Areas – An Empirical Observation"*, Paper submitted to the National Seminar on "Political Economy of Tribal Development", held in Warangal during April.

11. Madhura Swaminathan (2007): *"The Micro Credit Aleternative?"*, Economic and Political Weekly, March 31.

12. Michael Chu (1995): *"Building Bridges: Financing Small and Medium Enterprises"*, Economic Reform Today, No. 3, p. 9.

13. Mishra R.K (1974): *"Some Problems of Developmental Administration of Tribal Area in India"*, in *"Perspectives on Tribal Development and Administration"*, - Proceedings of the Workshop held at NICD, Hyderabad, 18-20, April, pp. 93-94.

14. Morduch Jonathan (1999): *"The Micro finance Promise"*, Journal of Economic Literature, Vol. 37, No. 4.

15. Nayar, D.P. (1974): *"Education for Tribals"*, - Kurukshetra, 1st October, pp. 38-39.

16. Nair, T.S. (2000): *"Rural Financial Intermediation and Commercial Banks: Review of Recent Trends"*, *Economic and Political Weekly*, January 29, pp. 300- 301.

17. Nair, T.S. (2000): *"Rural Financial Intermediation and Commercial Banks: Review of Recent Trends"*, *Economic and Political Weekly*, January 29, p.304.

18. Narayana Prasad Sharma (1990): *"Bonded Agricultural Labourers and Their Working Conditions"*, - Kurukshetras, November, pp.18-20.

19. Pallavi Chavan and R Ramakumar (2002): *"Micro Credit and Rural Poverty –An Analysis of Empirical Evidence"*, *Economic and Political Weekly*, March 9.

20. Paxton et all, (2000): *"Modeling Group Loan Repayment Behaviour: New Insights from Burkiner Faso"*, Economic Development and Cultural Change, Vol. 48, No.3, April, pp. 639-655.

21. Puhazhendl V (1995): *"Transaction Costs of Lending to the Rural Poor: Non- Governmental Organisations and Self-Help Groups of the Poor as Intermediaries for Banks In India"*, The Foundation for Development Cooperation, Brisbane, Australia.
22. Puhazhendhi V and KJ Satyasai (2000): *"Micro Credit for the Rural People: An Impact Evaluation"*, Study Report, National Bank for Agriculture and Rural Development, Mumbai.
23. Priya Basu, Pradeep Srivastava (2005): *"Exploring Possibilities: Microfinance and Rural Credit Access for the Poor In India", Economic and Political Weekly*, April 23.
24. Quraishi M.A. (1974): *"Tribal Development In the Fifth Plan"*, - Kurukshetra, 1st October, pp.13-15.
25. Rajaram Dasgupta (2005): *"Micro Finance In India Empirical Evidence, Alternative Models and Policy Imperatives", Economic and Political Weekly, March*, 19.
26. Ramaiah, P. (1981): *"Tribal Economy of India"*, Light and Life Publishers, Tilak Street, Paharaganj, New Delhi.
27. Ramakrishna R.2001: *"Credit Needs of the Rural Poor and the Role of SHGs"*, Indian Journal of Agricultural Economics Conference No. July-Sep, Vol. 56, No. 3, pp.459-460.
28. —————— 2003: *"Micro Credit for Rural Poor through SHGs"*, Cooperative Perspective (Journal of Cooperative Management) Oct-Dec, Vol. 38, No.3, pp.48-59.
29. ——————— 2004: *"Empowering Rural Women through Self Help Groups"*, Indira Devi M. (Ed), Strategies for Sustainability of Self Help Groups, Andhra University Press and Publications, Visakhaptnam, 2004, pp. 163-170.
30. Sampti Gupta, Goutam Gupta (2005): *"Micro Credit far Income Generation"*, The role of ROSCA *Economic and Political Weekly*, April, 2.
31. Satish P (2005): *"Mainstreaming of Indian Micro Finance", Economic and Political Weekly*, April.
32. Shylendra, H. S. (2006): *"Micro finance Institutions in Andhra Pradesh: Crisis and Diagnosis"*, Economic and Political Weekly, May 20.
33. Sinha, U.P. (1985): *"Demographic Profile of Tribal Population in India"* in *"Demography of Tribal Development"*, Inter India Publications, New Delhi.
34. Vasimalai M.P., Narender K. (2007): *"Micro finance for Poverty Reduction: The Kalanjam Way", Economic and Political Weekly*, March 31.
35. Wenner M.W (1995): *"Group Credit: A Means to Improve Information Transfer and Loan Repayment Performance"*, Journal of Development Studies, Vol. 32, No. 2, December.
36. Wydick Bruce (1999): *"Can Social Cohesion be Harnessed to Repair Mrket Failures? Evidence from Group Lending In Guatemala"*, The Economic Journal, Vol. 109, No.457.

37. Zeller (1995): *"Determinants of Credit Rationing: A Study of Informal Lenders and Formal Credit Groups in Madagascar"*, World Development, Vol. 22, No. 12, pp. 1885-1909.

38. ——— (1998): *"Determinants of Repayment Performance in Credit Groups: The role of Programme Design, Intra-group Risk Pooling and Social Cohesion"*, Economic Development and Cultural Change, Vol. 46, No.3, April, pp. 599-620.

39. 13th Report of the *"Commissioner for Scheduled Castes and Scheduled Tribes"*, Part I (1963-64) Manager Publications, New Delhi, p. 71.

40. 21st Report of *"The SC, ST Commission"*, 1971-72, 1972-73.

2

Credit Policy for the Tribal Poor and The Genesis of Micro Credit System in India

2.1. Introduction

The dependency of tribal poor on informal credit sources for meeting their production/consumption needs on exploitative terms is one of the causes which perpetuate poverty. Formal credit institutions, guided by the principle of growth with equity have disbursed huge credit which was channellsed towards the weaker sections of the community. The focus of this chapter is on critical examination of the policies of Government in relation to the credit needs of tribal poor. This chapter is organised into three sections. In the first section, an attempt is made to examine the credit policy for the poor, and tribal development in India under five year plans. In the second section an attempt is made to examine the magnitude of indebtedness among tribals based on data from Debt and Investment Survey (NSSO 48th Round). The Genesis of micro credit system and its progress in India is presented in the third section.

SECTION-I

2.2. Credit Policy for the Tribal Poor in India

An attempt has been made in this section to review the existing literature on the different dimensions of living conditions of tribals in India and credit policy for the poor. This section is again divided into two parts. Socioeconomic conditions of tribes in different parts of India are presented in part-A and Credit Policy for the poor is presented in Part-B.

PART-A

2.2.1. Socioeconomic Conditions of Tribes in India

Sociologists, anthropologists, politicians and economists have conducted lot of empirical research on the different dimensions of socioeconomic and living conditions of tribes in different parts of the Indian economy. To examine the insights of evolutionary changes in the living conditions of tribes, the research studies are classified and presented in chronological order.

(A) Studies Conducted in 1940s

Furer Haimondorf (1941) is a pioneer in the tribal development in Andhra Pradesh. He is a distinguished Austrian Anthropologist appointed as advisor on tribal matters to Nizam Government. He described some of the measures taken by the Madras Provincial Government to control the crime rate among the Chenchu tribes and the schemes implemented for their well being. He also described various changes taking place in the Chenchu tribal society due to intrusion of the contractors into Chenchu forests. He suggested the removal of contractors from forests and also employing tribals in the forest department. In another study, He listed out various changes that have come in the Reddy economy due to the entry of traders. He listed out certain recommendations for modifying the administrative structure in the interest of tribals.

Aiyappan (1948) dealt with various problems faced by the tribals due to forced labour, land alienation and forest regulation. The report discussed the true problems of exploitation and land alienation by shahukars and recommended for restricting their activities. The report suggested for separate tribal welfare authority and for taking up various welfare measures in the tribal areas of Andhra Pradesh.

(B) Studies Conducted in 1950s

Elwin, Varrier (1965) study is more an ethnographic study of Bondo. Hinglanders has planned to present one aspect of each tribe of Orissa. The character of Bondo is separately presented. Tribal myths of Orissa explained the common practices of all tribes of Orissa. Chatopadhya K. P.'s (1953) study has explained that substantial portion of the tribals in India is remained at a primitive level. The study identified the need for effective planning for tribal development. The study also identified the need for education promotion programmes for tribal development.

(C) Studies Conducted in 1960s

Raghaviah (1962) in his study on Yanadis stressed the need for scientific analysis of problems faced by the tribals and the need for cautious approach in dealing with them. The monograph on Madagada village in Araku Valley published in 1968 by the Tribal Cultural Research and Training Institute, Hyderabad dealt with various aspects of development programmes. Sexena (1964) followed the model of Nag and studied the tribals of Western hills in Madhya Pradesh and presented the economy of five tribes. Prior to these studies a number of aspects were given about tribal economy in different monographs. The studies of Vidyarthi (1963) and Rai (1967) pointed out the problem of getting the basic facts of economic life in a small, non monetary or partially monetary economy of the tribal people of specific nature. Chandramouli (1969) discussed in detail various socioeconomic changes that are taking place in the tribal areas of Andhra Pradesh over years. He suggested various administrative measures for the upliftment of the tribal communities on par with other people.

A study of Tribal economy of Gujarat undertaken by Shah (1967) was based on the Indian Rural Debt and Investment Survey of R.B.I. (1961-62). The survey has brought out that tribal economy in Gujarat still continues to be stagnant from all points of view. There is very little diversification in occupations. Agriculture continues to be the main occupation of tribal population, very little investment is taking place to modernize it, very few inputs are made to increase the productivity of land and many people depend upon traditional agencies for their credit requirements, which are mainly for meeting their household expenditure. All these are obvious characteristics of a subsistence economy.

(D) Studies Conducted in 1970s

Prasada Rao (1970) in his study on Jatapus of Srikakulam district analysed various aspects of tribal economy and the changes caused in the community due to the entry of merchants and moneylenders into the tribal inhabitants. In another study Prasad Rao (1971) described various exploitative practices adopted by moneylenders to alienate tribal lands. Raghava Rao (1971) analysed exploitative money lending activities of Shahukars in the tribal villages of Araku Valley and discussed the causes of indebtedness. He also examined the factors involved in the ineffective functioning of credit services rendered by banks and financial institutions. Murty (1972) discussed the malpractices of moneylenders, problems of cultivators and functioning of Muttader system and reviewed various measures to be taken for amelioration of tribal conditions in south India. The study of Nayhyer (1974) examined the tribal development under different Plans.

Pratap and Bose (1975) presented the implications of techniques followed in the identification of "Growth centers" in the tribal areas of

Visakhapatnam district and Andhra Pradesh respectively. He suggested for integration of the area planning for tribal development. Raghava Rao (1975) examined various changes that had taken place in the Konda Dora society due to the contacts with the non-tribal money lenders and shahukars and the introduction of modern technology by the developmental agencies. Subba Reddy (1977) traced the origin of naxalite and armed rebellion of the tribals in Srikakulam District of Andhra Pradesh. He attributed the prevalence of exploitation is due to ineffective implementation of protective legislation and failure of developmental schemes. Ratnaiah (1977) studied the educational development process among the tribals of Adilabad district and analysed various factors involved in the process of tribal development in Adilabad district. The study of Gopala Rao (1978) examined the process of transfer of land from tribals to non-tribals and various factors influencing such transfer in Mondomkhal, a mixed village of tribes and castes in the agency area of Parvatipuram taluk of former Srikakulam district.

(E) Studies Conducted in 1980s

Sharma (1980) tried to focus attention on the existing weak socio-cultural and economic linkages and also a solution there to, through a general settlement and linkages plan keeping in view of the different economic activities that might be acceptable to people and suitable for the tribal area. He also emphasized that frictions are likely to increase in economic spheres, particularly in recruitment and trading activities. Pradeep kumar Bose (1981) questioned the validity of observing stratification pattern among Indian tribes on the basis of caste hierarchy. He justified class as a valied principle for studying Indian tribes. Data were collected from seven districts of Gujarat through survey method and random sampling. He identified four distinct classes, rich peasant, middle peasant, poor peasent, poor peasant and agricultural labour. On the other hand Jaganathpathy (1981) analyzed classes and class relations in three villages of Orissa. He concluded that economically constituted class does not lead automatically to the self-conscious class.

Ramaiah (1981) analysed the economy of 408 Koya tribal families from 51 villages in Andhra Pradesh. He studied the problems of agriculture, forestry and indebtedness of tribals. The author critically discussed several approaches to the multi-dimensional development of Indian tribes. The study suggested that planners should not forget the basic characteristics of the tribal economy and the Government polices should not create feeling of isolation among the tribals Makhan Jha (1982) studied the socioeconomic and cultural dimensions of the Ollar tribes of Orissa. It is more an anthropological study which largely concentrated on cultural change. Bhagat (1983) attempted to quantify some of the socioeconomic factors determining the difference in the adoption of improved agricultural practices in tribal Bihar. Based on primary data, the multiple regressionmodel has been used for examining the relative contribution of different socioeconomic factors in explaining the variation, Farm size, economic status, education of the household. The study ultimately revealed that the economic factors are more important than the socio cultural factors in the case of tribal farms.

Kothari (1985) conducted enquiry about the tribal social change among the Bhils of South Rajasthan. The enquiry is concerned with the problem of the direction of social change. The tribals have shown their integration in the national mainstream. Maurya (1985) identified that, education can play a crucial role in inculcating awareness among the tribals about their legislative rights and thus help them to cope up with the challenges of modern life. He suggested that there is absolute need for an integrated approach for rapid expansion of education among tribals of Andhra Pradesh. Srivastava (1987) also focused on the education of tribals and stated that objectives of education in the tribal areas lead to production orientation, economic growth and value orientation. Sujatha (1988) viewed that for the fast development of tribal areas an integrated development approach is highly essential. Also the study suggested for further strengthening of the integrated approach towards education programmes in more effective manner. The study of Rama Rao (1988) also pointed out the need for integrated approach for tribal education development.

Ramaiah (1988) conducted a study on Konda Reddies in relation with their shift from traditional crops to commercial crops. The Konda Reddies are originally shifting cultivators. The introduction of cotton crop brought about fundamental change in the tribal economy. He stated that the crop fetched cash and economically they achieved better position and livelihood. The study of Rama Mani (1988)examined the tribal economy of Donubai Panchayat in Srikakulam district and stated that, the gap between tribals and non-tribals notwithstanding the fact of introducing protective measures, creation of new agencies and extension of credit by the institutional financing agencies. The study stated that tribal society is hierarchically organized.

Mahalingam (1989) has advocated that tribals in India form the very segment of the weaker sections of the country with their traditional skills and resources. He also explained the importance of different tribal groups and their marketable products, salient features of tribal marketing structure and institutional building for the development of tribal market. Obroi, Murty and Sharma (1989) conducted enquiry about agricultural development on tribal farms in Himachal Pradesh. The study mainly concentrated upon identification of constraints, which hinder agricultural growth and attempts to examine problems in the adoption of modern technology on tribals farms and to analyse the constraints in the agricultural development of the study area. The study revealed that the farmers were found to differ significantly among themselves for the constraints in the development of agriculture.

(F) Studies Conducted in 1990s

Shah (1990) observed that the tribals in India different from one another in many respects. She emphasized the different problems associated with the tribal education promotion programmes. She examined the difficulties and disparities in educational attainment of tribes, which are having the features of socio-cultural, religious, economic and ecological. Varma (1990), examined the different dimensions of the Indian tribal society through the ages. Khare (1991) examined the impact of economic development on the socioeconomic conditions of the Munda tribe of Bihar and Jarkhand States. The study identified a gap between the tribal welfare plans and their implementation. The original structure of the tribal society should be kept in view. Sivaramaiah (1991) examined the tribal development programmes in Adilabad district whose endeavor is to improve the socioeconomic conditions of the tribes duly protecting their cultural heritage and distinct identity.

Chowdry Budhadeb (1992) conducted a macro level study on Indian tribes. The dimensions of socio, cultural, religious and economic changes are highlighted in the study. The interrelationships among the different social dimensions are also examined. The study also analysed the socioeconomic and ecological development issues of Indian tribes. Heredia, Rudolf (1992) explained that the isolation of the tribal community from the mainstream of society is a much larger issue in which education as an agency of socialization is one important dimension. He advocated the need for promotion of non-formal education for the promotion of education in the interior tribal area. Bhange (1993) reviewed the recommendations of different tribal commissions and committees appointed by the Government of India. Mohan Rao (1993) reviewed the different dimensions of socio-cultural, profile of the tribes of Andhra Pradesh. The study examined the overall change in tribals of Andhra Pradesh. Syam Prasad Rao (1993) examined the changing tribal scene both in prospect and retrospect with reference to North Coastal Andhra Pradesh for the period 1950-90. The study pointed out that the tribal society of North Coastal Andhra has started moving.

Devendra Thakur and Thakur (1995) reviewed tribal development and planning in India. They studied indepth massive efforts that have been made for the socio economic development of the tribal people by the

Government through organized economic planning. Also the study suggested so many policy implications for future planning for tribal development. Mohan Rao (1999) examined tribal development in Andhra Pradesh with respect to their process, performance and prospects. The study reviewed the applied anthropological and sociological perceptiveness on the tribes in India in general and on the tribes of Andhra Pradesh in particular. Critical analysis of earlier efforts and present strategies of tribal development are highlighted in the study.

PART-B

2.2.2. Credit Policy

The credit policy in the pre-independence period concentrated largely on the farming community and the problem of the credit needs of the rural poor did not receive any worthwhile attention. The problem of credit in rural areas and the dominant role of moneylenders in rural economy were recognized nearly a century age by the Government (RBI, 1960). Since then, several committees have been appointed to suggest remedial measures to control the usurious lending practices of the moneylenders and to provide institutional credit to rural people (GOI, 1931).

Enactment of the Cooperative Credit Societies Act in 1904 marked the beginning of efforts to build an institutional financial system for agriculture. The Maclagan Committee on Cooperatives in 1951 recognised the need for the provision of capital for agriculture and to relieve farmers from indebtedness, if the Nation wanted to achieve agricultural growth. The Central Bank Enquiry Committee 1931, after a detailed investigation into the problem of agricultural credit, rural banking and again indebtedness, suggested linking agricultural finance with central banking functions. It is clear that right from the beginning, the Government of India made serious attempts to nurture the cooperative movement and until 1947, the general thinking was in favour of promoting Primary Agricultural Cooperative Societies (PACS) in rural areas. However, cooperatives largely catered to the credit needs of the farming community and could not pay any attention to the credit needs of the rural poor, as they were not considered creditworthy. The fact that cooperatives failed to deliver the goods even to the farming community was stressed by the All India Rural Credit Survey Committee (RBI, 1955).

Since the beginning of the planning era, Government of India has paid special attention to meet the credit needs of the rural people. Though the cooperative movement started in India with a view to provide loans for weaker sections in the farm sector at low rates of interest and protect them from the clutches of the moneylenders, its bias was towards affluent sections like large and big farmers.

The credit needs of rural poor were considered not credit worthy for want of security. This type of thinking was clearly exposed in the Draft First Five-Year Plan: "Being without land or other assets, agricultural workers have no security to offer. As a rule, therefore, they are ineligible for financial assistance from the Government. While loans for individuals may present administrative difficulties, it should be possible for State Governments to give financial assistance to cooperatives of landless workers to enable them to build houses, purchase bullocks and to start ancillary industries" (GOI, 1953).

First Plan (1951-56)

The first plan was of the order of Rs.1960 crores, out of which a lump sum provision for Rs.19.93 crore nearly one per cent of the total plan allocation as made for development of tribal areas. The Community Development Programme launched during the first year of the plan (1951-52), the community development blocks were constituted throughout the tribal areas in the country to implement certain sectoral programmes like agriculture, health, education, communication and so on for the promotion of all round development of the tribals. In 1954, the Special Multi-Purpose Tribal Development blocks constituted exclusively for the development of tribal areas supplemented the efforts of these blocks. The department of scheduled castes and tribes in the various states deals with the problem of education of tribal children. State programmes of tribal education included the creation of residential education ashrams, vocational and technical training schools and hostel for tribal students. A patent programme of health education with the assistance of mobile dispensaries and the gradual introduction of regular medical services introduced the advantages of scientific methods in dealing with problems of health and disease of the people.

Second Plan (1956-61)

In the second plan, total outlay was Rs. 4600 crores, particularly the allocation to tribal sector, was Rs. 49.92 crore again roughly over one per cent of the outlay. The Ministry of Education had earmarked Rs. 11.38 crore for post metric scholarships for Scheduled Tribes, Scheduled Castes and Other Backward Classes. The health services included the setting up of 600 dispensaries, mobile health units and sinking of 15000 drinking water wells in tribal areas. In addition, a number of schemes were sponsored by the central government with a view to tackle the special problems of Scheduled Tribes in a more intensive manner than in the past. These include multipurpose projects like colonization schemes, construction of houses, construction of new roads and improvement of existing means of communications in scheduled and tribal areas, the opening of new medical and health units to eradicate diseases such as leprosy, V.D. etc., construction of drinking water wells, development of cottage industries, vocational and technical training of welfare workers.

Third Plan (1961-66)

The third plan was of the order of Rs.8576 crores out of which a lump sum provision of Rs.50.53 crore (less than one per cent) was made for development of tribal areas. The broad policies for the development of the tribal population and tribal areas had been reviewed by the study team on social welfare. The scheduled areas and scheduled tribes commission, which was set up in April 1960, submitted an interim report based on its study of development in nine states (Andhra Pradesh, Assam, Bhiar, Gujarat, Madhya Pradesh, Maharashtra, Orissa, Punjab and Rajasthan and one union territory). The report emphasized that programmes should be undertaken in tribal areas for land improvement, land reclamation and soil conservation, minor irrigation, supply of improved seeds, manners, implements and bullocks, provision of facilities for training, demonstration of improved practices, development of cattle, etc. Regarding health services the working group suggested priority for preventive measures for diseases common in each area, provision of itinerant medical units, establishment of maternity and child welfare centers and provisions of drinking water in difficult areas were also considered in the interim report of the commission.

Fourth Plan (1969-74)

The Fourth plan was of the order of Rs.15902 crores out of which a lump sum provision of Rs.75000 crore (less than one per cent) was made for development of tribal areas. In the fourth plan an outlay of Rs.11 crores was provided for the award of post-matric scholarship to Scheduled Castes and Scheduled Tribes. The number of students of the Scheduled Castes and Scheduled Tribes awarded post-matric scholarships increased from 2180 in 1951-52 to 127684 in 1967-68. An outlay of Rs.1.5 crores was provided for research, training facilities and special projects. The planning commission has constituted a study team on tribal research institutes to examine their research and training activities.

Fifth Plan (1974-79)

The fifth plan was of the order of Rs.37250 crores out of which a lump sum provision of Rs.1182 core – approximately about 0.32 per cent was made for development of tribal areas. Tribal sub-plans incorporating programmes of particular significance to the tribal economy were prepared for areas with large concentration of scheduled tribes in 16 states and 2 union territories. These programmes were funded through provisions in the state plans and central assistance.

Sixth Plan (1980-85)

The sixth plan was of the order of Rs.97, 500 crores, out of which a lump sum provision of Rs.4193 crore was made for development of tribal areas, which was 4.30 per cent of the total plan allocation. The major objective of the sixth plan was to mobilize latent energies for the creation of a more dynamic and more equitable society through development of SC/ST. In view of this special component, plans were formulated as part of various programmes to enable Scheduled Caste / Scheduled Tribes families to cross over the poverty line within short periods. Separate sub plans were formulated covering 63 per cent of the tribal population in the country. The Tribal Sub Plan areas were divided into 180 integrated tribal developments for operational purposes. Other programmes included establishment of tribal research institutes for survey and research on tribal problems.

Tribal identity and the tribal way of life were preserved in a manner consistent with their aspirations for development. The main thrust of the policy thus for development of the scheduled Castes/Scheduled tribes during the sixth plan was fourfold viz., (a) Integration of services at the delivery point to the beneficiary with a view to develop self – reliance (b) Development of services from the bottom-upwards instead of top-downwards (c) Development of skills and (d) introduction of latest technology based on local materials and local skills to reduce drudgery of workers and also to remove the social stigma attached to their present profession.

Seventh Plan (1985-90)

The seventh plan was of the order of Rs. 180000 crores, out of which a lump sum provision of Rs. 6976 crores, which was 3.86 per cent of the total plan outlay was made for development of tribal areas. Special consideration was accorded to scheduled caste and scheduled tribe families in the Integrated Rural Development Programme (IRDP) in the county. The target of coverage of Scheduled Caste/Scheduled Tribe beneficiaries in the seventh plan was 30 per cent in the case of Scheduled Castes and 13.04 per cent in the case of Scheduled Tribe beneficiaries.

In the wage employment Programme of Jawahar Rozgar Yojana, preference was given to Scheduled Castes and Scheduled Tribes and bonded labourers. It has also been provided that at the village panchayat level, 15 per cent of the annual allocation must be spent on items of work that directly benefits the Scheduled Castes and Scheduled Tribes.

Eighth Plan (1992-97)

The eighth plan was of the order of Rs.314576 crores, out of which a lump sum provision of Rs.18311 crores (6 per cent) was made for development of tribal areas. The strategy of the special component plan for Scheduled Castes and Scheduled Tribes, the tribal sub plan were reviewed inter-alia to make them effective instruments of planning to ensure real and tangible flow of benefits to the target group, both individuals and families.

The attempts during the eighth plan were to rationalize the scheme to: (i) Provide guidance with reference employment opportunities and offering appropriate incentives for courses, which have a large market demand (ii) Improve the performance, if necessary by prescribing minimum standards and (iii) Identify causes of inter-caste/tribe variation in availing benefits under the scheme and chalk out appropriate remedial action.

Ninth Plan (1997-2002)

The main objective of the Ninth Plan was to intensify the efforts to bridge the gap between Scheduled Castes/Scheduled Tribes and the rest of the population. An outlay of Rs.775 crores was provided in the Ninth Plan for development of tribals.

In the field of economic development, financial assistance was offered to these communities from TAHDCO for undertaking economic activities. During 1998-99, the scheme of free supply of tools and appliances was modified as 'Kalvi Kudumba Thittam'. Under this scheme, family as a unit of development was recognized and poor SC/ST family having a member with a degree or diploma holder was assisted for self-employment. Existing training institutions were strengthened. Several innovative training programmes in fashion technology, plastic processing, footwear technology, driver training etc., were also conducted and placement was tied up with reputed institutions. Special coaching facilities for the SC/ST candidates were extended through Pre-examination centers to enable them to appear for civil service competitive examinations to get employment is State/Central Government offices and public sector undertakings.

Tenth Plan (2002-07)

An outlay of Rs.1200 crores is allocated in the Tenth Plan for the Welfare of Scheduled Castes and Scheduled Tribes. Out of Rs. 1200 cores an amount of Rs.1044 cores is allocated for SCs and the rest for STs for both ongoing and new schemes (Table 2.1). Details of Plan wise fund allocations and policies and programmes were presented to understand the importance given by the Government for tribal development (Table 2.2 and Appendix 2.1).

In the banking sector, many changes have taken place like Nationalisation of banks in 1969, the formulation of the Lead Bank Scheme and Village Adoption Scheme in 1972 and evolution of Agriculture Refinance and Development Corporation in 1975, which were some of the steps in this direction. All these measures have metamorphosed the orientation of the whole banking structure. In addition to these, progressive shifts in lending policies in favour of the poor and other weaker sections were undertaken. Also targets were set in terms of percentage of total credit to the weaker sections; norms of realization and adoption of lower interest rates for these vulnerable sections of society were some of the other steps. Two major changes were initiated in the Fifth Five-Year Plan period (GOI, 1974). Firstly, the number of projects was increased to 160. Secondly, the two programmes for small farmers, marginal farmers and agricultural labourers were combined to form SF/ MFALDA's. Each Agency on an average is expected to cover 70,000 small and Marginal farmers preferably in the ratio of 1:3 to conform to the All-India pattern.

The Government of India introduced 20-Point Economic Programme in 1975 for the economic upliftment of the poorest of the poor. Under this programme, a number of statutory measures have been introduced for enrolling members of the weaker sections into cooperatives and byelaws of cooperative institutions were also amended to give suitable representation to the weaker sections. The cooperative institutions have to ensure that the economic condition of the weaker sections is upgraded by providing them with suitable assistance by way of loans etc., for agricultural and allied activities. The Government of India, therefore, issued guidelines to the state governments to discharge and scale down the debt of the landless, small and marginal farmers and rural artisans obtained from non-institutional agencies. All these developments led to the creation of new institutions to cater to the credit needs of the poor and to issue policy directions to supply consumption credit to these sections.

2.2.3. Establishment of RRBs and FSSs

Despite the tremendous growth of cooperatives and commercial banks, they are not in a position to supply credit to weaker sections liberally. On account of the likely freezing of the non-institutional credit to the rural poor and the moratorium imposed under the 20 Point programme, new agencies like Regional Rural Banks (RRBs) and Farmers' Service Societies (FSSs) were introduced by the Government of India. The RRBs were set up on 2nd October 1975 with the main objective to develop the rural economy by providing credit and other facilities for the purpose of development of agriculture, trade, commerce, industry and other productive activities in the rural areas. These banks are expected to provide credit to small entrepreneurs and persons of small means.

The National Commission on Agriculture (NCA) (GOI, 1976) submitted an Interim Report on the credit needs and services for small and marginal farmers and agricultural labourers. The NCA had come to the conclusion that the existing cooperatives and commercial banks have failed to take care of the weaker sections. The commission noted that considering the overall constraints on credit, due weightage will have to be given to the small and marginal farmers, agricultural labourers and rural artisans in respect of quantum of credit and interest rates. In its Final Report submitted on January 1976, the NCA felt that for efficient utilization of credit by the weaker sections, an integrated and supervised credit structure would have to be built. This structure would consist of FSS at the grass-root level controlled by the small and marginal farmers and agricultural labourers, which would be linked to commercial banks or cooperative central banks for necessary financial and managerial support.

The FSS should also encourage and finance viable units of suppliers of inputs, custom services, storage, transportation and marketing in their respective areas. All types of credit should flow through the single agency to ensure appropriate control and use. According to the recommendation of the NCA, the FSS were established in 1976 in some selected states. Besides credit, they provide a package of services and guidance needed by the farmers and also cater to the credit needs of the agricultural labourers.

2.2.4. Consumption Loans

An Expert Committee had been appointed by the Government of India under the Chairmanship of Sri B. Sivaraman in 1976 (GOI, 1976) to go into the question of providing consumption credit to small and marginal farmers, landless labourers and rural artisans and to suggest ways and means for meeting the same. The Committee submitted its Report on 26th April 1976 and has made a number of recommendations. This Committee while discussing institutional arrangements for supplying consumption credit observed that barring the element of consumption credit included in the production loans, the banking institutions and the government do not make any arrangement at present to meet the consumption needs of the weaker sections and the relatively better off sections of the rural community. The Committee also observed the following difficulties in the disbursement of consumption credit by the existing agencies, viz., the commercial banks including the RRBs Government and PACS's:-

(a) Until the passing of the recent debt relief law, provision of credit to meet consumption needs even of those who had tangible security to offer, was not encouraged and

(b) The institutions do not also have the infrastructure necessary to reach the mass of people both for providing loans and more so for the recovery thereof.

Further, in view of these difficulties, the Committee also observed that any system that can effectively look after this type of lending business must be situated as close as possible to the borrower to facilitate his repaying in any small amount and over a period of time. The commercial banks came into the field during the last several years for extending rural credit but they have limitations in serving large number of individual loans of very small amounts directly. Keeping all the aspects of the situation in view, the Committee recommended that the PACS's should be merged with Farmers Service Societies (FSSs), Large size Multipurpose Societies (LAMPs) in the tribal areas each having a full time paid secretary. The committee further recommended providing automatic membership to all those agriculturists and non-agriculturists who wanted to join a society for production and for consumption credit facilities. In the opinion of the Committee, the universal membership concept should answer this requirement.

According to the recommendations of this Committee, the RBI permitted PACS's to issue consumption loans to members belonging to the weaker sections. The Committee suggested inter alia consumption loans of Rs. 250 for medical expenses, Rs. 100 for educational purposes, Rs. 250 for marriage and Rs. 75 for births, funerals and ceremonies. The overall credit limit, which was initially Rs. 250 per borrower was raised to Rs. 500 in the year 1976-77 (Khan, 1977). The Agricultural Credit Department of the RBI had advised the Registrars of Cooperative Societies, to advance consumption loans to a person up to 10 per cent of his short-term loan eligibility, subject to a maximum of Rs. 250 per individual and that preference in this behalf should be given to the weaker sections. The RBI did not prescribe any additional security for these consumption loans. However, it did not agree to refinance such operations and advised the banks and societies to use their own funds for this purpose.

All these efforts didn't solve the problem of providing consumption loans, to weaker sections through institutional agencies. The entire demand for consumption credit was met only by the informal sources at high exploitative interest rates that varied from 30 per cent to 90 per cent p.a. Due to the inability of the poor to offer any security for their small consumption loans, they were unable to take the short-term consumption loans from the formal banking system and thus remained outside the fold of the formal banking system.

2.2.5. Poverty Alleviation Programmes

Economists have shown in their studies that economic growth may be able to raise per capita incomes in developing countries, but reduction of poverty as well as elimination of unemployment and under-employment may not accompany it. To counter this situation, it was thought necessary to introduce various programmes for alleviating poverty by endowing the poor with productive assets or skills so that they can employ themselves usefully to earn greater incomes and cross the poverty line. The introduction of different poverty alleviation programmes like IRDP, Jawahar Rojgar Yojana, etc. had helped increased access of credit to weaker sections.

2.2.6. Tribal Sub Plan

The Tribal Sub Plan was introduced to ensure that all general development sectors at the State level earmark funds in proportion to ST population so that adequate benefits from all the concerned sectors flow to the tribal groups. The Consolidated Details of Plan wise Fund Allocations for Tribal Development and Plan-wise Development programmes were presented in Table 2.2 and Appendix 2.1. The objective is to assist the Tribal families in improving their socioeconomic and educational status. The expenditure incurred for implementing the Tribal Sub Plan including the Special Central Assistance has increased steadily from Rs. 94 lakhs in 1976-77 to Rs.17.55 crores in 2000-2001.

Tribal Sub Plan (TSP) strategy, which came into being in the Fifth Plan with the twin objectives of the area and sectoral approaches, envisages protection of the interests of the STs through legal and administrative measures and development and welfare activities through plan efforts. Empowerment of these tribal people requires more provision of the basic capabilities for integrating them into growth process.

The Tribal Sub Plan has been under implementations since 1976-77 with the aim of (1) helping the Scheduled Tribe families to cross the poverty line and (2) to provide basic amenities and facilities in their areas. The size of the Tribal Sub Plan should be in proportion to Scheduled Tribe population to the State's total population.

2.2.7. Strategy of Tribal Development

The strategy for tribal development should be to pull them out of perpetual poverty and relieve them from starvation throughout the year. This can be possible only through ensuring better returns for their farm and forest produce and also improve productivity in agriculture, horticulture, animal husbandry, forestry, cottage and small scale industries, etc. Though the efforts have been in the direction for development of tribals, since the inceptionof the planned development process in our country, particularly with the creation of special multi-purpose tribal blocks during the second plan period. However, a major breakthrough took place in the Fifth Plan in which a new strategy of Tribal Sub-Plan (TSP) for preparing micro plans for relatively vulnerably tribal groups requiring special attention was enunciated.

However, the broad approach to tribal development depends on the pattern of distribution of tribals in an area and the level of their economy. In the primarily tribal dominant, areas, approach is to focus on the development of tribal communities, such as restoring their traditional rights of forest-dwelling tribes as minor forest produce and involving in the development activities of the forest, as partners will be suitable. For displaced tribals: community oriented programmes such as, (a) restoring traditional rights of the tribal people over their Common Property Resource (CPR) and making tribal land a frozen asset, and its transfer, either through mortgage or sale both to no tribals and tribal be completely banned by law will have to be evolved, (b) in the case of primitive groups, which are facing special problems and are small in size, a very cautious individualized approach will have to be adopted for example, (i) in the organization of development activities priority should be given to those tribal families that have never received any benefit, (ii) the system of bonded-labour be abolished forthwish, lest their previous balance is irretrievably lost. The problem of tribal communities needs a systematic approach.

The development strategy suggested that the welfare programmes should be based on felt needs. The Planners have to be familiar with felt needs of tribes and find out ways to meet them by taking into consideration of available natural resources, existing human resources, existing technical know-how and infrastructure rearrangement. It is to ensure demand-driven development of the area and people. It appears that elaborate care has been taken during different five year plans to spell out tribal development strategies and budget allocations for the promotion of welfare and socioeconomic upliftment. However, these strategies and allocations proved to be a relief measure rather than solutions to unemployment and poverty eradication.

The micro level studies focused mainly on the impact of development programmes on tribal households. There were many reasons for the failure of tribal development programmes. There were delays in the implementation of the programs. Coordination at various levels was absent the state Governments did not ensure a reasonable share of benefits from the general development programs to the tribals. The developmental efforts increased the differences between tribal groups. The performance of the administrative machinery is not satisfactory. The remarks of the Planning Commission in this regard about the need of a fresh look at the tribal development are worth mentioning.

Various developmental agencies such as GCC, ITDA etc., have failed in improving the quality of life of the tribals and in the growth of their economy. Development of modern means of transport, roads and bus services has opened up the tribal areas in recent decades and several non-tribals came into contact with the tribals and contributed to the growth of tribal economy. For these changing agents and modern forces, tribals have shown fewer signals for transformation. The most important reason for their inability to respond to the continuous efforts of the government policies may be due to socio-cultural heterogeneity, low level of literacy and awareness, inadequate infrastructure and input supply and indifferent attitude of the tribals in general. Improvement in the quality of life and levels of socioeconomic conditions of tribals are sought to be examined in terms of endogenous and exogenous factors.

SECTION-II

2.3. Extent of Indebtedness

In the preceding section, an attempt is made to examine the policies of the Government of India as well as the State Governments, in relation to the credit needs of the poor. In this section, an attempt is made to examine the trends in indebtedness of Tribal poor households at the All India Level and to ascertain the contributing factors. Trends in indebtedness have been examined with reference to the magnitude of indebtedness, the purposes for which the loans are contracted, the sources of funds for these groups, on the basis of information available in the Debt and Investment Survey (NSSO 48th round). Further, the factors responsible for increase in indebtedness are also examined.

It is a well known fact that a household is required to borrow for a variety of reasons to satisfy its immediate needs arising out of the business undertaken by capital needs or to meet household expenditure which could not ordinarily be met out of its current income. In the case of families with low income, borrowings might have been incurred to bridge the gap between the income and the expenditure. Tribal households, unlike other sections of the society, are not privileged enough to rely on institutional agencies to meet their credit requirements. Therefore, they are forced to depend upon non-institutional credit agencies. Indebtedness to non-institutional agencies determine the destiny of Tribal households in many ways—Freedom to choose their employer, limits their bargaining capacity in the wage market and involves them in a host of obligations including the mortgage of the freedom of their family members.

In view of the changing trends in the significance of debt on the life pattern of Tribal households, indebtedness is examined with reference to Incidence of Indebtedness (IOI), Average Amount of Debt per household (AOD). The Average value of Assets (AVA) and Debt Asset Ratio (DAR) for the All India as of 30.6.91 and are presented in table 2.3.

In the table 2.3 "others" refer to those not belonging to either of the social groups SC or ST. The percentage distribution figures by social group is given in table, tells that, in 1991, the social group 'others' had a relatively higher share in the total debt (TD) than their numerical proportion among all rural households, while for the social groups SC or ST the picture was just the reverse. Rural households belonging to the social group 'others' accounted for nearly four-fifths of the aggregate debt in rural areas although they constituted only about two-thirds of all rural households. The survey figures tell that SC and ST households constituted respectively more than a fifth and more than a tenth of all rural households whereas they accounted for 16 per cent and 5 per cent respectively of the TD in the rural areas. In 1991, among the social groups, both the average amount of debt per household (AOD) and the burden of debt – as indicated by the debt-asset ratio-was the lowest for ST households. However, although the social group 'others' showed the highest AOD (Rs. 2,249), it was the SC households who were laden with the highest burden of debt (2.8 per cent). This value of the debt-asset ratio was substantially higher for SC households than for either ST (1.6 per cent) or 'other' (1.7 per cent). In 1991, among the three social groups, IOI was the lowest (17.4 per cent) for ST households and the highest (25.3 per cent) for SC households. IOI for other households was 23.6 per cent – 6 percentage points more than that for ST households but 2 percentage points less than that for SC households.

Detailed information about the per thousand distribution of households by household asset holding, Number of households reporting specified items of assets and cash loan outstanding and corresponding average values (Rs.) per household by household asset holding, per thousand distribution of amount of cash loans outstanding over credit agency, per thousand distribution of amount of outstanding cash loans by rate of interest, per thousand distribution of outstanding amount of cash loans over security of loan and per thousand distribution of amount of cash loans outstanding over purpose of loans for each social group as on 30.6.91, is presented in Appendix 2.2-2.7.

2.3.1. Credit Agencies and Social Groups

It would be interesting to study the variation in IOI in 1991 by different credit agencies for the three social groups. Table 2.4 presents these figures for rural areas. It may be noted that a number of estimates in this table are quite small. The comment made in the preceding section on small estimates being subject to large variability may be recalled. This observation holds true for such estimates in all tables presented subsequently.

Table 2.4 shows that for the three social groups, the pattern in the IOI, which in the preceding section covered all loans, continues to hold true even when loans taken only from institutional agencies and non-institutional agencies are considered separately. Thus, an overall low IOI is observed for both institutional agencies (12 percent) and non-institutional agencies (7 percent) for ST households. The corresponding figures of IOI for SC households are 17 percent and 11 percent of IOI which, incidentally, are the highest values among the three social groups for loans taken from institutional agencies and non-institutional agencies respectively. For ST households, relatively low IOI is observed for co-operative societies (4 per cent) among institutional agencies and for professional money lenders (1.5 per cent) and relatives and friends (1 per cent) among non-institutional agencies than among households belonging to any other social group. For SC households, on the other hand, for SC households, IOI was higher for commercial banks (9 per cent) among institutional agencies and, to an extent, for landlord (2 per cent) and agriculturist money lender (3 per cent) among non-institutional agencies than among households in any other social group.

The table reveals that in 1991, for all three social groups, the share of institutional agencies in the TD was quite substantial. However, not much difference is observed in this share between the three groups – it ranges between 61 per cent to 65 per cent. For ST households, although no substantial differences are noted in the shares of different institutional agencies for ST households, when compared with the other social groups, the share for banks (38 per cent) was a little higher. Similarly, among non-institutional agencies, share of relatives and friends was a little lower (2 per cent) as compared to the other social groups.

2.3.2. Type of Security and Social Groups

The differences by social groups regarding the percentage of indebted households (P) and percentage share (S) in the total amount of outstanding debt for the different types of security have been examined and presented in table-2.5. The table reveals that, so far as the pattern of incidence of indebtedness of different types of security is concerned, only minor differences existed between the indebted households in the three different social groups. However, in terms of actual values of P, while very little difference is observable in the social group 'others' compared to 'all social groups', some differences do occur when the social groups SC or ST are compared against 'all social groups'.

One prominent difference concerns the 'personal security'. For which P-value is just 11 per cent for ST but 18 per cent for SC and 15 per cent for all households. Further, the P-value for ST households is lower than those in the other social groups by about 2 percentage points for 'mortgage of immovable property'. With regard to percentage share, as brought out by table 2.5, the pattern of percentage shares of debt incurred against different types of security is broadly similar for indebted households belonging to any of the social groups, except for one notable difference. The share of debt against 'surety security' is clearly more than that against 'first charge on immovable property' of SC and ST households, which is not true for other households.

While the shares of debt by various security types were, by and large, close for social group 'others' and 'all social groups', some distinct differences are observable, for certain types of security, between the shares for ST or SC households and those for other households. For example, the share of 'personal security' for SC or ST households was substantially higher than that for other households- by 11 and 15 percentage points for ST and SC households respectively. Shares for debt incurred against 'mortgage of immovable property' for ST or SC households were significantly lower – by 10 percentage points for SC and 5 percentage points for ST – than that of other households. Similar is the case for debt incurred against 'first charge on immovable property' in rural areas. Share of such debt was 4 percentage points lower for SC or ST households than for other households.

2.3.3. Debt According to Purpose and Social Groups

The various purposes for which the loans were taken by the households as of 30.6.91, in terms of their incidence and the percentage shares in debt are discussed and presented in table 2.6. The table shows that, generally speaking, the pattern of incidence of indebtedness (P), in terms of the purposes for which loans were reportedly taken, was much the same for all the three social groups in rural areas. However, the actual values of P suggest that the category 'other expenditure' within 'household expenditure' was much less prevalent (6.5 per cent) among ST households than among SC households (13.4 per cent) or other households (11.1 per cent).

The table also reveals that the percentage share of 'capital expenditure', in the farm as well as non-farm business, was significantly lower among SC or ST households than among other households. It further brings out that ST households displayed a stronger propensity to incur 'other expenditure' in farm business (S value: 15 per cent) than SC households (S-value: 5 per cent) or other households (S-value: 11 per cent). The table also shows that a similar tendency was observable among SC households, on 'other expenditure' under 'household expenditure'. SC households incurred as high as 42 per cent of their debt for this purpose, compared to 27 per cent for ST and 31 per cent for other households.

SECTION-III

2.4. Genesis of Micro Credit System In India

2.4.1. Evolution

In this section, an attempt is made to examine as to what extent the policy developments have helped the flow of micro finance to poor households. The failure of formal institutions to serve the rural poor effectively led to a review and a look at the informal financial systems and lending groups (Humpi and Feder, 1990). The Share of the formal financial sector in the total rural credit was 56.6 per cent compared to informal finance at 39.6 per cent and unspecified sources at 3.8 per cent (RBI, 1992). At this juncture, it was apparent that there was an urgent need for the financial innovation in the credit markets in India. It was in such an environment that Micro finance emerged as an innovation all over the world. It was evolving into an effective system for the provision of financial services to the poor households, more specifically micro enterprises. Internationally several variants of micro finance technologies have evolved in the last two decades as also a wide range of institutions (Satish, 2005). A number of Non-Governmental Organisations (NGO) organize the poor into informal groups for mutual help and benefit. Many of these groups have been provided credit support. These NGOs are instrumental in promoting informal structures of the poor to help them save

---

*SHG concept

The concept of "SHG" is used to describe groups of people in different contexts. In the Indian context, a SHG can be defined as a "Homogeneous affinity group of rural poor, Voluntarily formed to save small amounts out of their emergent credit needs and revolving their resources among the members, both for consumption and production, at such rate of interest, period of loans and other terms, which the groups may decide. Such group may be informal or registered and should not have a membership of more than 20, if they were to be unregistered".

Characteristic Features of SHGs:

- Transparency in operations.

(Contd.)

and promote self-reliance in financing their needs through the concept of Self-Help Groups (SHGs).*

With the experiments conducted by Mohammad Yunus in Bangaladesh in 1979, which was popular by the name Grameen Bank (GB), micro-credit innovations got worldwide attention (Khandker, Khality and Z. Khan, 1995). In 1984, the main conclusion of the Third International Symposium on the Mobilisation of Personal Savings in Developing Countries organized by the united Nations, was that "the main means of improving the performance of the non-institutional sector were policies directed to enhancing its links with the institutional financial sector" (United Nations, 1986). By definition, micro-credit innovations can be said as "Programmes that provide credit for self-employment and other financial and business services (including savings and technical assistance) to very poor persons" (World Bank, 1997). Micro credit as an alternative source of credit for the poor has received wide attention in recent years and policies were formulated to link the informal system to the formal system.

The NABARD's involvement with SHGs came about in 1986, when the Sixth General Assembly of APRACA at Katmandu in Nepal considered a Proposal for promotion of Linkages between Banking Institutions and Self-help Groups in rural savings, mobilisation and credit delivery to the poor (Jayaraman, 2001). The first official interest in informal group lending in India took shape during 1986-87 when the NABARD supported and funded an action research project on 'Savings and Credit Management of Self-Help Groups' of MYRADA. In 1988-89 the NABARD undertook a survey of 43 non-governmental organizations spread over 11 states in India to study the functioning of SHGs and possibilities of collaboration between the banks and SHGs in the mobilization of rural savings and improving the delivery of credit to the

---

(Contd.)

- Intimate Knowledge of each other's intrinsic strengths, needs and problems.
- Have a common fund.
- Have simple and responsive rules.
- SHG route is one of the effective methods of delivery of credit to the unreached poor.
- Collective decision making.
- Market driven rates of interests and as decided by the group.
- Collateral free loans.
- External interference kept to the least and
- Conflict solving through collective leadership and mutual discussions.

poor (NABARD, 1995). In order to operationalise this concept, the NABARD launched a pilot project in February 1992 to link 500 SHGs with commercial banks across the Country. The pilot project was further extended to RRBs and Co-operative Banks in 1993 (Jayaraman, 2001). To formalize the mechanism further, the RBI constituted a working Group in November 1994 (NABARD, 1995) to review the functioning of NGOs and SHGs and make suitable recommendations for expanding their activities in the rural areas. Accepting the recommendations of the working group and integrated them with the mainstream of credit operation, the RBI had set up a micro credit cell in April 1999 (Jagadish Capoor, 2001). The Government of India bestowed national priority to the Programme through its recognition in the Union Budget, 1999.

2.4.2. Progress of SHGs in India

This analysis is entirely based on the secondary data available from the statistics supplied by the NABARD. Details relating to the cumulative progress of SHG-Bank linkage, highlights of the regional spread of physical and financial progress, agency-wise participation, model-wise cumulative position upto 31st March, 2006 were presented by using tabular analysis.

Though the promotion of SHGs by external intervention in India is of recent origin, there appears to be a fairly good progress in this regard. It is mainly the NGOs, which have taken a keen interest and initiative across the Country in promoting SHGs. It is evident from Table 2.7 that by March, 2006 about 22, 38,565 SHGs (cumulative) spread all over India have been linked with banks. Their growth was tremendous during 2001-2006 (Figure 2.2). 90 per cent of these groups were women groups which show the dominance of the participation of women in micro credit. There is an increasing trend even in the number of participating banks. Almost all the states and Union Territories were covered under this programme by the end of March 2006. Cumulatively 22,38,565 SHGs with refinance support of Rs. 41,597 million upto March, 2006 were instrumental in increasing bank finance to 32.98 million poor families (NABARD, 2006). The average loan per group as well as per family also increased during the period.

Model-wise per cent distribution of Self Help Groups and SHG credit in 2006 was presented in Table 2.8. Model-wise analysis shows that upto March 2006, 21 per cent of the total number of SHGs financed were under the Model-I. This showed an increase of 4 per cent over the position upto March 2003, reflecting an increased role of banks in promoting and nurturing SHGs. Model-II continues to have the major share, with 74 per cent of the total number of SHGs financed upto March 2006, falling under this category. The share of cumulative number of SHGs linked under the Model-III upto March, 2006 continued to be relatively small at only 6 per cent, but in years to come, this is expected to become a major delivery model (Table 2.8 and Figure 2.2). The details on region-wise and model wise progress of SHGs are presented in Appendix 2.8.

2.4.3. Spread of SHG-Bank Linkage Programme

It is evident from the Table 2.9A that many state governments, banks and other agencies accorded high-priority to the programme in their areas of operation, thereby increasing the absolute number of SHGs receiving bank credit. States selected under this programme were Andhra Pradesh (1,04,238), followed by Tamil Nadu (51,851), Karnataka (41,688), Orissa (35,316), Uttar Pradesh (25,514) and so on. Specific strategies were formulated by the NABARD to meet the requirement for widening the network and deepening the penetration of the programme in the States, which required special attention. In order to reduce regional imbalances in SHG-Bank Linkage, the NABARD devised region-specific strategies and intervention. Accordingly, special focus was given to the North-Eastern Region by encouraging collaboration with a large number of small NGO partners and micro finance agencies for enhancing the coverage of SHG-Bank Linkage. From Table 2.9.B it can be observed that in Andhra Pradesh, districts falling under above category were East Godavari (46,399), Srikakulam (25,654), Khammam (24,936) and so on.

2.4.4. Agency-wise Participation

The relative significance of various banking groups in the linking programme, is considered and presented in the study. At the National level, commercial banks are the major partners (49 per cent) followed by RRBs (36 per cent). The role of Co-operatives is minimized in the programme. A similar picture was noticed in Andhra Pradesh also (Table 2.10A and 2.10B).

During the year 2003-04, as many as 35,294 branches of 560 banks participated in the SHG-Bank Linkage Programme. The broad category-wise number of these banks, total branches participated and their percentage share to the total achievements is indicated below. The SHG-Bank linkage programme becomes a part of business for all the 27 public sector banks and 17 private sector banks. The NABARD's refinance support was available to all these banks against their loans to SHGs. Among the public sector banks, the SBI credit, linked the highest number of SHGs (48,473) during 2003-04, followed by Andhra Bank (20, 164) and Indian Bank (14,320). In the case of private sector banks, the ICICI Bank recorded the highest number of SHG (4,741) during 2003-2004, followed by the Vysya Bank Ltd., (1,202), Dhanalakshmi Bank (796) (See Appendix-2.9). The RRBs financed SHGs in a very significant way during 2003-04. Out of total 196 RRBs in the country, almost all the banks participated in the SHG-Bank linkage programme. The cumulative achievement of RRBs as a percentage of the total, registered an impressive increase in terms of loans disbursed and refinance availed from the NABARD. During the year 2003-04, the maximum number of SHGs have been linked by Pandian Grameen Bank (T.N), followed by Nagarjuna Grameen Bank (A.P.), Sri Visakha Grameen Bank (A.P) and so on (See Appendix-2.10). Though the number of partners to the SHG-Bank linkage in the co-operative sector increased to 316, upto March 2004, its role is the minimum compared to commercial banks and the RRBs (See Appendix 2.11).

On the whole, the performance of the SHGs is satisfactory. A major feature of the performance of the SHGs is coverage of the poor sections (Rajasekhar, 1994). This is possible mainly due to the emphasis of the NGOs in promoting SHGs to work mainly for the development of tribals, landless labour and especially the women from these categories. Secondly most of the SHGs have been able to successfully promote regular savings habits even among these poor households (Fernandez, 1994). These savings appear to be working towards making the SHGs self-reliant besides increasing the members' stake in their functioning. Thirdly, with funds mobilized through savings and borrowings from banks, the SHGs are able to meet diverse loan demand of the members for both production and house-hold purposes. In contrast to the formal agencies, the diversity in loan purpose appears to be their striking featres (Fernandez, 1994). Their autonomy as well as easy access to information about members' activities, seems to have enabled the SHGs to meet such diverse loan demands of the members. Fourthly, despite not following collateral-based lending, like formal agencies, the SHGs have been able to register high loan recoveries (Rajasekhar, 1994). A combination of factors like peer monitoring, easy and flexible loaning procedures, higher interest rates, effective screening, flexible repayment schedules, etc., seem to have positively influenced the loan recovery performance of his SHGs. Finally, the studies on SHGs also reveal that the SHGs promoted by the NGOs appear to be, from inception, dependent upon the NGOs for their various managerial and other requirements (Rajasekhar, 1994).

2.5. Summary

The credit policy in the pre-independence period concentrated largely on the farming community and the problem of the credit needs of the poor received only scant attention. In the first Three Five-year Plans, very little attention was paid to the credit needs of the poor. Because the planners believed in the theory of 'trickle down' effect and emphasis was laid on the overall development. From the Fourth Five-Year Plan onwards special agencies like SFDA and MFALDA were evolved to deal with the problems of the specific groups were evolved. In the banking sector also many changes have taken place and progressive shifts in lending policies in favour of poor and other weaker sections were undertaken. Some initiations were made to provide consumption loans to weaker sections and special target oriented programmes were designed to provide credit for the upliftment of the poor through promoting self employment.

The policy framework resulted in excessive target orientation in government-sponsored programmes. This resulted in high transaction costs and non-recovery problems to the formal credit institutions. All these weakened the strength of the financial institutions to serve the poor and further reduced their interest to transact such business. The failure of various programmes to address the root causes of the problem brought home the need to confront poverty on a sustained basis. Policy makers and the NGOs recognized that both the human capital and the productive capacity of the poor need to be improved in order to reduce poverty. To address these needs, SHGs were introduced in 1992 following the example of the Bangladesh Grameen Bank. To formalize the mechanism further, the RBI constituted a Working Group in November 1994 to review the functioning of the NGOs and the SHGs and make suitable recommendations for expanding their activities. Accepting the recommendations, the RBI advised the lending banks that the SHGs should be considered as an additional segment under priority sector advances and integrated them with the mainstream of credit operations. The Government of India bestowed national priority to the programme though its recognition in the Union Budget, 1999.

The progress of SHGs is very satisfactory in India. About 22,38,565 SHGs (cumulative) spread all over India, have been linked with banks by the end of March 2006. Model-wise analysis shows that upto March 2006, Model-II SHGs continued to have a major share of above 74 per cent of the total number of SHGs financed. Further, the spread of SHGs shows that the Southern Region occupied the first place in the Programme. Among the states of the Southern Region, Andhra Pradesh occupied the leading role. Agency-wise analysis shows that at the National level commercial banks are the major partners followed by the RRBs and the cooperatives' role is rather minimum in the programme.

The progress of SHGs is limited in term of spread, they certainly seem to hold a good potential in the field of credit for the poor. Precisely, based on such an assessment, the NABARD has an ambitious plan for expanding the SHGs all over the Country and promote them as instruments, which can supplement the institutional agencies in effectively reaching the poor.

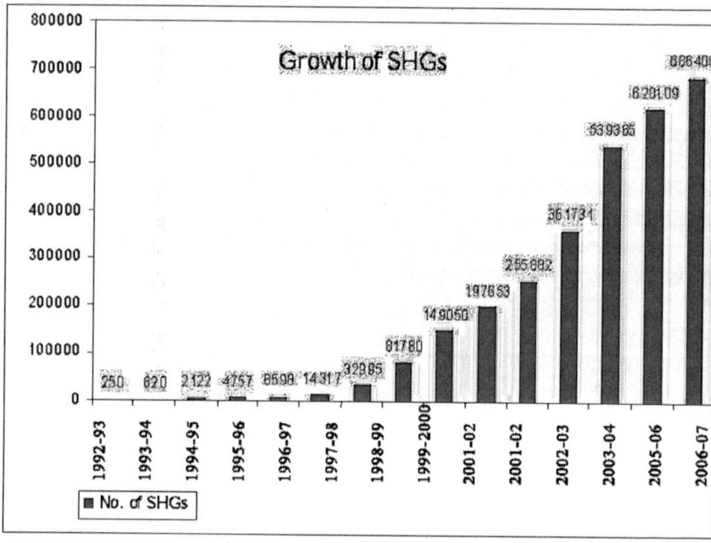

Growth of SHGs
800000
700000
600000
500000
400000
300000
200000
100000
0
250
620
2122
4757
8598
14317
32995
81780
149050
197653
255882
361731
539365
620109
686408
1992-93
1993-94
1994-95
1995-96
1996-97
1997-98
1998-99
1999-2000
2001-02
2001-02
2002-03
2003-04
2005-06
2006-07
No. of SHGs

Fig. 2.1.

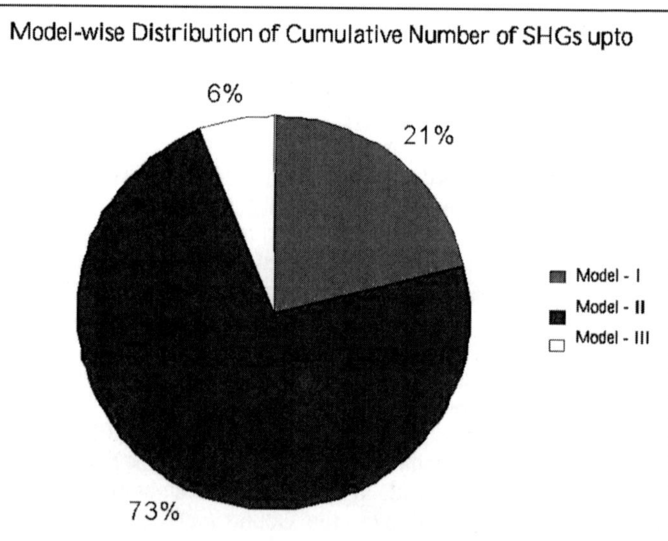

Model-wise Distribution of Cumulative Number of SHGs upto
6%
21%
73%
Model - I
Model - II
Model - III

Fig. 2.2.

Table 2.1. Details of Major Programmes in Tenth Plan Period

(Rs.In crores)

Sl. No	Programmes	On Going Schemes	New Schemes	Total
(A)	**Scheduled Castes:**	433.8	54.6	488.5
1.	Education	5.9	51.75	57.6
2.	Economic Development	364.3	96.45	460.8
3.	Housing and other Schemes	37.1	....	37.1
	Total: Scheduled Tribes:	841.2	202.8	1044.1
(B)	**Scheduled Tribes:**			
1.	Education	28.5	62.9	91.4
2.	Economic Development	0.4	1.8	2.2
3.	Housing and other Schemes	0.0	3.2	3.2
4.	Tribal Sub Plan	50.16	0.0	50.6
5.	Hill Area Development Programme	8.75	0.0	8.75
	Total: Scheduled Tribes	87.8	67.9	155.8
	Grand Total: A and B	929.1	270.8	1200.00

Source: Planning Commission Report on Welfare of SC/ST and other BCs Government of India, New Delhi.

Table 2.2 Consolidated Details of Plan Wise Fund Allocations
(1951-56 to 1997-2002)

Allocation of Tribal Development Sector in Total Budget

Plan	*Years*	*Total Budget*	*Rupees in Crores*	*Percentage*
I Plan	1951-56	1960.00	19.9	1.02
II Plan	1956-61	4600.00	49.9	1.08
III Plan	1961-66	8576.00	50.5	0.6
Annual Plan	1966-69	6756.00	32.3	0.4
IV Plan	1969-74	15902.00	75.0	0.4
V Plan	1974-79	37250.00	1182.0	0.3
Annual Plan	1979-80	12176.00	855.1	7.02
VI Plan	1980-85	97500.00	4193.0	4.3
VII Plan	1985-90	180000.00	6976.7	3.8
VIII Plan	1990-95	314576.43	18311.9	5.8
IX Plan	1997-02	859200.00	775.0	0.09
X Plan	2002-07		1200.00	

Table 2.3. Total Amount of Outstanding Cash Dues (TD), Average Debt (AOD) per Household, Average Value of Assets (AVA), Debt Asset Ratio (DAR), Incidence of Indebtedness (IOI) on 30.6.91 and Sample Size for each Social Group.

48th Round	*Social Group*			
	ST	*SC*	*Others*	*All*
TD (Rs. Crores)	1,077	3,503	17,616	22,211
p.c. share of debt	5	16	79	100
AOD (Rs.)	838	1,394	2,249	1,908
AVA (Rs.)	52,660	49,189	1,34,500	1,07,007
DAR (%)	1.6	2.8	1.7	1.8
IOI (S%)	17.4	25.9	23.6	23.4
No. of sample households	5,217	6,601	24,578	36,425

Note 1 : DAR is derived as follows: DAR = (AOD/AVA) * 100 Note 2 : Note as under table 1.

Table 2.4. Percentage of Households Reporting Cash Dues Outstanding (P) and Percentage Distribution of Outstanding total Debt (S) on 30.6.91 by Credit Agency for each Social Group.

Rural

Credit Agency	*Social Group*							
	ST		*SC*		*Others*		*All*	
	P	*S*	*P*	*S*	*P*	*S*	*P*	*S*
Govt Etc	1.7	7.2	2.5	9.2	1.4	5.5	1.7	6.1
Co-op. Society Bank	3.9	17.0	5.5	15.0	7.6	23.3	6.7	21.6
Commercial Bank including RRB	6.4	37.8	9.1	34.6	7.3	33.3	7.5	33.7
Insurance	0.0	0.0	0.1	0.2	0.1	0.3	0.1	0.3
Provident Fund	0.0	0.0	0.2	1.1	0.3	0.7	0.2	0.7
Other Institutional Agencies	0.3	2.9	0.4	1.0	0.4	1.6	0.4	1.6
All Institutional Agencies	12.0	64.9	17.1	61.1	15.8	64.6	15.6	64.0
Landlord	0.6	3.8	1.9	8.5	0.9	3.1	1.1	4.0
Agriculturist Money Lender	1.6	7.5	3.1	8.0	2.1	6.8	2.3	7.1
Professional Money Lender	1.5	11.0	3.2	10.4	3.3	10.5	3.1	10.5
Traders	0.4	2.2	0.6	2.4	0.7	2.5	0.7	2.5
Doctors, Lawyers etc.	0.0	0.0	0.1	0.3	0.1	0.2	0.1	0.2
Relatives and Friends	1.0	2.3	2.0	3.7	2.6	6.0	2.3	5.5
Others	1.6	7.0	1.2	3.3	1.0	2.6	1.1	3.0
All Noninstitutional Agencies	6.6	33.7	11.2	36.6	9.9	31.8	9.8	32.7
Unspecified Source	1.1	1.3	1.8	2.3	1.9	3.6	1.8	3.3
All Agencies	**17.4**	**100.0**	**25.9**	**100.0**	**23.6**	**100.0**	**23.4**	**100.0**

Note 1 As under Table 1. *Note 2* : As a household may report borrowings from more than one row (here credit agency), the sub-total/total figures in a column need not be the sum of its constituents.

Table 2.5. Percentage of Indebted Households (P) and Percentage Share (S) in Total Amount of Outstanding Debt on 30.6.91 by Type of Security for each Social Group.

Rural

Type of Security	*Social Group*							
	ST		*SC*		*Others*		*All*	
	P	*S*	*P*	*S*	*P*	*S*	*P*	*S*
Personal Security	11.0	55.5	17.7	59.8	14.3	44.6	14.7	47.6
Surely Security etc.	1.6	7.6	2.2	8.6	2.2	8.2	2.2	8.3
Crop	1.1	3.3	0.7	2.0	0.7	2.2	0.7	2.2
First Charge on	1.0	4.7	1.4	4.8	1.8	9.3	1.6	8.3
Immovable Property Mortgage of	2.7	23.7	3.9	18.4	5.1	28.4	4.6	26.6
Immovable Property	0.1	0.1	1.0	1.9	1.0	1.7	0.9	1.6
Bullion/Ornaments								
Share of Companies etc.	0.0	0.0	0.0	0.1	0.1	0.3	0.1	0.2
Agricultural Commodities	0.0	0.1	0.0	0.2	0.1	0.3	0.1	0.3
Other movable Property	0.1	0.4	0.1	0.3	0.2	0.2	0.1	0.2
Other Type of Security	0.6	2.4	1.1	3.3	1.2	4.0	1.1	3.8
Unspecified	1.2	2.3	1.3	0.5	1.1	0.8	1.1	0.8
Total	**17.4**	**100.0**	**25.9**	**100.0**	**23.6**	**100.0**	**23.4**	**100.0**

Note : As under Table 16 for 'P' Columns and as under Table 1 for 'S' Columns

Table – 2.6. Percentage of Indebted Households (P) on 30.6.91 by Purpose for each Social Group

Rural

Purpose	*Social Group*							
	ST		*SC*		*Others*		*All*	
	P	*S*	*P*	*S*	*P*	*S*	*P*	*S*
In Farm Business								
Capital Expenditure	1.7	6.9	1.9	7.0	3.0	13.3	2.6	12.0
Current Expenditure	0.4	1.0	1.0	2.0	1.2	2.9	1.1	2.7
Others	2.3	14.7	2.0	4.8	3.0	10.5	2.7	9.8
In Non-Farm Business								
Capital Expenditure	0.7	2.8	1.2	3.3	1.0	6.4	1.0	2.8
Current Expenditure	0.7	3.7	0.7	2.1	0.6	1.8	0.7	2.0
Others	1.4	7.3	1.4	4.4	1.6	5.1	1.5	5.1
In Household								
Capital Expenditure for Residential Buildings	0.6	7.6	1.7	7.2	1.3	6.3	1.3	6.5
Current Expenditure	0.0	0.0	0.2	0.3	0.2	0.6	0.2	0.5
Others	6.5	27.8	13.4	42.3	11.1	31.5	11.1	33.1
Unspecified	5.7	28.8	7.2	26.6	4.8	21.7	5.4	22.8
Any	**17.4**	**100.0**	**25.9**	**100.0**	**23.6**	**100.0**	**23.4**	**100.0**

Note . As under table 16.

Table 2.7 SHG-Bank Linkage – Highlights March 2001 to March 2006

Sl. No.	Items	March 2001	March 2002	March 2003	March 2004	March 2005	March 2006	March 2007
1.	No of new SHGs provided with bank loan during the year	1,49,050	1,97,653	2,55,882	3,61,731	5,39,365	6,20,109	6,86,408
2.	No of SHGs provided with bank loan (cumulative)	2,63,825	4,61,478	7,17,360	10,79,091	1618456	2238565	2,924,973
3.	% of women's groups	90	90	90	90	90	90	90
4.	No. of participating banks	314	444	505	560	545	545	498
	(i) Commercial Banks	43	44	48	48	47	47	50
	(ii) Regional Rural Banks	177	191	192	196	158	158	96
	(iii) Co-operative Banks	94	209	265	316	340	340	352
5.	No. of States /UTs	27	30	30	31	31	31	31
6.	No. district covered	412	488	502	563	N.A	583	587
7.	No. of NGOs	1,030	2,155	2,800	3,024	N.A	4896	-

(Contd.)

(Contd. Table 2.7)

Sl. No.	Items	March 2001	March 2002	March 2003	March 2004	March 2005	March 2006	March 2007
8.	Bank Loan (cumulative)	4,809	10,263	20,487	39,042	68985	113.98	180.41
9.	Refinance (Cumulative)	4,007	7,965	14,188	21,247	N.A	41.60	54.59
10.	No. of families assisted (in million)	4.5	7.8	11.6	16.7	N.A	32.98	40.95
11.	Average Loan/SHG (Rs)	18,227	22,240	28,559	36,179	N.A	50917	78693
12.	Model - wise linkage (cumulative)							
	(i) SHGs formed and financed by banks	13%	16%	20%	20%	20	20	17
	(ii) SHGs formed by formal agencies and NGOs but directly finance by banks	76%	75%	72%	72%	74	74	75
	(iii) SHGs financed by banks through NGOs	11%	9%	8%	8%	6	6	08

Source: Progress of SHG-Bank Linkage in India 2005-06, MICD, NABARD, New Delhi, 2006.

Table 2.8

States	Model I SHG (Number)	Model II SHG (Number)	Model III SHG (Number)	Model-I SHG Credit (Amount)	Model-II SHG Credit (Amount)	Model-III SHG Credit (Amount)
Haryana	12.5	87.5	0	9.6	90.4	0
Himachal Pradesh	2.5	96.9	0.6	2.6	97.3	0.1
Punjab	12.9	86.6	0.5	12.8	86.4	0.8
Jammu & Kashmir	0.8	99.2	0	0.3	99.7	0
Rajastan	10.2	89.8	0	9	91	0
Assam	79.4	11.9	8.7	89.4	7.3	3.3
Bihar	1.9	97.6	0.5	1.2	98.4	0.4
Orissa	37.1	51.7	11.2	37.7	54.8	7.5
West Bengal	33.5	34.5	7.2	65.4	25.3	9.1
Madhya Pradesh	30.1	68.8	1.1	28.6	70.5	0.9
Uttar Pradesh	17.6	79.7	2.7	15.7	82.8	1.5
Gujarat	6.9	66.9	26.2	7.4	61.1	31.5
Maharashtra	38.1	61.7	0.2	38.0	61.9	0.1
Goa	29.9	70.1	0	32.8	67.2	0
Andhra Pradesh	0.3	98.4	1.3	0.1	98.7	1.2
Karnataka	55.3	32.7	12	62.8	29.4	7.8
Kerala	16.8	51.6	31.6	16.9	54.7	28.4
Tamil Nadu & UTP	4.4	87.8	7.8	4	89.9	6.1

(Contd.)

(Contd. Table 2.8)

States	Model I SHG (Number)	Model II SHG (Number)	Model III SHG (Number)	Model-I SHG Credit (Amount)	Model-II SHG Credit (Amount)	Model-III SHG Credit (Amount)
REGION						
North	8.8	91.1	0.1	7.6	92.3	0.1
North-east	75.8	16.1	8.1	83.2	13.7	3.1
East	32.9	58	9.1	36.5	56.5	7.0
Central	19.6	0	1.9	17.4	81.5	1.1
West	31.7	62.8	5.5	30.7	61.8	7.5
South	12.7	80.2	7.1	9.6	85.3	5.1
All-India	21.0	72.7	6.3	14.3	80.8	4.9

Source: Same as Table- 2.7.

Table 2.9.A SHG-bank linkage – Regional Spread of Physical and Financial Progress as on 31 March 2006

(Rs. Million)

Sl. No	Region/State	No of SHGs provided with bank loan during 2005-06	Cumulative no of SHGs Provided with bank loan upto 31 March 2006	Bank Loan during 2005-06@	Cumulative bank loan upto 31 march 2006@
(A)	**Northern Region**				
1.	Himachal Pradesh	7233	22920	298.95	863.98
2.	Rajasthan	39622	98171	1033.90	2447.94
3.	Haryana	1696	4867	115.38	316.01
4.	Punjab	1740	4561	93.10	238.86
5.	Jammu & Kashmir	967	2354	43.90	100.48
6.	New Delhi	99	224	5.44	18.58
	Total (A)	51387	133097	1590.67	3985.85
(B)	**North Eastern Region**				
7.	Assam	25327	56449	482.17	1423.98
8.	Meghalaya	554	735	8.41	16.19
9.	Tripura	559	1996	12.05	31.12
10.	Sikkim	85	127	0.51	1.66
11.	Manipur	672	1468	41.75	71.85
12.	Arunachal Pradesh	66	346	1.52	13.49
13.	Nagaland	337	422	29.69	34.38
14.	Mizoram	946	974	61.30	64.14
	Total (B)	28546	62517	637.40	1657.01

(Contd.)

(Contd. Table 2.9 A)

Sl.No	Region/State	No of SHGs provided with bank loan during 2005-06	Cumulative no of SHGs Provided with bank loan upto 31 March 2006	Bank Loan during 2005-06@	Cumulative bank loan upto 31 march 2006@
(C) Eastern Region					
15.	Orissa	78468	180896	2236.71	4754.65
16.	Bihar	18816	46221	370.33	1052.19
17.	Jharkhand	9288	30819	399.87	1114.60
18.	West Bengal	60819	136251	1161.75	2424.52
19.	UT of A & N Island	66	164	2.47	8.23
	Total (C)	167457	394351	4171.13	9354.19
(D) Central Region					
20.	Madhya Pradesh	12931	57125	556.09	1666.86
21.	Chhatisgarh	12752	31291	165.86	337.81
22.	Uttar Pradesh	47887	161911	1997.75	5153.54
23.	Uttar Pradesh	4333	17588	315.81	891.86
	Total (D)	77903	267915	3035.51	8050.07

(Contd.)

(Contd. Table 2.9 A)

Sl.No	Region/State	No of SHGs provided with bank loan during 2005-06	Cumulative no of SHGs Provided with bank loan upto 31 March 2006	Bank Loan during 2005-06@	Cumulative bank loan upto 31 march 2006@
(E) Western Region					
24.	Gujarat	11806	34160	558.07	1244.51
25.	Maharashtra	70332	131470	1717.56	3951.67
26.	Goa	284	624	24.99	55.21
	Total (E)	82422	166254	2300.62	5251.39
(F) Southern Region					
27.	Andhra Pradesh	294341	587238	15994.25	43455.18
28.	Karnataka	93618	224928	4426.00	9927.53
29.	Kerala	34957	86988	2325.95	4821.48
30.	Tamil Nadu	131486	312778	10342.87	27121.87
31.	UT of Pondicherry	2494	2499	166.43	350.86
	Total (F)	556896	1214431	33255.50	85676.92
GRAND TOTAL		964611	2238565	44990.83	113975.43

Source: Same as Table- 2.7.

Table – 2.9B SHG-bank Linkage – District-Wise Physical and Financial Progress In Andhra Pradesh

(Rs. Million)

Sl.No.	Name of the District	No. of SHGs provided with bank loan during 01 April 2005 to 31 March 2006	Cumulative No. of SHGs provided with bank loan upto 31 March 2006	Bank Loan disbursed during 01 April 2005 to 31 March 2006@	Cumulative bank loan disbursed upto to 31 March 2006@
1.	Adilabad	2002	19001	322.58	1112.39
2.	Anantapur	4424	23349	579.57	1528.18
3.	Chittoor	4626	30814	1181.99	3117.76
4.	East Godavari	8163	67037	1645.37	5291.14
5.	Guntur	4876	26311	790.82	2286.39
6.	Kadapa	6018	16239	696.65	1476.94
7.	Karimnagar	3955	24894	300.78	1269.39
8.	Khammam	2641	33625	618.00	1683.65
9.	Krishna	5072	27033	830.47	2007.31
10.	Kurnool	2914	24266	687.32	1733.93
11.	Mahbubnagar	3587	27083	448.98	1850.95
12.	Medak	4844	27008	728.04	1775.46

(Contd.)

(Contd. Table 2.9 B)

Sl.No.	Name of the District	No. of SHGs provided with bank loan during 01 April 2005 to 31 March 2006	Cumulative No. of SHGs provided with bank loan upto 31 March 2006	Bank Loan disbursed during 01 April 2005 to 31 March 2006@	Cumulative bank loan disbursed upto to 31 March 2006@
13.	Nalgonda	8829	25334	622.34	1682.46
14.	Nellore	3288	14613	575.41	1273.08
15.	Nizamabad	4872	21244	449.65	1236.00
16.	Prakasam	3356	20888	696.33	1910.61
17.	Rangareddy	1513	14149	597.13	1325.54
18.	Srikakulam	1530	29362	1050.01	2965.40
19.	Visakhapatnam	6413	29319	1048.20	2252.79
20.	Vizianagaram	1515	19056	356.93	1064.86
21.	Warangal	3724	31455	525.97	1770.53
22.	West Godavari	6149	35158	1241.71	2840.42
23.	**Total**	**94311**	**587238**	**15994.25**	**43455.18**

Source: Same as Table- 2.7.

Table 2.10A Agency-wise Distribution of Number of SHGs Financed upto 31 March 2006

Agency	*During the year (2005-06)*			
	SHGs		*Bank Loan*	
	No.	*%*	*Amount*	*%*
Commercial Banks	344,567	55.6	28,284	62..87
Regional Rural Banks	176,178	28.4	12,226	27.17
Cooperatives	99,364	16.0	4,481	9.96

Source: Same as Table- 2.7.

Table 2.10B Agency-wise Distribution of Number of SHGs Cumulative upto 31 March 2006

Agency	*Cumulative upto 31st March 2006*			
	SHGs		*Bank Loan*	
	No.	*%*	*Amount*	*%*
Commercial Banks	1188040	53.07	6987.45	61.31
Regional Rural Banks	740024	33.06	3322.15	29.15
Cooperatives	310501	13..87	1087.95	9.55

Source: Same as Table- 2.7.

References

1. Aiyappan. A (1948): *"Report on the socioeconomic conditions of the Aboriginal tribes of the province of Madras"*, Govt., of Madras.
2. Aloysius P and Fernandez (2007): *"A Microfinance Institution with a Difference"* Economic and Political Weekly, March 31.
3. Bhagat L.N. (1983): *"Factors determining adoption of new Agricultural practices in Tribal Areas – A quantitative Analysis"*, Agricultural situation in India, June.
4. Bhange N.P. (1993): *"Tribal Commissions and Committees in India"*, Himalaya Publishing House, New Delhi.
5. Chandramoli (1969): *"A New deal for Tribals of Andhra Pradesh"*, ST cooperative finance and Development Corporation, Visakhapatnam.
6. Chatopadhya K.P. (1953): *"Tribal Education"*, Man in India, A quarterly Anthropology Journal.
7. Chaudhuri Budhadeb (1992): *"Socioeconomic and Ecological Development"*, Inter India Publication, New Delhi.
8. Devendra Thakur, DN (1995): *"Tribal Development and Planning"* (Tribal Life in India-9), Deep and Deep Publications, New Delhi.
9. Elwin Varrier (1965): *"Bondo Highlander"*, Oxford University Press, Bombay.
10. Fernandez A.P. (1994): *"The Myrad Experience: Alternate Management Systems for Savings and Credit of the Rural Poor"*, Bangalore, MYRADA.
11. Gopala Rao N. (1978): *"Land Alienation – A Menace to Tribal Economy"*, Tribe, Vol. X, No. 4.
12. Government of India (1931): *The Indian Central Banking Enquiry Committee*, Central Publication Branch, Culcutta, pp. 81-84.
13. —————————— (1953): First Five-Year Plan 1951-56, Planning Commission, New Delhi, p. 96.
14. —————————— (1974): Draft Fifth Five Year Plan 1974-79, Planning Commission, New Delhi. pp. 88-89.
15. —————————— (1976): *Report of the National commission on Agricultural*, Ministry of Agriculture and Irrigation, New Delhi.
16. —————————— (1976): *Report of the Expert Committee on Consumption Credit*, Department of Revenue and Banking (Chairman. B. Sivaraman), New Delhi.
17. Haimondorf Furer (1941): *"Seasonal Nomadism and Economics of the Chenchu of Hyderabad"*, Journal of Royal Asiatic Society of Bengal Vol.7.
18. Heredia Rudolfc. *"Tribal Education in India"*, New Frontiers in Education Vol. XXII, No. 9, 1992.
19. Humpi M. and G. Feder (1990): *"The Role of Groups and Credit Co-operatives in Rural Lending"*, The World bank Research Observer, Vol. 5, No. 2, July.

20. Jagannath Pathy (1981): *"Class structure in Rural Orissa"*, Sociological Bulletin, Vol. 30, No. 2.
21. Jayaraman B. (2001): *"Micro-Finance: Retrospect and Prospect"* Occasional Paper-20, NABARD, Mumbai.
22. Jagadish Capor (2001): *Address at the Asia Pacific Region Micro Credit Summit Meeting of Councils* at New Delhi, on February 3.
23. Khan F.H. (1977): *"Consumption Credit: Cooperatives in New Perspective"*, Cooperative News Digest, Vol. 28, p. 92, June.
24. Khandker S.R., B. Khality and Z. Khan (1995): *"Grammeen Bank: Performance and Sustainability"*, World Bank Discussion Paper 306, The World Bank, Washington, D.C., U.S.A.,
25. Khare P.K. *"Social Change of Indian Tribes"*, Deep and Deep Publications, New Delhi.
26. Kotari K.L. (1985): *"Tribal Social Change in India"* Himamsu Publications, Delhi.
27. Mohan Rao K (1993): *"Socio-Cultural Profile of Tribes of Andhra Pradesh"*, Hyderabad.
28. ——————— (1999): *"Tribal Development in Andhra Pradesh – Problems, Performance and Prospects"*, Book lines Corporation, Hyderabad.
29. Mahilingam S. (1989): *"Tribal groups and Market Development in India"*, Journal of Rural Development., NIRD, Hyderabad., Vol.8 (3).
30. Makhan Sha (1982): *"Readings in Tribal Culture"*, Inter – India Publications, New Delhi.
31. Murty DK (1972): *"The tribal situation in South India"*, in Suresh Singh (ED), Tribal situation in India pp.213-27, 1972.
32. Maurya R.D. (1985): *"Education for Tribals in A.P. Problems and Prospects"*, Kurukshetra, Vol. 33, No. 4.
33. NABARD (1995): *Report of the working group on Non-Governmental Organisations and Self-Help Groups*, Mumbai.
34. —————— (2006): *NABARD and Micro Finance 2005-2006*, Mumbai, p.3.
35. National Sample Survey Organisation (1998): *Debt and Investment Survey*, 48 the round.
36. Nayer D. P. "Education for Tribals", Kurukshetra, Vol. 23 No. 4 pp. 35-40, 1974.
37. Obroi R.C., Moorti T.V. and Sharma RK (1989): *"Agricultural Development on Tribal Farms"*, Indian Journal of Regional Science, Vol. XXI, No.2.
38. Prasada Rao DL (1970): *"The Jatapus – A Scheduled Tribe in Andhra Pradesh"*, Unpublished Ph.D. thesis, A.U., Waltair.

39. —————————— (1971-72): *"Shahukars and Tribal Society"*, Tribe Vol. III Nos. 3 & 4.
40. Pratap and Bose (1975): *"A Study of Andhra Pradesh Scheduled Tribes"*, Tribal Cultural Research and Training Institute, Hyderabad.
41. Pradeep Kumar Bose (1981): *"Stratification among Tribals of Gujarat"*, Economic and Political Weekly, Vol. 26, No.6.
42. Raghaviah V.C.T. *"Tribal Revolts"*, Andhra Rashtriya Adimajati Sevak Sangh, Nellore, 1962.
43. Raghava Rao D.V. (1971): *"Marketing of produce and indebtness among Tribals"*, A report on the study of Visakhapatnam District, AER Center, A.U., Waltair.
44. —————————— (1975): *"Konda Dora's – A Study in Socio-Cultural Change"*, unpublished Ph.D. Thesis, A.U., Waltair.
45. Rai B.K. (1979): *"Man and Forest in Chota Nagpur"*, unpublished Ph.D. Thesis, Renchi University.
46. Rajasekhar D. (1994): *"Savings and Credit Systems of Poor as a Strategy of Economic Development: Some N.G.D.O. Experiences in India"*, Bangalore: NOVIB and HIVDS.
47. Ramaiah P. (1981): *"Tribal Economy of India"*, Life and Light publications, New Delhi.
48. —————— (1988): *"The economic problems of Konda Reddies"*, Life and Light Publications, New Delhi.
49. Rama Rao V. (1988): *"Tribal Education and the role of the Teacher"*, Man and Life, Vol.14, No's 1 & 2.
50. Ratniah EV (1977): *"Structural Constraints in Tribal Education"*, Sterling Publishers, New Delhi.
51. Rama Mani V. S. "Tribal Economy-problems and prospects", Ph.D thesis, Andhra University, Waltair, 1988.
52. Reserve Bank of India (1955): *All India Rural Credit Survey 1951-52*, Bombay.
53. —————————— (1960): *Report Regarding the Possibility of Introducing Land and Agricultural Banks into the Madras Presidency (1985)*, (Chairman: Nicholson), Bombay, p.465.
54. —————————— (1992): *'All India Debt and Investment Survey'*, Reserve Bank of India, Mumbai.
55. Satish P (2005) *"Mainstreaming of Indian Micro Finance"*, Economic and Political Weekly, April 23, pp. 1731-1739.
56. Sexena R.P. (1964): *"Tribal Economy in Central India"*, Calcutta, K.L. Mukhopadya.
57. Shah B. (1990): *"Research on Tribal Education"*, Perspectives in Education, Vol. 6, No. 3.

58. Shah Vimal (1967): *"Tribal Economy in Gujarat"*, Paper published in 'Tribal' Vol. IV, No. 2.

59. Sharma BK. (1980): *"Tribal Employment and Linkages"*, ICSSR Research Abstracts, Quarterly, Vol. XX, No. 1 and 2 pp. 73-82.

60. Siva Ramaiah C. (1991): *"Tribal Development Programmes in Adilabad District"*, Inter India publications, Dew Delhi.

61. Srivastava LRN *"Education and Tribal Development"*, Journal of Rural Development, NIRD, Hyderabad.

62. Subba Reddy N. (1977): *"Crisis of confidence among tribal people and the Naxalite Movement in Srikakulam District"*, Human Organization 36.

63. Sujatha K. (1988): *"Tribal Education in India"*, Perspectives in Education, No. 4, Vol. 4.

64. Syam Prasad Rao C.(1993): *"Changing Tribal Scena Prospects and Retrospect- A case study of North Coastal Andhra Pradesh"*, Unpublished Ph.D thesis, Andhra University.

65. United Nations (1986): *"Savings for Development"*: Report on the Third International Symposium on the Mobilisation of Personal Savings in Developing Countries, New York.

66. Varma R.C. (1990): *"Indian Tribes through the Ages"*, Publications Division, Ministry of Information and Broadcasting, Govt. of India.

67. Vidyarhi L.P. (1963): *"The Maler – A case study in nature man–spirit complex of a hill tribe in Bihar"*, Book Land, Calcutta.

68. World Bank (1997): *"Introducing Savings in Micro Credit Institutions: When and How?"* CGAP Focus Note, Consultative Group to Assist the Poorest of the poor, Washington, D.C., U.S.A.

3

Socio-economic Profile of the Study Area and Sample Respondents

3.1. Introduction

A review of the secondary database of Srikakulam District forms the basis of the Study. It can help to assess the level of institutional and infrastructural base and to understand the various infrastructural bottlenecks that seek to restore the institutional and infrastructural balance. In addition, a study of the socioeconomic profile in which the tribal poor live may serve as an indicator of the roles, responsibilities and opportunities in their interface with participation in the development process. The present chapter is organised into two sections. Section – I focussess on the profile of the Srikakulam District and in Section – II, an attempt is made to present a profile of the socioeconomic status of sample respondents in relation to age, family size, occupation pattern, employment, income and assets.

SECTION-I

3.2. District Profile

Srikakulam District is a part of the North Andhra Coastal plain and lies in the extreme northeastern corner of Andhra Pradesh situated within the geographical co-ordinates of 18°20′ and 19°10′ of northern latitude and 83°50′ of eastern longitude. Srikakulam District was carved out in 1950 by bifurcating it from Visakhapatnam District. Again in November

1969 the district lost 63 villages from Saluru Taluk and 44 villages from Bobbili Taluk on account of their transfer to the then newly constituted Gajapathinagaram Taluk of Visakhapatnam District. Again in may 1979 the district had undergone major territorial changes on account of the formation of new district with head guarters at Vizianagaram which involved transfer of Saluru, Bobbili, Parvatipuram and Cheepuruupalli taluks (partly) to the new District. The district is skirted to a distance by Kadivalasagedda, Vamsadhra and Bahuda at certain stretches of their courses, while a line of hights of the great Eastern Ghats run from North East to South West. Vizianagaram District flanks in the south and west, while Orissa bounds it on the north and Bay of Bengal on the East. The district derived its name from Srikakulam which is its headquarters town. (Sources: Glimpses of District, Andhra Pradesh, Srikakulam, Directorate of Economics and Statistics Government of Andhra Pradesh, Hyderabad).

3.2.1. Administrative Features

For administrative convenience, the district is divided into 3 divisions with 38 mandals. There are 1715 revenue villages including 99 un-inhabited villages and gram panchayats. There are 6 towns in Srikakulam district. Out of these, 4 are Municipalities (Srikakulam, Amadalavalasa, Ichapuram and Palasa) and 2 (Sompet and Kasibugga) are notified Panchayats.

3.2.2. Demographic Characteristics

The people inhabiting the district may be classified into two categories namely (1) people of the plains and (2) people of the agency areas. The people of the plains, who are mostly Telugus, generally resemble the Telugu speaking population of the other Northern circars in their customs. Regarding the religious rituals, they are said to follow semi-Brahminical ceremonies. The people of the agency areas are, however, altogether different. Their customs and religious beliefs have remained virtually untouched by outside influences, as they live in isolation.

In the agency tracks, the Savaras constitute for the largest tribe. The origin of the Savaras is traced to the ancient sabaras who had migrated to this part of the country from the lower reaches of the Ganges. The Gazetteer on Visakhapatnam district (1907) records that the Savaras, like the Ghonds, consist of two classes, namely, (i) the primitive race which lives in the hills and (ii) the Kapu Savaras who dwell on the plains. The hill Savaras also known as the jati Savaras, regard themselves as superior to their counterparts on the plains. The villages inhabited by these people are generally I smaller I. The Savaras live on cultivation and hunting, besides collecting minor forest produce.

The total area of the district is 5,837 Sq. Kms. As per 2001 Census the Population of Srikakulam District is 25,37,593 (Table 3.1). The male population is 12,60,020 while the female population is 12,77,573. The decennial growth rate from 1991 to 2001 is 8.93 per cent for the district as against 14.44 per cent of the State, which is significantly lower than the State average. Regarding sex-ratio the district has 1014 females for every 1000 males while the state average is 978 females for 1000 males. Thus the District has the highest sex-ratio in the state. The density of the Population for the district is 438 persons per sq.km. as against the State average of 277. The Scheduled Caste and Scheduled Tribe population of the District is 2,29,609 and 1,51,249 respectively. This forms 9.05 per cent and 5.96 per cent respectively of the total population of the district as per 2001 census. There are 7,31,778 male literates and 4,85,881 female literates. The literacy rate is 67.2 per cent among males and 43.7 percent among the female population of the district (Table 3.2). The workforce participation rate is 47 per cent in the district (Table 3.3 and Figs. 3.1, 3.2). The urban population in the district is 2,78,659 which works out to 10.98 per cent of the total population as against 27.3 per cent of the state (Appendix 3.1).

3.2.3. Rivers

The Nagavali, Vamsadhara, Suvarnamukhi, Vegavathi, Mahendratanaya, Gomukhi Champavathi, Bahuda and Kumbikotagedda are the important rivers of the District. The vamsadhara river rises in the Eastern Ghats of Orissa state and enters Srikakulam district in Bhamini Mandal and finally falls into the Bay of Bengal, near kalingapatnam. The Nagavali and Suvarnamukhi rivers also originate in the Eastern Ghats while Nagavali in Vangara Mandal and the confluence joins the Bay of Bengal at Kallepalli, near Srikakulam. Rising in Pachipenta hills, the Vegavathi river flows from west to east, ultimately joining the river Suvarnamukhi, Gomukhi joins Suvarnamukhi at Siriam Village of Vizianagaram district, Mahendratanaya which is a tributary of the Vamsadhara joins the later at a Komanpally village in Hiramandalam Mandal. Another river of the same eastern Ghats flows through Madasa and Sompeta Mandals and falls into the Bay of Bengal at Baruva. The Bhada river also rises in the Eastern Ghats enters Srikakulam District at Boddabada village of Ichapuram Mandal and flows through Ichapuram, kaviti, mandasa and enters into the Bay of Bengal at Donkuru. The District has a sea coast of 193 kms.

3.2.4. Climate and Rainfall

Throughout the year, the climate is characterized by humidity. The South West monsoon which follows the summer season lasts upto to

September. North-East monsoon starts from 1st October to the end of November. The period from December to mid February is generally a fine weather. As against the normal rainfall of 1162 mm, the annual rainfall is 804 mm during the year 2002-03, with a deficit of 30.8 per cent.

3.2.5. Flora

The forest in the district exhibits a variety of local changes in quality, composition and density. The forests are of varying types greatly differing in nature, intermixed and interrupted by superior or inferior types. This shows much diversity in the representation and combination of the main species. The forests can be broadly classified as follows: The South Indian moist deciduous which includes mixed forests, Sal forests and hilly Savannahs. The South-India dry evergreen miscellaneous forests. The South Indian dry deciduous which includes mixed forests and thorn forests.

3.2.6. Fauna

The land fauna in Srikakulam District is very little. In the past, the district might have been the resort of several wild animals. Human habitation and the indiscremate destruction of forests resulted in the disappearance of the many species. Among the carnivore the tiger is almost extinct, but leopard hyena and wolf are occasionally seen in the forests. The jackal fox, wild cats and dogs are other carnivorous animals found in the district. The herbivorous class is represented by the samber and spotted deer or chital, while wild goat and wild bears are the other common ones. The black buck, the blue bull and the bison are conspicuously absent in these parts. Among the birds, the peafowl, peacock, jungle fowl, pigeon, parrot, myna, partridges, goose, doves etc., is common.

3.2.7. Agriculture

Agriculture is an important occupation of the people in the district. The soil types are mainly Rega or Black Cotton, Red Ferruginious, Alluvial and Sandy loams. The main crops grown in the district are Rice, Groundnut, Sesamum, Cashew nut, Coconut, Chillies and Green Gram. The total geographical area of the district is 584290 hectares of which the arable area is 369175 hectares, which accounts for 63.2 per cent. The Net area irrigated as a percentage of gross area is 76.6 per cent (Tables 3.4, 3.5, Appendix 3.1 and Figs. 3.3, 3.4).

In the district the total number of operational holdings is 484354 for all social groups, inclusive of Institutional, Joint and Individual holdings with 351410 hectares of area operated (Tables 3.6, 3.7, 3.8). The number of holdings and area operated for Scheduled Castes and Scheduled Tribes is 27964 holdings and 13629 hectares and 27618 holdings, 21358 hectares respectively.

3.2.8. Irrigation

The projects and reservoirs cater to the irrigation needs of the farmers. The Gross area irrigated is 1.6 lakh hectares with a net area irrigated of 1.5 lakh hectares (Table 3.9). The irrigation intensity is about 1.06 during the year 2002-03. The Gross Area Irrigated as a per cent to Gross Cropped Area is 45.51 percentage. As per Minor Irrigation Census 2001, there are 36,389 dug wells, 6,720 tube wells, 57 deep tube wells, 7,744 surface flow sources and 33 lift irrigation sources.

3.2.9. Animal Husbandry

The total livestock population of the district is 12,67,064 and the poultry 12,39,621 as per 1999 Census, of which 6,37,109 are cattle, 163853 buffaloes, 2,35182 sheep and 1,45,462 goats (Table 3.10 and Fig. 3.5).

3.2.10. Minerals

The district is endowed with Manganese, Quartz, Lime Kankar and Coloured Granite among major minerals. Among Minor Minerals large quantities of Road metal and sand are found in the district.

3.2.11. Industries

The district is industrially backward. There are 434 factories under organized manufacture sector as per Annual Survey of Industries of Government of India 2000-01 with an input of Rs. 781.16 crores in 2000-2001 with value of output of Rs. 1047.05 crores with net value added of Rs. 234.81 crores and employment generation is 32,88,000 mandays. As per the Economic Census 1997, the total number of enterprises and persons working in these enterprises is 74,834 and 1,64,003 respectively under un-organized sector.

3.2.12. Infrastructure

The distribution of households with source of drinking water indicates 48.2 per cent are with wells, 10.2 per cent with tap water and 36.4 per cent are having hand pumps and tube wells, 4.5 per cent are using rivers, canals as source of drinking, 0.8 are depends on spring and other sources (Table 3.11).

The distribution of households with sanitary facilities available shows that out of that total households 12.6 per cent households only having bathroom facility within the house and 14.2 per cent of households with latrine facility within the house and by type of water outlet is 4.8 per cent in closed drainage 37.8 per cent with open drainage and remaining 57.4 [Plz Join] percent are without drainage (Table 3.12).

The distribution of households by type of fuel used for cooking indicates that 68.4 per cent households are using firewood and 16.5 per cent households are using crop residue, cow dung and coal combined as fuel and 2.0 per cent of households are using Kerosene and 11.9 per cent of households are using LPG as fuel for cooking (Table 3.13).

The distribution of households availing banking services and households having each of the specific assets shows that 22.8 of total households use banking services. The percentage of households having radio is 14.5 per cent 16.0 per cent having TV, 3.3 per cent having Telephone, 20.2 per cent having Bicycle, 3.8 per cent having Scooter/ motor cycle, 0.4 per cent having a car and none of the specified assets is 64.9 percent of the total (Appendix 3.1).

SECTION-II

3.3. Socio-economic Profile of the Sample Respondents

The different features such as age, literacy, family size, caste, members by earning status, occupation, income and expenditure of the sample borrowers are studied to assess the socioeconomic situation of the selected tribal poor households and is presented in this Section. The survey was conducted during the period from 1st April 2007 to 31st May 2007 to study the above aspects. In all, 300 households were selected for the study. While 150 of these households are New Micro Finance Borrowers (NMFB) i.e. membership in SHG is two years from the data of the survey, the remaining 150 households are Old Micro Finance Borrowers (OMFB) i.e. membership in SHG is five years. The reference period for OMFB households is 2001-02 and for NMFB households is 2004-05. These two groups of sample borrowers have been chosen, keeping in view the OMFB borrowers are in a better position compared to the NMFB borrowers. The rationale for selecting Seethampeta Mandalam is that it has the maximum coverage of the SHG programme in the Srikakulam District and also it has one of the highest percentages of tribal poor in the District (Appendix 1.2).

3.3.1. Age Composition

The age of the head of the household may influence his decision-making and productive capacity of the household. If he is too young, he lacks experience in decision-making and if he is very old, he cannot take decision in time and this may influence the production capacity of the household. Data on the age composition of the heads of households and family members are given in tables 3.14A and 3.14B. The age of the Heads and Family members are classified into (a) below 18 (b) 18-39 (c) 40-49 (d) 50-59 (e) 60 and above.

Table 3.14A presents the age wise distribution of the Heads of the households for NMFB and OMFB categories. It can be seen from the table that almost half of the heads of households are in the age group of 18-39 for both the categories. On the other hand, the age composition of the family members (Table 3.14 B) shows that around 30 per cent are in the age group of below 18 and around 35 per cent are in the age group of 18-39 in both the categories.

3.3.2. Family Size

Data relating to the size of the family is given in table 3.15A. It can be seen from the table that the majority of the households in NMFB (48 per cent) and OMFB (63 per cent) is having a family size of 4 & below. This implies that households have an awareness of the two child norm and family planning techniques. We further analyse the average size of the family and is presented in Table 3.15B. In OMFB households, the average size of the family is only 4.05 whereas it is 4.51 in the case of NMFB.

3.3.3. Educational Status

In the present day scenario, education and health are recognised as important components of human resource development. In view of this, Government of India has undertaken a number of measures to promote educational level, especially among the poor. Apart from increasing the enrolment ratio, measures are also taken to check the dropouts. The data relating to the educational status of the heads of households are presented in table 3.16 A. The proportions of illiterate heads are very high among NMFB (75.3 per cent) and OMFB (84 per cent). To have a complete understanding one has to examine the educational status of all the members of the family. Data relating to the educational status of all family members are presented in table 3.16B. It could be observed from the table that the proportion of illiterates is very high in both the categories i.e. 50 percent in NMFB and 60 per cent in OMFB. It implies that micro finance doesn't help much in increasing the educational status of the heads of households as well as other family members in the family.

3.3.4. Caste Composition

Caste can determine the social status of the households to some extent. The data relating to the caste composition of the households is given in table 3.17. It could be seen from the table that more than half of the households in NMFB belong to Jathapu caste and in case of OMFB Savara caste constitute higher proportion i.e. 84 per cent.

3.3.5. Value of Assets

The value of assets will explain the economic status of the households. The assets include all physical assets like land, house, furniture, ornaments, utensils etc. The distribution of sample households according to the total value of assets is presented in table 3.18.

It may be observed from the table that the percentage of households having assets worth below Rs. 25000 is high i.e. around 80 per cent in both the categories. The high percentage of households in the asset group of less than Rs. 25000 is due to lack of empowerment.

3.3.6. Occupational Pattern

The earners in the NMFB and OMFB households are found in a variety of occupations. However, we grouped all the different activities of our sample into seven broad categories and is presented in table 3.19. It may be observed from the table that in NMFB out of 396 earners 67 per cent is doing cultivation, 30 per cent are agricultural labourers. In OMFB households, out of 368 earners 60 per cent are doing cultivation and 36 percent are agricultural labourers.

The age wise distribution of NMFB earners shows that out of 396 earners 60 per cent are in the age group of 18-39, 30 per cent is in the age group of 40-59, followed by other groups. The age wise distribution of OMFB earners shows that out of 368 earners 62 per cent is in the age group of 18-39, 25 per cent are in the age group of 40-59 followed by others. From the above analysis, we can summarize that majority of earners in both categories are engaged in cultivation followed by agricultural labour. The age wise distribution shows that the majority of the earners in both the groups is in the active age group of 18-39.

3.3.7. Income

The increase in employment opportunities will lead to increase in the earnings. Puhazhendhi and Satya Sai. (2000) in their study, found that the average net income/household income increased from Rs. 20177 to Rs. 26889 or by about 33 per cent in pre and post group formation situation. Another study conducted by Puhazhendhi in 2001 in Tamil Nadu covering 70 SHGs and 1041 members, found that net incremental income due to the programme implementation was Rs. 2,424 for all groups and it was relatively more in best performance groups (Rs. 2,697) than in average and poor performance groups (Rs. 1,650 and Rs. 1,299 respectively).

Sebastian Titus in the year 2001, conducted a survey of 340 SHG members, drawn from SHGs functioning under NGOs in Central Tamil Nadu and found that the overall average incremental income for all households who took loans for productive purposes, was Rs. 376.75 per month. More than 60 per cent of the respondents reported a monthly increase in income of above Rs. 300 arising out of income generating activities. Studies on Grameen Bank have, in general shown a positive change in the income of the beneficiaries. However, all these studies use recall method and therefore suffer from memory bias. Further, these studies have not attempted to isolate the income flows from assets acquired through loans. Therefore, comparing the beneficiary income with a control group's income, rather than its own income will be a reliable method. Pallavi Chavan and R. Ramakumar, (2002) in their analysis concluded that both NGO-led micro-credit and state-led credit institutions have led to positive but only marginal increases in the earnings of their beneficiaries. However, given the methodological problems associated with studies on income changes, more empirical evidence is required in order to substantiate such a conclusion.

In general, the income of the households indicates the economic status of the households. In tribal areas, households are engaged in diversified occupations for their livelihood. Therefore, in arriving at the total annual income, income from cultivation, income from agricultural labour etc., are considered. To overcome the problem of recall, the income from agricultural labour for seven days preceding the data of survey, has been taken up as the basis. The annual income from cultivation as declared by sample households has been taken up, as there are no problems of recall in this regard. The details of the distribution of the households by income groups and average annual income and average per capita income by source are presented in Tables 3.20A, 3.20B and 3.20C.

It could be seen from the Table 3.20A and Fig. 3.6 that around 50 per cent of the households are in the income range of below Rs. 20,000 per year indicating that the micro finance has marginal impact on their income levels. The distribution income by source as indicated in Table 3.20B shows that in case of NMFB and OMFB households, income from agricultural labour is major one accounting for around 50 per cent followed by income from cultivation. The per capita income of the households is estimated separately for NMFB and OMFB households and is presented in Table 3.20C. It may be observed from the table that the average per capita income of the OMFB households is relatively higher than that of the NMFB.

3.3.8. Expenditure

An attempt is made to examine the expenditure pattern of the NMFB and OMFB households to understand the consumption levels of the households. The household expenditure is divided into two categories viz., recurring expenditure and non-recurring expenditure. Recurring expenditure is the amount spent on food and non-food items like clothing, housing, fuel, education, etc. nonrecurring expenditure is the amount spent on events like birth, sickness, marriage, death, etc. Data on recurring expenditure was collected on daily, weekly, monthly, and annual basis for different items. To assess the non-recurring expenditure, the amount spent on birth, sickness, marriage, death, etc. during the past three years preceding the reference period, was considered. The annual non-recurring expenditure was arrived at by making an average for the three-year period. Accordingly the total annual expenditure was arrived. The details of distribution of the households according to annual expenditure are presented in Table 3.21A and Fig. 3.7. It could be observed from the Table 3.21A that the percentage of households reporting an annual expenditure of Rs.20,000 and above is around 50 in both NMFB and OMFB households. The average annual amount of recurring and non-recurring expenditure in presented in Table 3.21B. It could be noticed that the per capita recurring and non-recurring expenditure for the OMFB households is greater compared to the NMFB households. This may be due to the OMFB households having access to formal credit institutions for several years.

3.3.9. Income–Expenditure Relationship

Duesenberry and Engle widely discussed the relationship between income and expenditure of the households in the economic literature. In fact, the relationship between income and expenditure on food and non-food items has assumed much more importance in the thinking of many economists. Engle's hypothesis regarding income-consumption relationship (popularly known as Engle's law) is "as income of a family increases, the proportion of its income spent on food falls and that spent on non-food items increases". Against this backdrop of Engle's hypothesis, the income consumption relationship of the sample households is analysed. The consumption pattern over the period indicates that with an increase in the per capita income, there is a decline in the share of food expenditure and vice versa. Details of the pattern of the relationship between expenditure (recurring) and income of the sample households are given in the Table 3.21C and Figs. 3.8A and 3.8B.

All the sample households, category wise, are classified into different income groups and the average per capita expenditure on food and non-food items are estimated. The share of expenditure on food is high for the sample as a whole. There is a decline in the share of food expenditure as the income-size increases indicating an inverse relationship between per capita income and share of food expenditure. This phenomenon is similar for both the NMFB and OMFB households. But the decline is more in the OMFB households compared to the NMFB households. This may be due to the fact that OMFB households are having access to formal institutions for several years.

3.3.10. Earning Status and Dependency Ratio

Earning status of the family members is an important concept that will define the family income of the household. Data regarding the distribution of family members by earning status and dependency ratio is presented in Table 3.22. It could be observed from the table, that more than half of the total members in both the households, are non-earners and among the earners, the percentage of earners in OMFB is higher than that in NMFB households but it is marginal. Among the earners, the children's contribution in the workforce in both the groups is insignificant. Sex–wise the contribution of males is higher than that of females, among both the groups. The non-earners among the school going children constitute a higher percentage in both the groups. From the table, it could also be observed that in both the households there is a higher dependency ratio of 1.06 (OMFB) and 1.05 (NMFB) respectively.

3.4. Summary

The socioeconomic profile of the sample households shows that a majority of the heads of the households is in the age group of 18-39, for both the groups of households. The family size of the households is less than four members of both the groups of households. Regarding literacy levels of the heads of households, the proportion of literates is less in both OMFB and NMFB households. Similar picture was noticed among the family members of both the groups.

The high percentage of households are in the asset range of less than Rs.25000 in the both the households. This shows that there is no impact of micro finance on the sample households. More than half of the total members in both the households are non-earners. Among the earners, the percentage in NMFB is higher than that in OMFB households. The dependency ratio is lower in NMFB households than in the OMFB households but it is marginal. In both the households around 50 per cent are in the income range of below Rs.20000 per year indicating that the micro finance has marginal impact on their income levels. The distribution income by source as indicated in Table 3.20B shows that in case of NMFB and OMFB households, income from agricultural labour is major one accounting for around 50 per cent followed by income from cultivation.

It was observed that the per capita expenditure (Recurring and Nonrecurring) for the OMFB households is greater, compared to the NMFB households. This may be due to the fact that the OMFB households are having access to the formal institutions for several years. In order to observe the income-consumption relationship, the Engle's Law is tested. It was observed that there is a decline in the share of expenditure on food items as income size increases. This decline is so sharp in the OMFB households compared to the NMFB households. This may be due to the fact that the OMFB households are having access to formal institutions for several years.

To sum up, in both the households the performance is not satisfactory in terms of literacy, value of assets, earning status and dependency ratio, occupational pattern, and income-consumption relationship. This may be due to the lack of impact of micro finance among tribals.

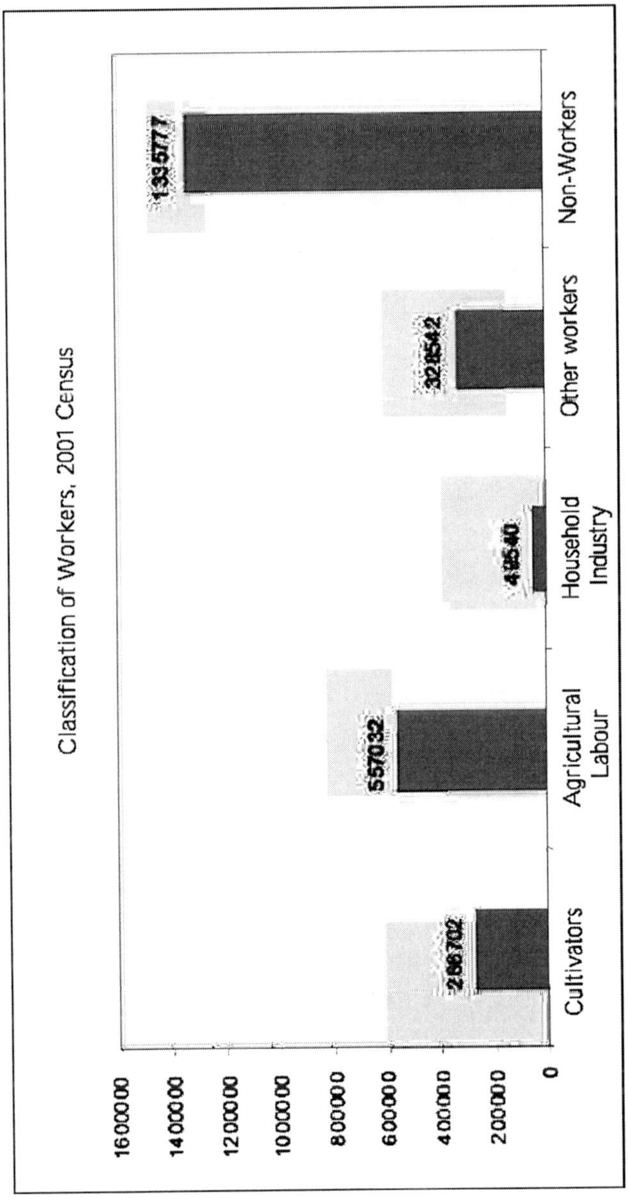
Classification of Workers, 2001 Census
1600000
1400000
1200000
1000000
800000
600000
400000
200000
0
286702
557032
48540
328542
1335777
Cultivators
Agricultural Labour
Household Industry
Other workers
Non-Workers

Fig. 3.1.

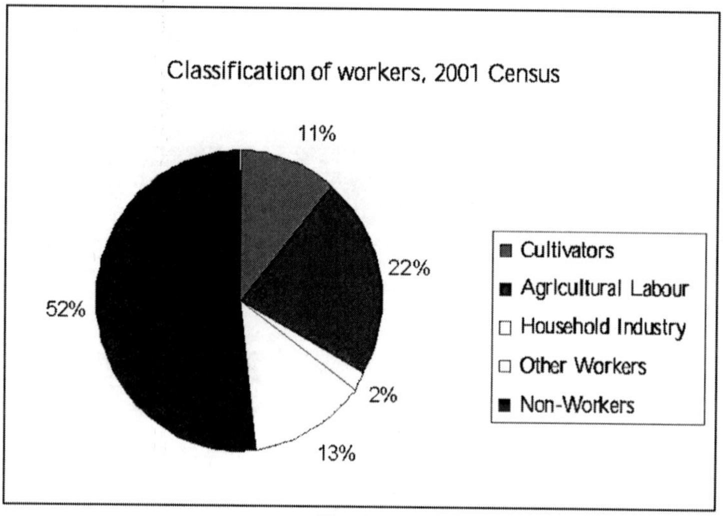
Classification of workers, 2001 Census
11%
22%
2%
13%
52%
Cultivators
Agricultural Labour
Household Industry
Other Workers
Non-Workers

Fig. 3.2.

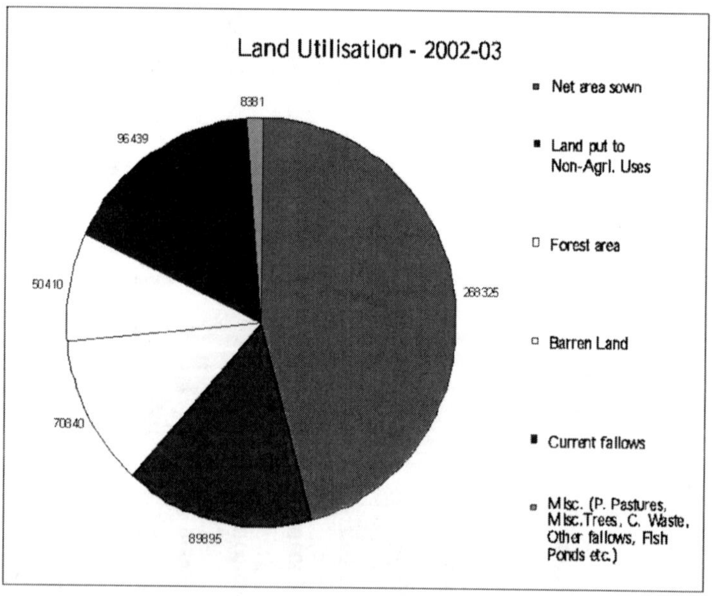
Land Utilisation - 2002-03
8381
96439
50410
268325
70840
89895
Net area sown
Land put to Non-Agrl. Uses
Forest area
Barren Land
Current fallows
Misc. (P. Pastures, Misc.Trees, C. Waste, Other fallows, Fish Ponds etc.)

Fig. 3.3.

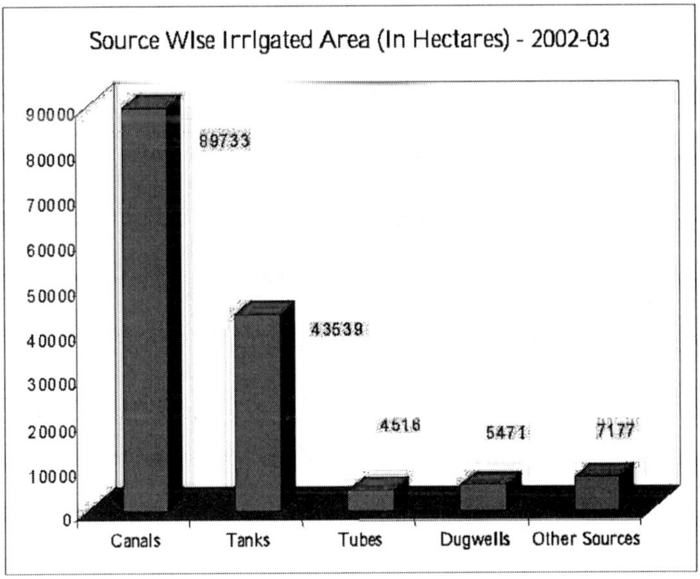
Source WIse Irrigated Area (In Hectares) - 2002-03
90000
80000
70000
60000
50000
40000
30000
20000
10000
0
89733
43539
4516
5471
7177
Canals
Tanks
Tubes
Dugwells
Other Sources

Fig. 3.4.

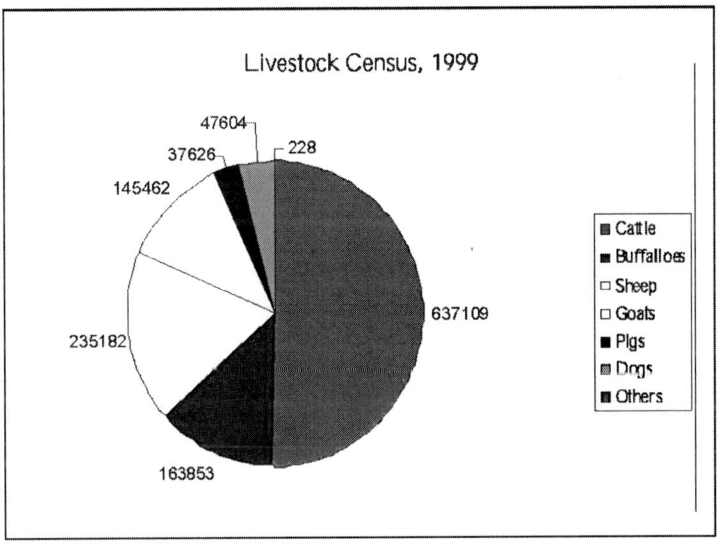
Livestock Census, 1999
47604
228
37626
145462
235182
163853
637109
Cattle
Buffalloes
Sheep
Goats
Pigs
Dogs
Others

Fig. 3.5.

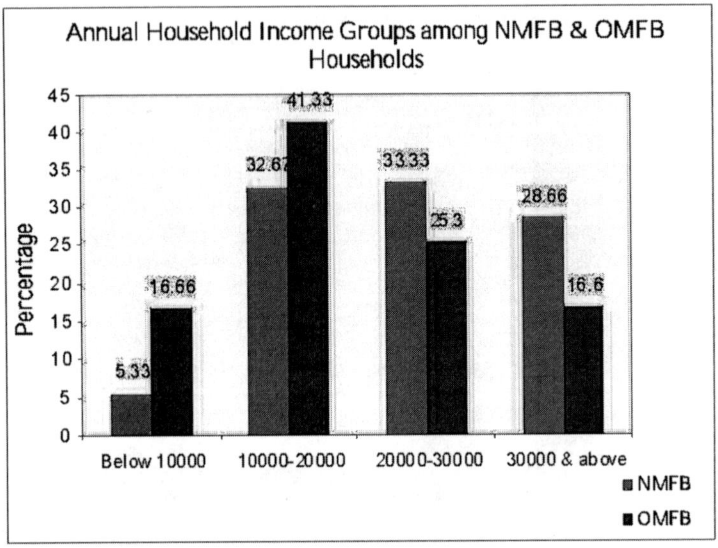
Annual Household Income Groups among NMFB & OMFB Households
Percentage
45
40
35
30
25
20
15
10
5
0
5.33
16.66
32.67
41.33
33.33
25.3
28.66
16.6
Below 10000
10000-20000
20000-30000
30000 & above
NMFB
OMFB

Fig. 3.6.

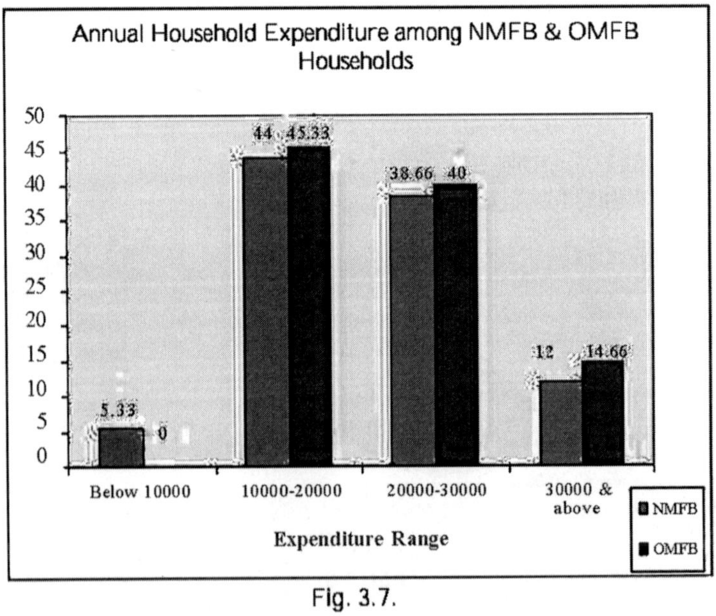
Annual Household Expenditure among NMFB & OMFB Households
50
45
40
35
30
25
20
15
10
5
0
5.33
0
44
45.33
38.66
40
12
14.66
Below 10000
10000-20000
20000-30000
30000 & above
Expenditure Range
NMFB
OMFB

Fig. 3.7.

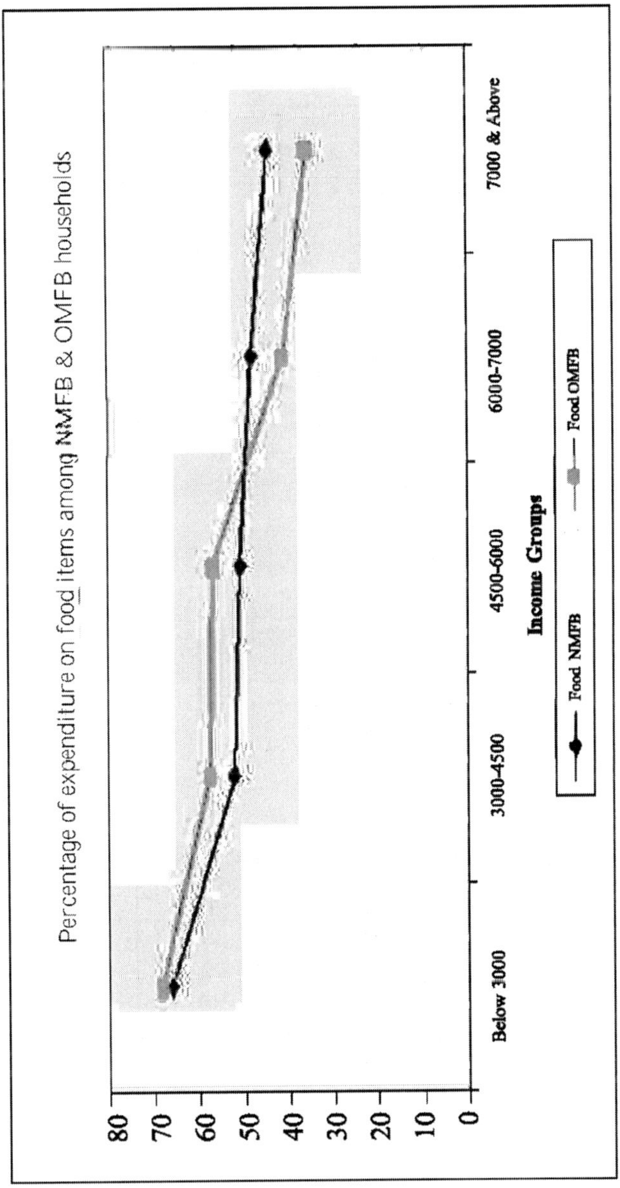
Percentage of expenditure on food items among NMFB & OMFB households
80
70
60
50
40
30
20
10
0
Below 3000
3000-4500
4500-6000
6000-7000
7000 & Above
Income Groups
Food NMFB
Food OMFB

Fig. 3.8A.

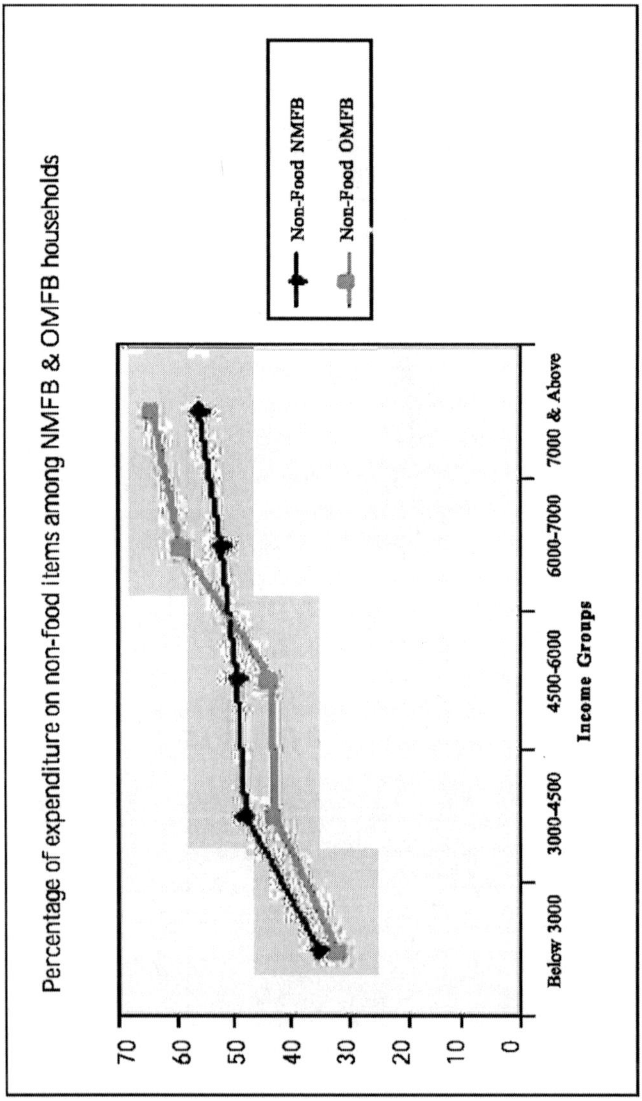
Percentage of expenditure on non-food items among NMFB & OMFB households
70
60
50
40
30
20
10
0
Below 3000
3000-4500
4500-6000
6000-7000
7000 & Above
Income Groups
Non-Food NMFB
Non-Food OMFB

Fig. 3.8B.

Table 3.1. Population Variations in the District – 1901 to 2001

SL No	Year	Population (Persons)	Variation (Increase (+) or Decrease (-)) No. of Persons	Percentage	Density of Population Per Sq.Km.
1	2	3	4	5	6
1.	1901	1071182	-	-	183
2.	1911	1102168	30986	2.89	189
3.	1921	1126549	24381	2.21	193
4.	1931	1222937	96388	8.56	209
5.	1941	1333249	110312	9.02	228
6.	1951	1405904	72655	5.45	241
7.	1961	1555586	149682	10.65	266
8.	1971	1769968	214382	13.78	303
9.	1981*	1959352	189384	10.70	336
10.	1991	2321126	361774	18.46	397
11.	2001	2537593	216467	9.33	435

*Percentage of Growth of Population is decreased due to formation of Srikakulam District.

Table 3.2. Literate Population and Literacy Rates, Census 2001.

	Mandal	*District*
Literacy Rate		
Persons	37.22	55.31
Male	47.49	67.19
Female	26.98	43.68
Literates		
Persons	16502	1217659
Male	10510	731778
Female	5992	485881
0-6 Population		
Persons	7942	336093
Male	3921	170831
Female	4021	165262
Total Population	52282	2537593

Table 3.3. Classification of Workers, Census 2001.

	Mandal	*District*
(Main + Marginal) Workers category		
Cultivators	9649	266702
Agricultural Labour	16853	557032
Household Industry	87	49540
Other Workers	1606	328542
Non-Workers	24087	1335777
Total Marginal Workers	7709	331192
Total Main Workers	20486	870624
Total Workers	28195	1201816
Population	52282	2537593

Table 3.4. Classification of Land Use in the District and State – 2002-03.

(Area in Hectares)

Sl. No.	Category	District	State
1.	Geographical area	584290	27440049
2.	Forest	70840	6199225
3.	Barren and uncultivable land	50410	2083664
4.	Land put to non-agri.use	89895	2588384
5.	Permanent pastures & other grazing lands	930	676062
6.	Misc. Trees, groves not included	2619	277032
7.	Culturable waste	470	700651
8.	Other fallow lands	3941	1678843
9.	Current fallows	96439	3506800
10.	Net area sown for the year	268325	9614539
11.	Fish ponds	421	114849
12.	Area sown more than once	81943	1944090
13.	Total cropped area	350268	11558629

Table 3.5. Area, Yield and Production of Principal Crops in the District-2002-03.

Sl. No.	Name of the Crop	Normal Area (In Hect.)	Area (In Hectares)	Yield (In Kgs/Hect.	Production (In Tonnes)
1.	Rice	192477	153780	1750	269152
2.	Jowar	522	358	385	138
3.	Bajra	3670	3476	1297	4508
4.	Maize	312	900	4278	3846
5.	Ragi	4910	2823	1021	2881
6.	Horse gram	17039	13692	429	5874
7.	Green gram	25246	23120	262	6059
8.	Bengal gram	0	0	0	0
9.	Redgram	1665	1523	350	533
10.	Black gram	33999	28658	300	8591
11.	Chillies	3215	2167	1965	4259
12.	Onions	1166	1262	9173	11577
13.	Turmeric	0	229	5362	1228
14.	Sugarcane*	5169	3149	65815	207251
15.	Cotton (Lint)**	1620	1522	302	2704
16.	Groundnut	41586	33253	764	25404
17.	Seasamum	6444	4515	147	663
18.	Sunflower	81	56	1094	61
19.	Castor	0	0	0	0

* Area coming for harvest has been taken into account.

** Production in bales of 170 kgs. Lint.

Table 3.6. Size Class Wise Number of Operational Holdings and Area Operated in the District and Andhra Pradesh – 2001 (Provisional)

Sl. No.	*Size of Holding*		*No. of Operational Holdings*		*Area Operated (In Hectares)*	
			Srikakulam	*Andhra Pradesh*	*Srikakulam*	*Andhra Pradesh*
1.	Marginal	M	296951	5421904	111941	2415568
		F	84997	1599421	29510	687850
		T*	382107	7023118	141509	3104194
2.	Small	M	58653	2060846	80934	2922998
		F	10834	456551	14756	640752
		T*	69541	2518124	95770	3564785
3.	Semi-Medium	M	22081	1202817	59039	3218548
		F	3568	219895	9477	574412
		T*	25699	1423500	68654	3795193
4.	Medium	M	5646	436903	30857	2492379
		F	823	63036	4473	355455
		T*	6516	501109	35620	2855419
5.	Large	M	375	57306	7357	910271
		F	59	7624	927	123234
		T*	491	66094	9857	1079666
	All sizes	M	383706	9179776	290128	11959764
		F	100281	2346527	59143	2381703
		T*	484354	11531945	351410	14399257

* Total includes Institutional Holdings also.

Table 3.7. Size Class Wise Number of Operational Holdings and Area Operated In the District-Scheduled Tribe-2001.(Provisional)

Sl. No.	Size of Holding (Hect)		No. of Operational holdings				Area operated (in Hectares)			
			Individual	Joint	Instinational	Total	Individual	Joint	Institutional	Total
1.	Below 0.5	M	11091	0	0	11091	2800	0	0	2800
		F	2514	0	0	2514	598	0	0	598
		T	13605	0	0	13605	3398	0	0	3398
2.	0.5 – 1.0	M	6134	0	0	6134	4465	0	0	4465
		F	1193	0	0	1193	873	0	0	873
		T	7327	0	0	7327	5338	0	0	5338
	Marginal	M	17225	0	0	17225	7265	0	0	7265
	(1+2)	F	3707	0	0	3707	1471	0	0	1471
		T	20932	0	0	20932	8736	0	0	8736
3.	1.0 – 2.0	M	4084	1	0	4085	5538	2	0	5540
		F	723	0	0	723	966	0	0	966
		T	4807	1	0	4808	6504	2	0	6506
	Small (3)	M	4084	1	0	4085	5538	2	0	5540
		F	723	0	0	723	966	0	0	966
		T	4807	1	0	4808	6504	2	0	6506
4.	2.0 -3.0	M	1069	0	0	1069	2503	0	0	2503
		F	153	0	0	153	357	0	0	357
		T	1222	0	0	1222	2860	0	0	2860

(Contd.)

(Contd. Table 3.7)

Sl. No.	State of Hoding (Hect)		No. of Operational holdings Individual	Joint	Institutional	Total	Area operated (in Hectares) Individual	Joint	Institutional	Total
5.	3.0 - 4.0	M	305	0	0	305	1039	0	0	1039
		F	38	0	0	38	126	0	0	126
		T	343	0	0	343	1165	0	0	1165
	Semi-Medium	M	1374	0	0	1374	3542	0	0	3542
	(4+5)	F	191	0	0	191	483	0	0	483
		T	1565	0	0	1565	4025	0	0	4025
6.	4.0 - 5.0	M	119	0	0	119	525	0	0	525
		F	11	1	0	12	49	0	0	54
		T	130	1	0	131	574	0	0	579
7.	5.0 - 7.5	M	107	0	0	107	634	0	0	634
		F	19	0	0	19	109	0	0	109
		T	126	0	0	126	743	0	0	743

(Contd.)

(Contd. Table 3.7)

Sl. No.	State of Hoding (Hect)		No. of Operational holdings Individual	Joint	Institutional	Total	Area operated (in Hectares) Individual	Joint	Institutional	Total
8.	7.5 - 10.0	M	26	0	0	26	221	0	0	221
		F	2	0	0	2	19	0	0	19
		T	28	0	0	28	240	0	0	240
	Medium	M	252	0	0	252	1380	0	0	1380
	(6+7+8)	F	32	1	0	33	177	5	0	182
		T	284	1	0	285	1557	5	0	1562
9.	10.0 - 20.0	M	19	0	0	19	233	0	0	233
		F	4	0	0	4	50	0	0	50
		T	23	0	0	23	283	0	0	283
10.	20.0 and	M	5	0	0	5	246	0	0	246
	Above	F	0	0	0	0	0	0	0	0
		T	5	0	0	5	246	0	0	246
	Large (9+10)	M	24	0	0	24	479	0	0	479
		F	4	0	0	4	50	0	0	50
		T	28	0	0	28	529	0	0	529
	All Sizes	M	22959	1	0	22960	18204	2	0	18206
		F	4657	1	0	4658	3147	5	0	3152
		T	27616	2	0	27618	21351	7	0	21358

Table 3.8. Size Class Wise Number of Operational Holdings and Area Operated Scheduled Tribes-2001 (Provisional)

	Mandal	*District*
Marginal (Upto 1.00 Hect.)		
No. of Holdings	6300	20932
Area Operated	2694	8736
Small (1.00-2.00 Hect.)		
No. of Holdings	1778	4808
Area Operated	2446	6506
Semi-Medium(2.00-4.00 Hect.)		
No. of Holdings	792	1565
Area Operated	2033	4025
Medium(4.00-10.00 Hect.)		
No. of Holdings	145	285
Area Operated	790	1562
Large(10.00 Hect & above)		
No. of Holdings	15	28
Area Operated	309	529
All Sizes		
No. of Holdings	9030	27618
Area Operated	8272	21358
Average Size of Area Operated	0.92	0.77

Table 3.9. Source Wise Net Area Irrigated- 2002-03

(Area In Hectares)

	Mandal	*District*
Tube Wells		
Kharif	0	3172
Rabi	0	1344
Total	0	4516
Tanks		
Kharif	101	43462
Rabi	0	77
Total	101	43539
Canals		
Kharif	0	89733
Rabi	0	0
Total	0	89733
Dug Wells		
Kharif	0	1887
Rabi	0	3584
Total	0	5471

Table 3.10. Livestock Population-Census 1999

	Mandal	*District*
Cattle	15683	637109
Buffaloes	3417	163853
Sheep	2123	235182
Goats	6195	145462
Pigs	1870	37626
Dogs	1443	47604
Others	0	228
Total Live Stock	30731	1267064
Poultry	24131	1239621

Table 3.11. Distribution of Households by Sources of Drinking Water Census-2001

	Mandal	*District*
Tap	374	74934
Hand Pump	67	24952
Tube Well	172	42079
Well	155	17308
Tank, Pond, Lake	11047	509011
River, Canal	461	28565
Spring	5069	224257
Any Other	5911	340528
Total No. of Households	11441	593350

Table 3.12. Distribution of Households having Sanitary Facilities-Census-2001

	Mandal	*District*
Number of Households having bathroom facility within the house	374	74934
Type of Latrine within the House		
Pit Latrine	67	24952
Water closet	172	42079
Other Latrine	155	17308
No. Latrine	11047	509011
Type of connectivity for water outlet		
Closed Drainage	461	28565
Open Drainage	5069	224257
No Drainage	5911	340528
Total No. of Households	11441	593350

Table 3.13. Distribution of Households by Availability of Separate Kitchen and A Type of fuel used for Cooking

	Mandal	*District*
Fire Wood	10712	405692
Crop Residue	225	48377
Cow dung cake	0	47906
Coal, Lignite Charcoal	8	1457
Kerosene	64	11844
LPG	414	70528
Electricity	1	244
Bio-gas	9	3775
Any other	1	2241
No Cooking	7	1286
Total No. of Households	11441	593350

Table 3.14.A. Distribution of the Heads of Households by Age Composition

Age in Years	*NMFB*	*OMFB*	*All*
Below 18	0	0	0
18-39	44.6	47.3	46.00
40-49	30.6	30.00	30.33
50-59	20.00	18.00	19.00
60 & above	4.6	4.6	4.66
Total	100.00 (150)	100.00 (150)	100.00 (300)

Table 3.14.B. Distribution of the total Family Members by Age Composition

Age in Years	*NMFB*	*OMFB*	*All*
Below 18	28.8	33.8	31.20
18-39	35.5	34.6	35.0
40-49	17.8	15.95	16.96
50-59	10.9	8.22	9.6
60 and above	6.79	7.23	7.00
Total	100.00 (677)	100.00 (608)	100.00 (1285)

Note: Figures in brackets are the Heads of the Households.

Table 3.15A. Distribution of the Households by Size of the Family

Size of the family	*NMFB*	*OMFB*	*All*
4 and Below	48.00	63.33	55.6
5 – 6	40.00	26.6	33.3
7 and Above	12.00	10.00	11.00
Total	100.00 (150)	100.00 (150)	100.00 (300)

Note: Figures in brackets are Households.

Table 3.15B. Distribution of the Households of Average Family Size

	NMFB	*OMFB*	*All*
No. of Households	150	150	300
No. of Family Members	677	608	1285
Average Family Size	4.51	4.05	4.28

Table 3.16A. Distribution of the Heads of Households by Literacy Level

Literacy Level	*NMFB*	*OMFB*	*All*
Illiterate	75.3	84.00	159.33
Primary	10.6	10.66	21.33
Secondary	11.33	4.66	16.00
Higher Secondary	2.66	0.6	3.33
Total	100.00 (150)	100.00 (150)	100.00 (300)

Note: Figures in brackets are Heads of Households.

Table 3.16.B. Distribution of the Heads of Households by Literacy Level

Literacy Level	*NMFB*	*OMFB*	*All*
I. Illiterate	**49.48**	**60.03**	**54.47**
Male	42.6	43.0	42.85
Female	57.31	52.8	55.00
II. Primary	**30.57**	**29.44**	**30.03**
Male	51.6	46.92	49.48
Female	48.3	53.07	50.51
III. Secondary	**12.70**	**10.85**	**11.82**
Male	58.1	69.6	63.15
Female	41.8	30.3	36.84
IV. Higher Secondary	**6.64**	**2.13**	**4.51**
Male	60.00	61.53	60.34
Female	40.00	38.46	39.65
V. Technical	**0.59**	**0**	**0.31**
Male	50.00	0	0.15
Female	50.00	0	0.15
Total	**100.00**	**100.00**	**100.00**
	(677)	**(608)**	**(1285)**

Note: Figures in brackets are total Family Members.

Table 3.17. Distribution of the Households by Caste

Caste	*NMFB*	*OMFB*	*All*
Jathapu	53.33	16.00	34.6
Savara	46.6	84.00	65.33
Total	**100.00** **(150)**	**100.00** **(150)**	**100.00** **(300)**

Note. Figures in brackets are Households

Table 3.18. Distribution of the Households by Value of Assets

Value of in Rupees	*NMFB*	*OMFB*	*All*
Less than 25000	77.33	89.3	83.3
25000-50000	9.33	2.00	5.6
50000-100000	4.00	7.3	5.6
100000-150000	4.6	0.00	2.3
More than 150000	4.6	1.3	2.9
Total	**100.00** **(150)**	**100.00** **(150)**	**100.00** **(300)**

Note: Figures in brackets are Households.

Table 3.19. Distribution of Workers by Main Occupation and Age

Occupation	*NMFB*					*OMFB*				
	Age Group					*Age Group*				
	Below 18	*18-39*	*40-59*	*60 & Above*	*All*	*Below 18*	*18-39*	*40-59*	*60 & Above*	*All*
Cultivation	4.01	42.17	18.68	3.38	**67.17**	3.26	38.04	17.11	1.90	**60.32**
Agricultural Labour	2.27	16.16	9.84	1.51	**29.79**	2.44	22.82	7.88	2.98	**36.14**
Construction Labour	0	0.25	0.50	0	**0.75**	0	0.50	0	0	**0.54**
Livestock and Allied Activities	0	0.25	0	0.25	**0.50**	0	0	0	0.50	**0.54**
Petty Trade	0	0.50	0.50	0	**1.01**	0	0.50	0	0	**0.54**
Household Industry	0	0	0	0	**0**	0	0.50	0	0	**0.54**
Salaried people	0	0.25	0.25	0.25	**0.75**	0	0.75	0.50	0	**1.35**
Total	**6.31**	**59.59**	**29.79**	**4.29**	**100.00 (396)**	5.70	**62.5**	**25.54**	**5.43**	**100.00 (368)**

Note: Figures in brackets are Workers.

Table 3.20 A. Distribution of the Households by Annual Household Income Groups

Amount In Rupees	*NMFB*	*OMFB*	*All*
Below 10000	5.33	16.66	11.00
10000-20000	32.67	41.33	45.66
20000-30000	33.33	25.3	26.00
30000- and above	28.66	16.6	17.33
Total	100.00 (150)	100.00 (150)	100.00 (300)

Note: Figures in brackets are Households.

Table 3.20 B. Average Annual Household Income of the Sample Households by Source

Source of Income	*NMFB*	*OMFB*
Cultivation	45.88	33.23
Agricultural labour	51.41	52.75
Livestock and Allied activities	2.20	0
Trade and commerce	0.26	0.16
Household Industry	0	0.13
Salary	0.22	7.25
Others	0	0
Total	100.00 (16597)	100.00 (15012)

Note: Figures In brackets are Household Income.

Table 3.20 C. Average Per Capita Income by Source

(In Rupees)

Source of Income	*NMFB*	*OMFB*
Cultivator	46.16	33.23
Agricultural labour	51.48	52.75
Livestock and allied activities	2.21	6.44
Trade and commerce	0.13	0.16
Household Industry	0	0.13
Salaried people	0	7.2
Others	0	0
Total	100.00 (9567)	100.00 (9758)

Note: In New SHGs total Workers are 396 and in Old SHGs total Workers are 368 Figures in brackets are Per Capita Income.

Table 3.21 A. Distribution of the Households by Annual Household Expenditure

Amount in Rupees	*NMFB*	*OMFB*	*ALL*
Below 10000	5.33	0.00	2.66
10000-20000	44.00	45.33	4.66
20000-30000	38.66	40.00	39.33
30000 and above	12.00	14.66	13.33
Total	100.00 (150)	100.00 (150)	100.00 (300)

Note: Figures in brackets are Households.

Table 3.21 B. Average Annual Recurring and Nonrecurring Expenditure

(In Rupees)

Nature of Expenditure	*Groups of Households* *NMFB*	*OMFB*
Recurring	68.34	73.12
Nonrecurring	31.65	26.87
Total	100.00 (41645)	100.00 (51345)
Per Capita Expenditure	10266	11055

Note: Figures in brackets are Expenditure.

Table 3.21 C. Percentage Distribution of Annual Per Capita (recurring) Expenditure on Food and Non-Food Items

Per Capita Income Groups	*Groups of Households*			
	NMFB		*OMFB*	
	Food	*Non-food*	*Food*	*Non-food*
Below 3000	66.00	34.99	68.06	31.93
3000-4500	52.06	47.93	57.22	42.71
4500-6000	50.74	49.25	56.43	43.56
6000-7000	47.93	52.06	41.07	58.92
7000 and Above	44.41	55.58	35.18	63.81
Total	53.14	46.85	57.75	42.24

Table 3.22. Distribution of the Family Members by Earning Status

Groups of House-holds	*Earner/Workers*				*Non-Earner/Non-Workers*				*All*	*Dependency Ratio*
	Male	*Female*	*Children*	*All*	*Male*	*Female*	*Children*	*All*		
(I) NMFB	24.07	14.62	9.89	48.59	29.83	12.99	8.56	51.40	**100.00 (677)**	**1.05**
(II) OMFB	27.30	11.18	10.03	48.51	30.09	12.33	9.04	51.48	**100.00 (608)**	**1.06**

Note. Figures in brackets are Family Members.

References

1. Puhazhendhi V and KJS Satyasai (2000): *"Micro Credit for the Rural People: An Impact Evoultion"*, Study Report, National Bank for Agriculture and Rural Development, Mumbai.
2. Puhazhendi V (2000): *"Evaluation study of Self-Help Groups in Tamil Nadu"* National Bank for Agricultural and Rural Development, Mumbai.
3. Sebastoam Titus A.P. (2001): *"Impact of Micro Credit Programmes of NGOs on Rural Women"*, IASSI Quarterly Vol. 20, No.2, pp.136.
4. Pallavi Chavan and R. Ramakumar (2002): *"Micro credit and Rural Poverty – An Analysis of Empirical Evidence"* Economic and Political Weekly, March 9. pp. 958.

4

Factors Determining Borrowing and Indebtedness

4.1. Introduction

In this Chapter, an attempt has been made to study the structure of borrowings among the tribal poor households. In order to enhance their participation in micro credit programmes and to make appropriate changes in the policies, one has to analyse the structure of their borrowings and their participation in different sources of credit. This Chapter has been divided into four sections. Section-I present the theory of Asymmetric Information. In Section-II the structure of borrowings of sample respondents in relation to purpose of borrowing, borrowings by agency, borrowings by rate of interest and borrowings by type of security offered among NMFB and OMFB households is analysed. In Section-III, by applying the qualitative response models, an empirical analysis was carried out to find out the determinants of participation of the individuals in borrowings. Finally, in Section-IV, the factors influencing the access to different sources of credit are examined. As done in the previous chapter, a comparative analysis between NMFB and OMFB households is carried out to identify the specific factors that influence the success of micro credit programmes in reaching the poor.

SECTION – I

4.2. Theory of Asymmetric Information

The theory of asymmetric information states that informal sector lending thrives due to the advantage it has over formal sector regarding the sources of information, about its prospective clients and the credit worthiness of clients. An attempt to explain the puzzle of rural poor borrowing at very high rates of interest from the local moneylender rather than from the local bank at a much lower interest rate, led to the emergence of the theory of asymmetric information (Hoff Karla and Joseph E. Stiglitz, 1990). As pointed out by Stiglitz and Weiss, due to asymmetric information, the targeted loans may fail to reach target households (Stiglitz – Joseph E. and Anren Wesis, 1973, 1981). Therefore, financial institutions may need to address "the concern of imperfect information to reach the rural poor" (Hoff Karla and Joseph E. Stiglitz, 1990). Financing through groups can be used by the formal credit market to overcome its informational disadvantage to lend successfully to the poor borrowers (Madheswaran and Amita Dharmadhikary, 2001).

Many micro credit programmes rely on group based lending to resolve the problem of imperfect information. Using a group-based approach to lending, the country's small-scale micro credit programmes provide more credit than the traditional financial institutions in rural areas (World Bank, 1996). A group based lending may help to identify target households better than individual lending. Individual lending can "perpetuate and reinforce the existing socioeconomic inequities and access to scarce financial resources" (Yaron Jacob, 1992). In contrast, group lending can help the poor self-select programs, making it a powerful instrument of identification and targeting (Khandker Shahidur, et.al., 1995). In the available literature, it is well documented that many micro credit programs have attained the out reach objective of reaching a large number of clients with small amounts of resources (Hussain,1988., Dersing Market, 1990., Bernett Lynn, et.al 1996., Hulme David, et.al., 1996).

Government-directed financial institutions have been developed in order to provide the poor with access to credit. One of the examples for this is SHG-Bank Linkage Programmer sponsored by the NABARD. What factors are crucial in order to provide the poor with access to credit from formal sources, are well discussed from the angle of the rationing mechanism (Manfred Zeller, 1994). The most important factor is the physical collateral such as land, which will be considered by the formal lender assessing the borrowers' credit worthiness. In other words, the demand for physical collateral, limits the access of the rural poor like landless farmers, wage laborers, small holders and small-scale rural entrepreneurs to formal sources of credit. On the other hand, informal lenders substitute third-party guarantees, tied contracts, usufructuary rights etc for physical collateral. The rural poor due to their social contacts provide these substitutes which reflect easy access towards informal sources. These collateral substitutes depend on the ability of the lender to obtain information about the creditworthiness of the borrower at a lower cost.

The recent innovative policy of group lending by the formal sources has taken into consideration the joint liability in place of physical collateral. Hence, the disadvantage of the poor i.e., lack of physical assets, has been overcome by the group lending. Now, the interesting aspect is, Which factors influence the group members' access to the group loan? Can the micro credit be an alternative to informal credit in rural and urban areas? The access of the poor is limited by the mismatch between the demand and supply of credit structures. The poor generally demand credit in small amounts for un-productive purposes such as consumption, health, education, marriages, petty production, petty trade, etc. This does not match with the supply menu of banks, which consists of large amounts of loan for productive purposes. It is not the rigidity of the banks but their constraints due to high transaction costs and risk on account of asymmetric information that they cannot extend such credit to individual borrowers. Individual borrowers on the other hand, face the problems of absorbing large amounts of credit for some unwanted purpose.

Loan contract therefore does not take place between an individual small borrower and a formal lender basically because of a mismatch between demand and supply of credit structure. Through group lending, this mismatch between demand and supply is reduced because the bank extends credit in lump sum amounts and the group uses the amount according to its own needs (Rajaram Dasgupta, 2001). Hence the questions are (i) what factors will influence the access of tribal poor for formal credit through groups? (ii) Can micro credit supplement the formal credit in meeting the credit needs of poor? And (iii) whether micro credit increased access to institutional credit, thereby reducing borrowing from informal sources?. In the succeeding sections an attempt is made to answer the above questions by a comparative analysis between formal, informal and micro credit.

SECTION –II

4.3. Structure of Borrowings of the Sample Respondents

An attempt is made in this section to examine the borrowings of the sample households with reference to the purpose of borrowing, borrowings by the agency, the interest rates at which loans are borrowed and the nature of security offered, etc. In studying the above aspects the sample households are divided into two groups, those whose membership in SHG is two years from the data of the survey and those whose membership in SHG is five years. For the sake of convenience, whose membership in SHG is two years are termed as 'NMFB' and borrowers whose membership in SHG is five years are termed as 'OMFB'. The major objective behind this classification is to assess whether OMFB is in a better position than NMFB in reducing dependency of the tribal poor households on informal credit agencies.

4.3.1. Distribution of Households by Levels of Deficit

After arriving at the deficit of income over expenditure, one can estimate the burden of debt of the households. Generally, in poor families the income and expenditure gap is a time-lagged phenomena. Past expenditures and /or liabilities are met with the surplus of the present income. The borrowings will act as a bridge to meet this time-lagged gap between income and expenditure. As it is the deficit of income over expenditure that largely reflects the need to borrow by the poor households, the distribution of borrowers by level of deficit have been worked out both for NMFB and OMFB. The details are shown in Table 4.1 and Fig. 4.1. It could be observed from the table that the percentage of households without any the deficit is only 20 per cent among NMFB and OMFB households and it is 30 per cent among OMFB and 10 per centt among NMFB. Further, the proportion of households in the higher deficit range is more among NMFB and OMFB households.

4.3.2. Extent of Indebtedness

The data relating to borrowings of the sample households during the past three years were collected from different sources and are presented in Table 4.2. From the table 4.2 it can be observed that the average amount of credit per household was reported at Rs. 15584 for the OMFB households and Rs. 9347 for the NMFB households. In both the households more than half of the credit was from micro credit institutions. The maximum credit from micro credit institutions in OMFB households, i.e. around 70 per cent may be due to households positive response to micro finance. The SHG Bank Linkage Programme will be a good supplement to the existing former credit services, which could do much to improve the welfare of the tribal poor.

4.3.3. Distribution of Borrowings by Agency

The relative share of micro credit, formal and informal credit in the borrowings of tribal households, has been examined and the details are shown in Table 4.3. In both the households among micro credit, commercial banks have provided the entire credit, i.e. 100 per cent. Among the formal credit, regional rural banks have provided the highest percentage of the borrowings, i.e. 53 per cent of NMFB households and 63 per cent in OMFB households. Among informal sources of credit money lenders have provided the highest percentage of the borrowings i.e. 70 per cent of NMFB households and 54 per cent in OMFB households followed by friends and relatives, i.e. 20 per cent of NMFB households and around 40 per cent of OMFB households.

4.3.4. Distribution of Borrowing by Purpose

A deficit of income over expenditure reflects the need to borrow by poorer households. For this purpose, borrowings for existing outstanding loans are only considered to overcome the problem of recall. Borrowings from different sources of credit are examined to bring in sharply the differences in the relative share of various purposes in the total borrowings and are shown in Table 4.4. An analysis of borrowings from micro credit agencies shows that more than 70 per cent of the borrowings by both NMFB and OMFB households are for productive purposes. An analysis of borrowing from formal credit sources shows that around 60 per cent of total borrowings by both the households are for productive purposes. An analysis of borrowing from informal credit agencies shows that more the 50 per cent of total borrowings by the both the households are for unproductive purpose. Borrowings for productive purposes are higher among micro credit and formal credit sources compared to informal credit sources in both the households.

4.3.5. Distribution of Borrowings by Rate of Interest

The emergence of micro credit to the poor, should have reduced the interest burden on NMFB and OMFB households. In both the households, the credit borrowed from micro credit sources is in the interest range of less than 12 percent and 12-24 per cent and the credit borrowed from informal credit sources is in the highest interest range of 36 per cent and above (Table 4.5).

4.3.6. Distribution of Borrowings by Security

Information has been collected on borrowings by security and is presented in Table 4.6. It could be observed from the table that group security is the means for getting micro credit and pledge of land and house are the important means for getting formal credit. For getting informal credit, promissory note, borrowed previously and known since fathers' time plays a major role in both the households.

To sum up, through micro credit intervention, the formal credit can reach the poor for their betterment. The NMFB and OMFB households still depend upon the informal source of credit for productive activities, which reflects the inadequacy of micro finance. In case of micro finance, the personal security took another form as group security and the poor are getting benefit from micro finance by monitoring one another and getting loans at lower rates of interest.

SECTION -III

4.4. Determinants of Participation in Borrowings

In order to enhance borrowers' participation in micro credit programme, at the first stage it will be useful to examine the following two questions: (1) who are the individuals really participating in borrowing? And (2) What are the factors that determine their participation in borrowing? In this section, an attempt has been made to answer the above two questions by an empirical study. The data based on the survey of 300 households regarding their borrowings during the past three years from different sources is used for the analysis. The borrowings made by every member (if he/she has borrowed) of the household are recorded by their name separately. The assets held by the individual members and the individual's earnings were recorded separately. In the analysis, the unit of study is the individual member of the household (members aged 18 years and above). The rationale behind considering the individual member, as a unit of study, is firstly, the total borrowings of the households are nothing but sum of the borrowings made by the individual members. Secondly, the individual characteristics as well as household characteristics influence the access to credit. The participation of the individuals in borrowing is analysed with help of Probit model (Qualitative Response Model).

4.4.1. Qualitative Response Model

In regression models, the dependent variable or the regressend is a quantitative variable. In case where the regressend is qualitative in nature, such as a 'yes or no' type, the conventional regression methods are inappropriate to apply. The models which deal with such type of response variables, which take only two values, i.e., the regressend is a binary or dichotomous variable, are known as Qualitative Response (QR) models. These models are widely used in various areas of social sciences and medical research.

In regression models, we estimate the expected value of the regressend given the values of the regressors. In qualitative response models we find the probability of the happening of the same event. Hence, qualitative response models are often known as probability models. There are three approaches to develop a probability model for a binary response variable.

1. The Linear Probability Model (LPM)
2. The Logit Model
3. The Probit Model

4.4.2. The Linear Probability Model (LPM)

If we consider the following regression model

$$Y_i = \beta_0 + \beta_1 x_i + u_i \quad \ldots (4.1)$$

Model 4.1 looks like a typical linear regression model, but because the regressend is binary or dichotomous, it is called a linear probability model.

$E(Y_i/x_i)$ gives the probability of occurrence of an event. Therefore the model is as follows

$$E(Y_i/x_i) = \beta_0 + \beta_1 x_i \quad \ldots (4.2)$$

Suppose if P_i = **Probability that Y-i** = 1 (i.e., the event occurs),

$$P_i = E(Y=1/x_i) = \mathbf{F(x, \beta)} = \beta_0 + \beta_0 + \beta_1 x_i \quad \ldots (4.3)$$

Then 1-P_i = Probability that Y_i = 0 (i.e., that the event does not occur)

$$(1-P_i) = \text{Prob}(y=0) = 1-F(x, \beta) \quad \ldots (4.4)$$

Where the set of parameters β reflects the impact of changes in x on the probability of occurrence of an event.

The major problems associated with the LPM to mention are the:

(i) Non-fulfillment of $0 < E(Y_i / x_i) < 0$

(ii) Assumption of $P_i = E(Y=1/x_i)$ increases linearly with x, that is, the marginal or the incremental effect of x remains constant throughout.

Therefore, later on the probability models, which are developed to resolve these two problems, used the Cumulative Distribution Function (CDF) approach. There are two types of CDFs commonly used for 0-1 response models. They are the logistic and the normal, the former giving rise to Logit Model and the latter to the Probit Model.

4.4.3. The Logit Model

In the Logit Model

$$P_i = E(y=1/x_i) = \frac{1}{1+e^{-(\beta_0+\beta_1 x_0)}} \quad \ldots (4.5)$$

Where 'e' is the familiar base of the natural logarithm in other way

$$P_i = 1/1 + e^{x_i} \quad \ldots (4.6)$$

Where $Z_i = \beta_0 + \beta_{i\,xi}$

This equation 4.6 represents what is known as the logistic distribution function P_i represents the probability of occurrence of an event, 1-P_i represents the probability of non-occurrence of an event.

$$1\text{-}P_i = \frac{1}{1+e^{Z_i}}$$

$$\frac{P_i}{1\text{-}P_i} = e^{Z_i} \qquad \because (1+e^{z}_{i} / 1+e^{-z}_{i})$$

Where $\frac{P_i}{1\text{-}P_i}$ Is the odds ratio

Taking natural log on both the sides

$\ln(P_i / 1\text{-}P_i) = \ln(e^{Z_i}) = \beta_0 + \beta_i x_i$
$L_i = \beta_0 + \beta_i x_i$

i.e., L, the log of the odds ratio is called the Logit*

4.4.4. The Probit Model

The estimating model that emerges from the normal CDF is popularly known as the Probit Model. Given the assumption of normality.

$$Pi = Prob(y=1) = \frac{1}{\sqrt{2\pi}} \int_{-\infty}^{\beta_0 + \beta_i x_i} e^{-t^{2/2}} dt$$

Where t is a standardized normal variable i.e., $t \sim N(0,1)$.

Since P_i represents the probability than an event will occur, it is measured by the area of the standard normal curve from $-\infty$ to Z_i where $Z_i = \beta_0 + \beta_i x_i$

The chief difference between logistic and normal distribution lies in the trails. The logistic distribution has slightly fatter tails. This is to say that the conditional probability P_i approaches to zero or one at a slower rate in Logit Model than in Probit

Model (Damodar N. Gujarati, 2000). The logistic distribution is very similar to the t- distribution with seven degrees of freedom, while the normal distribution is a t- distribution with infinite degrees of freedom (Eric Hanushek and John Jackson, 1997).

* Note: In LPM $y_i = \beta_0 + \beta_i x_i$ ———— where y_i are known values. In Logit Model L_i $\beta_0 + \beta_i x_i$ where the values of L_i should be calculated. $L_i = \ln(1/0)$ where y=1 and $L_i = \ln(0/1)$ where y=0; Therefore, in estimating $L_i = \beta_0 + \beta_i x_i$ were cannot use OLS (Ordinary Least Squares) and we should use Maximum Likelihood Method.

The question of which distribution to use is unresolved, because it is difficult to justify the choice of one distribution or another on theoretical grounds. In most applications it seems not to make much difference (William H. Greene, 2000). Therefore, the choice between the two is one of convenience and ready availability of computer programs or statistical techniques.

4.4.5. The Marginal Effect

In the LPM, the slope coefficient measures directly the change in the probability of an event occurring as a result of a unit change in the value of a regressor, with the effect of all other variables held constant.

In the Logit Model the slope coefficient of a variable gives the change in the log of the odds associated with a unit change in that variable, again holding all other variables constant. In this Model the rate of change in the probability of an event happening is given by $B_j P_i (1-P_i)$, where B_j is the (partial regression) coefficient of the Jth regressor. In evaluating P_i, all the variables included in the analysis are involved. In the Probit Model, the rate of change in the probability is given by $B_i f(Z_i)$, where $f(Z_i)$ is the density function of the standard normal variable and

$$Z_i = \beta_0 + \beta_1 x_1 + \beta_2 x_2 + \text{———————} + \beta_i x_i$$

Thus, in both the Logit and Probit Models all the regressors are used in computing the changes in probability. In interpreting the estimated model, it will be useful to calculate the marginal effects or slopes at the means of the regressors (William H. Greene, 2000).

4.4.6. Specification of the Model and Variables

Based on the theoretical background, an attempt is made here to assess the factors affecting the individual participation in borrowing by applying the Probit Model. The participation in borrowing, which is measured by the probability of an event that an individual borrows, can be explained by a set of explanatory variables. The variables such as age, education, sex, working status, earnings, events of food expenditure, non- food expenditure, having a responsible position in the house as well as in the society, which determine the participation in borrowing of an individual. The following equation is used for estimating the probability of participation in borrowing.

Prob (BORROW) = F (IC, HC)

Where Prob (BORROW) is the probability of an individual borrowing and IC is a vector of Individual Characteristics and HC is a vector of Household Characteristics.

Individual Characteristics

SEX = Sex of the Individual

AGE= Age of the individual (18 years of age and above)

REL=Dummy variable, whether the individual is relationship of the head of Household

EDU= Number of Years of Education of Individual

WP =Dummy variable, whether the individual is working participation.

IINC=Annual Earnings of the individual

Household Characteristics

FINC=Annual family income of the household

FEXP=Annual food expenditure of household

NPEXP =Annual non-food expenditure of household

The individual borrowing, BORROW is a dichotomous dependent variable, which takes values either 0 or 1, 1 for those who borrow, 0 for those who do not borrow.

SEX, males are expected to have more responsibility than the females, the variable takes the value 1 for male and 0 for female.

AGE, age of the individual is expected to have a negative relation. The hypothesis is, younger individuals are more likely to borrow since they have a capacity to repay.

REL, is a dummy variable, and takes the value 1 for the relationship of the head of the household 0 for other household members. It is expected to have a positive relation because head has more responsibility in the family.

EDU, years of schooling is expected to have a negative relation.

WP, is a dummy variable and specifies the working status of the individual. It takes the value 1 for workers and 0 for non-workers. It is expected to have a positive relation since workers are expected to participate in borrowings as they have higher repayment capacity.

IINC, which represents individual earnings of the member is expected to have a negative relation with the probability to borrow because the increase in earrings decreases the need to borrow.

FINC, the annual income of the household family is expected to have a negative relation with the probability to borrow. As the household income increases, the need for raising credit decreases.

FEXP, represents the expenditure on food items of the households that are expected to have a negative effect on NMFB households and positive effect on the OMFB households. The identified incident of more food expenditure leads to less borrowing capacity in the case of NMFB whereas in the case of OMFB it is reversible.

NFEXP, represents the number of household events that are expected to have a positive effect on credit demand. The identified events are sickness of the family members, death and birth ceremonies, marriage, and puberty functions. This variable takes a value according to the number of events happened in household. This variable is expected to have a positive effect on probability of participation as it increases the demand for credit.

4.4.7. Results of the Probit Model

The regression results concerning the participation in borrowings are presented in Table 4.7 both for the NMFB households and the OMFB households. The calculations, means, standard deviations and odds – ratio are presented in Appendix 4.1 for the NMFB households and Appendix 4.2 for the OMFB households.

In the NMFB households the estimated Model shows that the unrestricted log – likelihood is 68.7945. The chi-squared statistic (for 13 of freedom) is 334.5426. The calculated value is greater than the critical value, so the joint hypothesis that the coefficients are all zero is rejected. The estimated model predicted 95.58 per cent of the observations correctly for BORROW = 1 correctly for BORROW = 0. Therefore, the estimated model is highly significant.

In the OMFB households the estimated model shows that the unrestricted log-likelihood is – 2348.546. The chi – squared statistic (for 13 degrees of freedom) is 256.3846. The calculated value is greater than the critical value, so the Joint hypothesis that the coefficients are all zero is rejected. The estimated Model predicts 89.76 per cent of the observations correctly for BORROW = 1. Therefore, the estimated Model is highly significant.

The results point out that it is the relationship of the head, REL, who participates more in borrowing among all the members of the household. In NMFB households the probability of participation in borrowings by the relationship of the head is 0.21 per cent whereas in the case of OMFB households the probability of participation in borrowings by the relationship of the head is 0.02 percent. In both NMFB and OMFB households may be benefited from group activity, which in turn reduces the burden of obtaining a loan, by the relationship of the head. This factor is statistically significant.

The variable IINC, has got positive in the case of NMFB and negative sign in the case of OMFB households. The hypothesis is that higher the income lower will be the borrowing. In NMFB household the probability of borrowing is high which 42 per cent is and in OMFB household the probability of borrowing is low which is 8.2 supporting the above hypothesis. This is significant at the 1 per cent level.

The parameter SEX, is negative in NMFB and OMFB households, the probability of females' participation in borrowing is higher by 85.4 per cent than men in the NMFB and is higher by 0.095 per cent in the OMFB households. Therefore, by encouraging more and more female groups their participation may be improved, for the overall development of the family. This factor is statistically significant at the 1 per cent level.

The variable work participation WP, has got a positive sign, as expected, which implies that participation of worker participation in borrowing is higher in OMFB households by 70.48 per cent and 23.27 per cent in NMFB households. That means the demand for credit by work participation is higher in OMFB households. Therefore, by providing more credit to work participation we can meet the credit the credit needs of the poor in an effective manner. However, this is not statistically significant.

The variable school education EDU, has got to expect negative sign in NMFB households and positive sign in OMFB households. The higher the education lower will be the borrowing. The results indicate that in NMFB households due to group formation most of the individuals are becoming literates and thereby have got job opportunities, which automatically reduce the access to credit. This factor is not statistically significant. The other variables AGE, FINC, FEXP, FEXP and NPEXP are not statistically significant in determining the individual's participation in borrowing. The marginal effects of these variables are also very negligible.

To sum up, the data based on the survey of 300 households regarding their borrowing during the past three years is used for the analysis. In the analysis, the unit of study is the individual member of the household (member aged 18 and above years). The results of the Probit analysis indicated that factors like the position of the individual in the family as head (REL), individual earnings (IINC) and sex of the individual (SEX) are significant. The probability of participation in borrowing by the relationship of the head is higher in OMFB than the NMFB. It is 0.02 percent of his OMFB households and only 0.002 per cent in NMFB households. Regarding the variable IER, the hypothesis is that higher the income lower will be the borrowing. In NMFB households the probability for borrowing is high which is 42 per cent and in OMFB households the probability of borrowing is low which is 0.082 supporting the above hypothesis.

SECTION – IV

4.5. Determinants of Access to Different Sources of Credit

In the previous Section, by using the Probit Model, the factors which influence an individual's participation in borrowings was analysed. In this Section an attempt is made to assess the determinants of access to different sources of credit, by using the Tobit Model.

4.5.1. The Tobit Model

An extension of the Probit Model is the Tobit Model which was originally developed by James Tobin. In the Tobit Model the main interest is in finding out the amount of borrowing by an individual from different sources in relation to socioeconomic variables, which influences their access either positively or negatively. Now the problem is if an individual does not borrow from a particular source, obviously we have no data on the amount borrowed from that particular source. We have such data only on an individual who actually borrowed from a particular source.

Thus individuals are divided into two groups, one consisting of n_1 individuals about whom we have information on the regressors as well as the regressand and another consisting of n_2 individuals about whom we have information only on the regressors but not on the regressand. A sample, in which information on the regressand is available only for some observation, is known as a censored sample. Therefore, the Tobit Model is also known as a Censored Regression Model. Some authors call such models as limited dependent variable regression models because of the restriction put on the values taken by the regressand (Williams H Greene, 2000). When data are censored, the distribution that applies to the sample data is a mixture of discrete and continuous distribution. To analyse this distribution, we define a new random variable y transformed from the original one y^*, by

$Y = 0$ if $y^* \leq 0$

$Y = y$ if $y^* > 0$

The distribution that applies if $y^* \sim N[\mu, \sigma^2]$ is Prob $(y = 0)$ = Prob

$$(y^* \leq 0) = \Phi\left(-\frac{\mu}{\sigma}\right) = 1 - \Phi\left(\frac{\mu}{\sigma}\right)$$, **and if $y^* > 0$, then y** has the Density of y^*.

This distribution is mixture of discrete and continuous parts. The total probability is 1, as required, but instead of scaling the second part, we simply assign the full probability in the censored region to the censoring point (Willam H Greene, 2000).

$$\therefore \; E\left[y_i / x_i\right] = \Phi\left(\frac{\beta^{\circ}x_i}{\sigma}\right)\left(\beta^{\circ}x_{i} + \sigma\lambda_i\right)$$

$$\text{where} \quad \lambda_i = \frac{\varnothing\left(\beta^{\circ}x_i + \sigma\right)}{\Phi\left(\beta^{\circ}x_i + \sigma\right)}$$

For the standard case with censoring at zero and normally distributed disturbances, the marginal effects are (Willam H Greene, 2000).

$$\frac{\partial E\left[y_i / x_i\right]}{\partial x_i} = \beta\,\Phi\left(\frac{\beta x_i}{\sigma}\right)$$

In the estimation process, the maximum Likelihood Method is followed. The coefficients in this model can be interpreted like any other regression coefficients. As done by the Shahidur R. Khandker the probability of borrowing by a particular source is given by the cumulative density function evaluated at the means of the explanatory variables (Shahidur and Khandker, 1998). In order to obtain the marginal changes, the Tobit coefficients are multiplied by the probability of borrowing from a particular source (Mc Donald Joh F., et. al., 1980).

4.5.2 Specification of the Model and Variables

The amount borrowed from a particular source is determined by the factors like Age of the individual (18 years of age and above) AGE, Sex of the individual SEX, Number of Years of Education of individual EDU, Working status of the individual WP, Position of the individual is relationship of head of Household REL, Annual Earnings of the individual IINC, Annual income of the household family FINC, Events of food expenditure FEXP, and non-food expenditure happened in family NFEXP. The factors AGE, SEX, EDU, REL, EXP, NFEXP will have an influence on the amount demanded and factors like WP, IINC, FINC, will have an influence on the amount borrowed. These factors are crucial in assessing the credit worthiness of the individual and other aspects, which limit his access to credit.

The following function is used for estimating the amount borrowed from different sources of credit.

AMT = f (SEX, AGE, REL, EDU, WP, IINC, FINC, FEXP, NFEXP)

The function is applied for all the three sources as well as the two categories of households. The following equations are estimated separately for Formal, Informal and Micro credit and for the NMFB and the OMFB households.

$$AMT_{nmfbf} = \beta + \beta_{AGE} + \beta_{SEX} + \beta_{EDU} + \beta_{WP} + \beta_{REL} + \beta_{IINC} + \beta_{FINC} + \beta_{FEXP} + \beta_{NFEXP} \quad (4.7.1)$$

$$AMT_{nmfbif} = \beta + \beta_{AGE} + \beta_{SEX} + \beta_{EDU} + \beta_{WP} + \beta_{REL} + \beta_{IINC} + \beta_{FINC} + \beta_{FEXP} + \beta_{NFEXP} \quad (4.7.2)$$

$$AMT_{nmfbmc} = \beta + \beta_{AGE} + \beta_{SEX} + \beta_{EDU} + \beta_{WP} + \beta_{REK} + \beta_{IINC} + \beta_{FINC} + \beta_{FEXP} + \beta_{NFEXP} \quad (4.7.3)$$

$$AMT_{omfbf} = \beta + \beta_{AGE} + \beta_{SEX} + \beta_{EDU} + \beta_{WP} + \beta_{REL} + \beta_{IINC} + \beta_{FINC} + \beta_{FEXP} + \beta_{NFEXP} \quad (4.7.4)$$

$$AMT_{omfbif} = \beta + \beta_{AGE} + \beta_{SEX} + \beta_{EDU} + \beta_{WP} + \beta_{REL} + \beta_{IINC} + \beta_{FINC} + \beta_{FEXP} + \beta_{NFEXP} \quad (4.7.5)$$

$$AMT_{omfbmc} = \beta + \beta_{AGE} + \beta_{SEX} + \beta_{EDU} + \beta_{WP} + \beta_{REK} + \beta_{IINC} + \beta_{FINC} + \beta_{FEXP} + \beta_{NFEXP} \quad (4.7.6)$$

Where

AMT_{nmfbf}, AMT_{nmfbif}, AMT_{nmfbmc}, AMT_{omfbf}, AMT_{omfbif} AMT_{omfbmc} represents the amount borrowed by the NMFB and the OMFB households from formal, informal and micro credit sources.

SEX = Sex of the Individual

AGE = Age of the individual (18 years of age and above)

REL = Dummy variable, whether the individual is relationship of the head of household

EDU = Number of Years of Education of the individual

WP = Dummy variable, whether the individual is working status

IINC = Annual Earnings of the Individual

FINC = Annual income of the household family

FEXP = Annual food expenditure of household

NFEXP = Annual non-food expenditure of household.

SEX, is a dummy variable, the variable takes value 1 for male; 0 for female.

AGE, age of the individual is expected to have a negative relation. The hypothesis is, younger individuals are more likely of borrowing since they have the capacity to repay.

REL, is a dummy variable, and takes the value 1 for the individual who, is the head of the households and 0 for the others. Head of the households is expected to have more responsibility in the family and are expected to have a positive relation with demand for credit.

EDU, years of schooling is expected to have a negative relation. It is expected that literacy improves the performance of an individual and there is no need to borrow.

WP is a dummy variable and specifies the working status of the individual. It takes the value 1 for workers and 0 for non-workers. It is expected to have a positive relation as worker will have more assessing the credit worthiness.

IINC, which represents individual earnings of the members has both positive and negative types of influence. If earnings are more the demand for credit will be less. At the same time if earnings are more the amount that can be borrowed will be more by showing his earnings as a security.

FINC, the annual income of the household family, similar to IINC, has also both positive and negative influences. If the household income increases, the demand for credit is expected to decrease. If any household has demand for credit, the FINC has a positive influence on access to credit, more particularly towards informal sources.

FEXP, represents the expenditure on food items of the households that are expected to have a negative effect on NMFB households and positive effect on the OMFB households. The identified incident of more food expenditure leads to less borrowing capacity in the case of NMFB whereas in the case of OMFB it is reversible.

NFEXP, represents the number of household events, that are expected to have a positive effect on credit demand. The identified events are sickness of the family members, death and birth ceremonies, marriage, and other functions. This variable takes value according to the number of events happened in a household. This variable is expected to have a positive effect on the demand for credit.

4.5.3. Results of the Tobit Model

The regression results concerning the amount borrowed from different sources by the NMFB households is presented in table 4.8. For the OMFB households they are presented in Table 4.9. The calculations, means and standard deviations are presented in Appendix 4.3, Appendix 4.4, Appendix 4.5, Appendix 4.6, Appendix 4.7 and Appendix 4.8.

The results indicate that for both categories of households the estimated equations are a good fit since the log likelihood for the micro credit, formal and informal credit of the NMFB households it is -213.1431, -203.0430 and -225.2264 and for the micro credit, formal and informal credit of the OMFB households are found to be -347.2361, -149.2162 and 1248.346 respectively.

A preliminary investigation of the results indicates that the probability of borrowing is 0.23 for micro sources, 0.23 for formal sources and 0.24 for informal sources in the case of the NMFB households. In contrast it is 0.35 for micro credit, 0.36 for formal credit and 0.24 for informal credit in the OMFB households. It clearly indicates that the existence of the micro credit programme brought down the probability of borrowing from formal sources. The informal sources are still playing a major role in their borrowings.

Out of the 9 factors identified three are turned out to be significant factors that determined the amount borrowed from different sources. They are age of the individual, the position of the individual as head of the households, individual income and food expenditure were statistically significant.

In the OMFB households, heads of the households have got positive relation with micro credit and negative relation with formal and informal source in both the groups of households. This reveals that in micro credit the participation of family members other than heads is high compared to other sources that means micro credit facilitates other family member of households to participate in borrowings. A comparison between the NMFB and the OMFB households shows that the persons, who are heads of households participate in borrowings and borrow low from informal sources, which they can get easily and could be the best alternative for formal source. However, it is not statistically significant only in micro credit and informal credit of OMFB and informal credit of NMFB.

SEX got a negative sign in NMFB households for micro credit, and also for informal credit in both the groups of households. This indicates that female's borrowings are more from micro and informal sources than men's borrowing. The variable sex is statistically significant at the 1 per cent level in OMFB in the case of micro credit.

AGE is negatively to informal credit source but positively related to micro credit and formal credit source in OMFB households where as in NMFB households it is vice versa. From this no specific inference could be drawn, but this variable is statistically significant in the case of informal sources in NMFB households.

However, the other variables like Year of school education (EDU), Working participation of individual (WP), the Annual income of the individual (IINC), the Annual income of the family (FINC), Annual expenditure of food (FEXP), Events of Annual expenditure of non-food (NFEXP) are not statistically significant.

To sum up, to assess the level of borrowings form different source of credit, by poor households the Tobit model is used. A sample, in which information on the regressand is available only for some observations, is known as a censored sample. Therefore, the Tobit model is also known as a censored regression model. Some authors call such models as limited dependent variable regression model because of the restriction put in the values taken by the regressand. The results indicate that for both categories of households, the estimated equations are good fits since the loglikelihood for the micro credit, formal and informal credit of the NMFB households it is -213.1431, -203.0430 and -225.2264 and for the micro credit, formal and informal credit of the OMFB households are fund to be -347.2361, -149.2162 and 1248.346 respectively.

A preliminary investigation of the results that the probability of borrowing is 0.23 for micro credit, 0.23 for formal and 0.24 for informal credit sources in case of the NMFB households. In contrast it is 0.35 for micro credit, 0.36 for formal credit and 0.24 for informal credit in the OMFB households.

4.6 Summary

In general, the poor need credit for various requirements and raise credit from different sources. The above aspects were observed by analysing the structure of borrowings of tribal households. The analysis of borrowing between the NMFB and OMFB households reveal that the percentage of borrowing from informal sources of the NMFB households account for 36 per cent whereas it is 11 per cent in OMFB households. In both the households the formal credit accounts for more than half and in which micro credit constitutes around four-fifth of the total. This clearly indicates that group lending could be a good supplement for the formal credit system.

The agency wise analysis shows that rural banks play a vital role in providing formal credit and commercial banks play a major role in implementing the new innovative group lending approach. The purpose wise analysis shows that in both the households the percentage of formal and micro credit in productive purposes is high. The analysis of borrowing according to the rate of interest shows that formal and micro credit carries interest rates lower than informal credit. The analysis of borrowings by nature of security shows that by group security, the formal credit made available to the tribal poor without any physical collateral. Finally the above analysis confirmed that micro credit supplements the informal sources of borrowings of the tribal poor households.

In order to enhance the tribal household's participation in micro credit programmes, the analysis was carried out to analyse the determinants of the participation in the borrowing of the individuals. While analysing the determinants the attention was shifted from the household level to the individual level. The participation of the individuals in borrowing is analysed with the help of Probit Model. The results of the Probit analysis indicated that factors like the position of the individual relationship of the family head (REL), the income of the individual (IINC) and sex of the individual (SEX) are significant. The probability of participation in borrowing by the head of the household is higher in OMFB than the

NMFB. It is 0.002 percent in the OMFB households and only 1.123 percent in NMFB households. The parameter sex is positive in the NMFB and OMFB households, and it implies that the probability of female's participation in borrowing is higher by 0.095 percent than men in the OMFB and is higher by 10 percent in the NMFB households. Regarding the variable IINC, the hypothesis is that higher the income lower will be the borrowing. In NMFB household the probability for borrowing is higher which is 0.42 per cent and in OMFB. To assess the level of borrowings from different sources of credit by the poor households, the Tobit model is used.

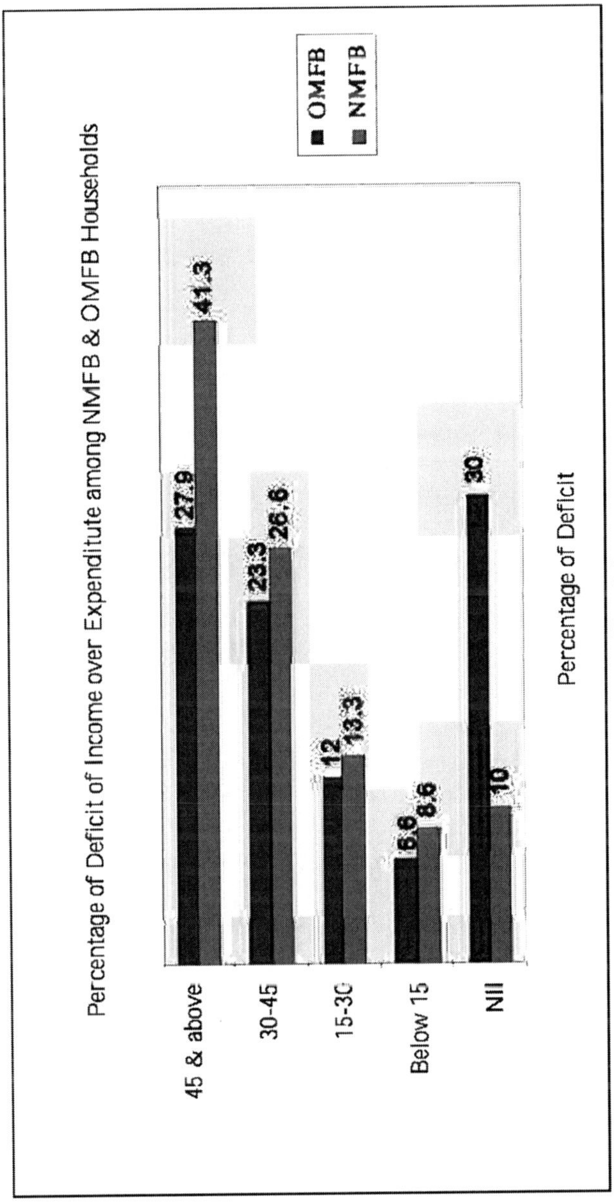
Percentage of Deficit of Income over Expenditute among NMFB & OMFB Households
OMFB
NMFB
45 & above
30-45
15-30
Below 15
Nil
27.9
41.3
23.3
26.6
12
13.3
6.6
8.6
30
10
Percentage of Deficit

Fig. 4.1

Table 4.1. Distribution of the Households by Percentage of Deficit

Percentage of Deficit of Income over Expenditure	*Groups of Households*		
	NMFB	*OMFB*	*All Households*
Nil	10.0	30.0	20.0
Below 15	8.6	6.6	7.6
15- 30	13.3	12.0	12.6
30-45	26.6	23.3	25.0
45 and above	41.3	27.9	34.6
Total	**100.0**	**100.0**	**100.0**
	(150)	**(150)**	**(300)**

Note: Figures In brackets are Households.

NMFB: New Micro Finance Borrowers

OMFB: Old Micro Finance Borrowers

Table 4.2. Distribution of Average Amount of Borrowing by Source

Source	*NMFB*	*OMFB*
Micro Credit	52.50	69.55
Formal Credit	11.27	19.15
Informal Credit	36.22	11.29
Total	100.0	100.0
	(9347)	(15584)

Note: Figures in brackets are Average Amount of Borrowings.

Table 4.3. Distribution of Average Amount of Borrowings by Agency

Source	*Total*	*Commercial Bank*	*Rural Bank*	*Co-operative Bank*	*Land lord*	*Private chit funds*	*Money lenders*	*Friends and relatives*
				NMFB				
(A) Micro Credit	(4907) 100.0	100.0	-	-	-	-	-	-
(B) Formal Credit	(1054) 100.0	25.9	53.1	20.6	-	-	-	-
(C) Informal Credit	(3386) 100.0	-	-	-	5.6	4.9	69.6	19.7
Total (A+B+C)	(9347) 100.0	55.4	5.9	2.3	2.04	1.7	25.2	7.16
				OMFB				
(A) Micro Credit	(10839) 100.0	100.0	-	-	-	-	-	-
(B) Formal Credit	(1760) 100.0	20.0	62.8	17.04	-	-	-	-
(C) Informal Credit	(2985) 100.0	-	-	-	2.7	4.3	53.8	38.9
Total (A+B+C)	(15584) 100.0	71.8	7.10	1.92	0.53	0.83	10.31	7.4

Table 4.4. Distribution of Average Amount of Borrowings by Purpose

Source	*Total*	*Purchase of productive asset*	*Land Development*	*Agrl. Investment*	*Live stock*	*Health*	*Children education*	*House construction and repair*	*Domestic consumption*	*Marriage and other ceremonies*
					NMFB					
(A) Micro Credit	**(4907) 100.0**	-	30.7	21.6	20.2	0.6	0.95	-	9.91	15.8
(B) Formal Credit	**(1054) 100.0**	29.05	15.19	-	22.76	-	-	9.48	17.07	6.32
(C) Informal Credit	**(3386) 100.0**	10.23	3.62	9.96	21.75	16.14	-	-	6.76	31.50
Total (A+B+C)	**(9347) 100.0**	**6.98**	**19.16**	**14.97**	**21.05**	**6.17**	**0.50**	**1.06**	**9.57**	**20.48**
					OMFB					
(A) Micro Credit	**(10839) 100.0**	5.53	26.69	26.08	19.46	4.13	0.35	1.41	14.65	1.62
(B) Formal Credit	**(1760) 100.0**	11.36	21.9	26.51	-	3.78	-	3.78	2.27	30.3
(C) Informal Credit	**(2985) 100.0**	12.17	13.24	8.55	-	8.71	-	2.34	8.73	46.23
Total (A+B+C)	**(15584) 100.0**	**7.46**	**23.57**	**22.77**	**13.55**	**4.9**	**0.25**	**1.86**	**12.11**	**13.41**

Note: Figures in brackets are Average Amount of Borrowings.

Table 4.5. Distribution of Average Amount of Borrowings by Rate of Interest

Source	*Total*	*Less than 12 per cent*	*12-24 per cent*	*24-36 per cent*	*36 per cent and above*
		NMFB			
(A) Micro Credit	**(4907)**				
	100.0	68.4	31.5	-	-
(B) Formal Credit	**(1054)**				
	100.0	100.0	-	-	-
(C) Informal Credit	**(3386)**				
	100.0	-	25.4	4.13	70.33
Total (A+B+C)	**(9347)**				
	100.0	**47.2**	**25.7**	**1.49**	**25.5**
		OMFB			
(A) Micro Credit	**(10839)**				
	100.0	93.07	6.92	-	-
(B) Formal Credit	**(1760)**				
	100.0	100.0	-	-	-
(C) Informal Credit	**(2985)**				
	100.0	-	13.9	18.64	67.35
Total (A+B+C)	**(15584)**				
	100.0	**69.60**	**7.49**	**3.57**	**12.89**

Note: Figures in brackets are Average Amount of Borrowings.

NMFB: New Micro Finance Borrowers.

OMFB: Old Micro Finance Borrowers.

Table 4.6. Distribution of Average Amount of Borrowings by type of Security

Source	*Total*	*Promissory Note*	*Borrowed Previously*	*Pledge of Land*	*Pledge of House*	*Group Security*	*Know since father time*	*Friends and Relatives*
				NMFB				
(A) Micro Credit	**(4907)**	-	-	-	-		-	-
	100.0					100.0		
(B) Formal Credit	**(1054)**	-	-			-	-	-
	100.0			92.40	7.5			
(C) Informal	**(3386)**					-	-	
Credit	**100.0**	66.48	7.10	7.18	12.5			6.71
Total (A+B+C)	**(9347)**						-	
	100.0	**24.08**	**2.56**	**13.02**	**5.39**	**52.49**		**2.42**
				OMFB				
(A) Micro Credit	**(10839)**	-	-	-	-		-	-
	100.0					100.0		
(B) Formal Credit	**(1760)**	-	-			-	-	-
	100.0			56.43	43.5			
(C) Informal	**(2985)**					-		
Credit	**100.0**	44.3	27.13	1.78	0.22		15.18	11.3
Total (A+B+C)	**(15584)**							
	100.0	**8.49**	**5.19**	**7.86**	**4.96**	**69.55**	**2.90**	**2.16**

Note: Figures in brackets are Amount of Borrowing.

Table 4.7. Estimated Co-efficient and Slopes of the Explanatory Variables of Individual Borrowing for the NMFB and OMFB households – Probit Estimates

Item	*NMFB* *Individual Borrowings*	*NMFB* *Slope*	*OMFB* *Individual Borrowings*	*OMFB* *Slope*
Constant	1.4379	0.1123	-0.2127	0.75205
SEX	0.5261 (1.854)	0.8545	1.1640 (3.306)	0.00095
AGE	0.2438 (0.854)	0.1285	0.8542 (0.347)	0.72845
REL	1.4489 (5.656)	0.0021	1.8547 (4.329)	0.00002
EDU	-0.1866 (1.391)	0.1626	0.4502 (0.171)	0.86410
WP	0.6864 (1.963)	0.2327	0.4252 (0.379)	0.70482
HINC	0.3955 (2.125)	0.4252	0.6291 (1.736)	0.08252

(Contd.)

(Contd. Table 4.7)

Item	NMFB		OMFB	
	Individual Borrowings	Slope	Individual Borrowings	Slope
FINC	0.2354 (1.125)	0.1456	0.1852 (0.379)	0.70482
FEXP	2.6485 (9.127)	0.0010	0.5624 (1.736)	0.08252
NPEXP	0.8145 (1.856)	0.2185	0.2122 (0.379)	0.70482
No. of Observations	385		356	
Log-Likelihood	68.7945		-2348.546	
Chi-squared Percentage	334.5426		256.3846	
Predicated correctly	98.56		89.76	

NMFB: New Micro Finance Borrowers
OMFB: Old Micro Finance Borrowers

Table 4.8. Estimated Co-efficient and Slopes of the Explanatory Variable of Amount of Borrowing for the NMFB households – Tobit Estimates

Item	*NMFB*					
	Micro Credit		*Formal Credit*		*Informal Credit*	
	Amount borrowed	*Slopes*	*Amount borrowed*	*Slopes*	*Amount borrowed*	*Slopes*
Constant	-1.2168	1.1112	-0.2035	0.0002	-0.22346	0.64204
SEX	-1.3851 (-1.466)	1.1134	-0.3520 (-0.433)	0.0024	-2.2530 (-2.205)	0.00084
AGE	1.1251 (1.113)	1.7274	0.0220 (0.003)	0.4244	-0.2400702 (-0.236)	0.62734
REL	1.1617 (4.115)	1.1231	0.0304 (4.002)	0.0000	2.4636 (3.228)	0.00002
EDU	-1.1175 (-1.261)	1.1615	-0.0042 (-0.230)	0.0.02	0.2434802 (0.262)	0.75320
WP	1.4175 (1.753)	1.1516	0.4042 (0.423)	0.0203	-0.22242 (-0.268)	0.60372

(Contd.)

(Contd. Table 4.8)

Item	*NMFB*					
	Micro Credit		*Formal Credit*		*Informal Credit*	
	Amount borrowed	*Slopes*	*Amount borrowed*	*Slopes*	*Amount borrowed*	*Slopes*
IINC	1.2284 (1.815)	1.1441	0.2254 (0.502)	0.0440	0.45283 (2.625)	0.07242
FINC	-1.1571 (-1.614)	1.3575	-0.0240 (-0.304)	0.3242	-0.22242 (-0.268)	0.60372
FEXP	1.6413 (11.576)	1.1213	0.3403 (00.243)	0.0000	0.45283 (2.625)	0.07242
NFEXP	1.1161 (1.235)	1.1674	0.0030 (0.232)	0.0344	-0.22242 (-0.268)	0.60372
Σ	246.7462		243.4432		208.2482	
No. of observations	168		143		74	
Log Likelihood	-213.1431		-203.0430		-225.2264	
Probability of Borrowing	0.234		0.230		0.242	

NMFB: New Micro Finance Borrowers
OMFB: Old Micro Finance Borrowers

Table 4.9. Estimated Co-efficient and Slopes of the Explanatory Variables of Amount of Borrowing for the OMFB Households – Tobit Estimates

Item	*OMFB*					
	Micro Credit		*Formal Credit*		*Informal Credit*	
	Amount borrowed	*Slopes*	*Amount borrowed*	*Slopes*	*Amount borrowed*	*Slopes*
Constant	-21137.0	0.13214	-22219.0	0.21224	-532.31	0.66174
SEX	3237.2 (0.242)	0.76742	1219.2 (0.242)	0.96942	-5131.7 (-4.662)	0.00000
AGE	-60.210 (-0.326)	0.72143	-60.220 (-0.126)	0.92241	18.402 (0.726)	0.24714
REL	6743.7 (1.101)	0.26101	6941.9 (2.202)	0.26202	-2852.0 (-2.176)	0.00140
EDU	-211.36 (-0.603)	0.23632	-222.16 (-0.601)	0.21612	-11.562 (-0.263)	0.51325
WP	-1732.1 (-0.212)	0.77770	-2912.2 (-0.222)	0.99990	-225.10 (-0.227)	0.52435

(Contd.)

(Contd. Table 4.9)

Item	OMFB					
	Micro Credit		Formal Credit		Informal Credit	
	Amount borrowed	Slopes	Amount borrowed	Slopes	Amount borrowed	Slopes
IINC	0.7003 (0.031)	0.46131	0.9001 (0.012)	0.46212	-0.1516802 (-0.004)	0.77511
FINC	-2222.3 (-0.234)	0.21473	-2222.1 (-0.214)	0.22491	1123.1 (1.242)	0.01713
FEXP	0.1123 (0.303)	0.76116	0.2221 (0.101)	0.96226	0.1047501 (2.067)	0.00113
NPEXP	0.7707 (0.630)	0.22230	0.9909 (0.610)	0.22210	0.3325401 (0.187)	0.55117
Σ	724.3713		924.1921		1273.208	
No. of observations	128		104		124	
Log Likelihood	-347.2361		-149.2162		1248.346	
Probability of Borrowing	0.354		0.362		0.243	

NMFB: New Micro Finance Borrowers
OMFB: Old Micro Finance Borrowers

References

1. Bernett Lynn, Mike Goldberg and Pamela Hunte (1996): *"Ownership and Sustainability: Lessons on Group-Based Financial Services from Five NGOs in South Asia"*, World Bank, Washington D.C.
2. Dersing Market (1990): *"Support for Micro Enterprises: Lessons for Sub-Saharan Africa"*: World Bank Technical Paper 122, Washington, D.C.
3. Damodar N. Gujarati (2000): *Basic Econometrics*, McGraw – Hill International edition, p. 614.
4. Eric Hanushek and John Jackson (1997): *Statistical Methods for Scientists*, Academic Press, New York, p.189.
5. Hoff Karla and Joseph E. Stiglitz (1990): *"Introduction: Imperfect Information and Rural Credit Markets – Puzzles and Policy Perspectives"*, The World Bank Economic Review, Vol.4, No.3, September, pp. 235-51.
6. Hossain Mahabub (1988): *"Credit for Alleviation of Rural Poverty: The Grameen Bank in Bangladesh"*, IFPRI Research Report 65 International Food Policy Research Institute, Washington, D.C.
7. Hulme David and Paul Mosley (1996): *Finance against poverty*, New York, Routledge Publishing.
8. Khandker Shahidur R., Baqui Khalily and Zahed Khan (1995): *"Grameen Bank: Performance and Sustainability"*, World Bank Discussion Paper 306, Washington D.C.
9. Madheswaran S. and Amita Dharmadhikary (2001): *"Empowering Rural Women through Self- help groups; Lessons from Maharashtra Rural Credit Project"*, Indian Journal of Agricultural Economics, Vol. 56, July- September 2001. p. 441.
10. Mc Donald joh F., and Robert A. Moffitt (1980): *"The Uses of Tobit Analysis"*, the Review of Economics and Statistics, 62(2): 318-21.
11. Manfred Zeller (1994): *"Determinants of Credit Rationing: A Study of Informal Lenders and Formal Credit Groups in Madagascar"*, World Development, Vol. 22, No.12, pp.1895-1907.
12. Rajaram Dasgupta (2001): *"An Informal Journey through Self-help Groups"*, Indian Journal of Agricultural Economics, July-September, Vol. 56, No.3, p. 377.
13. Stiglitz – Joseph E., and Anren Wesis (1981): *"Credit Rationing in Markets with Imperfect Information"*, American Economic Review, 71(3): 393-410-1983.
14. Stiglitz – Joseph E., and Anren Wesis (1973) *"Incentive Effects of Termination: Applications to the credit and Labour Markets"*, American Economic Review 73(5): pp. 912-27.

15. Shahidur R. Khandker (1998): *"Fighting Poverty with Micro Credit (Experience In Bangladesh)"*, Oxford University Press, Inc., p. 122.
16. William H. Greene (2000): *Econometric Analysis* Prentice – Hall, International Inc., p. 815. 14. *Ibid* – p. 816
17. World Bank (1996): *"Bangladesh: Poverty alleviation Micro Finance Project"* Staff Appraisal Report South Asia Region, Country Department –I, Private Sector development and Finance Division, Washington.
18. Yaron Jacob (1992): *"Assessing Development Finance Institutions"*. World Bank Discussion Paper 174, Washington D.C., p. 12.

5

Transactions Costs of Loans – Borrowers' Perspective

5.1. Introduction

Any attempt to increase access to credit by the poor, should be guided by how the poor and the policy makers perceive the constraining factors to be. One such constraining factor is the transactions costs. The common theme that runs through the majority of the studies done on transaction costs is that costs associated with transaction in the credit market led to market imperfections. (Stiglitiz, 1981; Herath, 1994; Roman, 1994). The majority of the studies (Saito and Villaneuva, 1981; Liedholm, 1985; Olomola, 1999) is viewed as generally accepting the hypothesis that higher the transaction costs, the greater is the extent to which they help increase access to credit by the poor. Acceptance of this hypothesis has generally led to the promotion of the micro finance schemes. The most significant feature of the micro credit lending through groups is a reduction in transaction costs both for the lenders and borrowers. In group lending, institutional variations are possible, based on how transactions are organized during various stages of credit delivery.

The viability of a group lending arrangement, largely depends on its ability to reduce both lender and borrower transaction costs, with specific social contexts (Bhatt and Tang, 1998; Alam, Mohammed Ferdous, 1981). The NABARD's linkage programme of self-help groups with banks is an effort in this direction. The efforts made to study the transaction costs in the credit system, are focused from lenders' viewpoint and it is found that transaction costs are reduced due to group lending. However, the studies attempted to study the costs of borrowing in a systematic manner from borrowers' viewpoint, are few in number. In this chapter, therefore, an attempt is made to study the transaction costs of borrowing of tribal poor from different sources of credit.

5.2. Transactions Costs of Borrowing

A concise definition of transaction cost, is provided together with a discussion on the sources of transaction costs and their variation. Two central views regarding credit markets have dominated academic and policy space between 1950 and 1990. The argument was that, interest rates should be kept low in order to speed up the accumulation of capital. The other view (McKinnon, 1973) was that credit markets work like classical competitive markets and observed that high interest rates are a reflection of the risks of default. The policy recommendation was basically to discourage any intervention in credit markets.

New Institutional Economists (Nabli and Nudent, 1989; North, 1992; Lin and Negent, 1995), in an attempt to overcome the limitations of mainstream neo-classical economics that take institutions as given, put forward an argument that accounts for institutions' characteristic of credit markets. Hoff and Stiglitz (1990) argue that with imperfect information, interest rates have sorting and incentive effects. For example, high interest rates adversely sort out good credit risks from bad credit risks. Alternatively, higher interest rates may induce borrowers to invest in riskier projects and may not exercise due diligence in reducing risks. It should also be highlighted that the supply of loanable funds is an increasing function of expected profits. Thus, unlike in the classical economic analysis where excess demand at a given interest rate is choked off by a rise in interest rates, the adverse selection and moral hazard literature propose that there is no tendency for the interest rate to rise, in order to choke off excess demand, as credit may be rationed through non price mechanisms.

The discussion made above, shows the limitations imposed on credit operations in administratively determined interest rates and full credit liberalization regimes. This underscores the importance of two basic problems that neo-classical economics overlook, that of transaction costs and imperfect information. These, together with the theory of collective action, constitute the main themes of New Institutionalist Economics (NIE). Transactions Costs are broadly referred to the costs involved in the exchange. These are the costs that prevent market from operating efficiently. Transactions Costs occur both from the lenders' side as well as from the borrowers' side. Transactions Costs of lenders can be termed as Transactions Costs of Lending (TCL) and transaction costs of borrowers can be termed as Transaction Costs of Borrowings (TCB). On the lenders' side, transactions costs involve costs of information gathering, loan administration, enforcement, etc. Where loanable funds are in limited supply, the use of non-price factors such as collateral quotas, compensating deposit balance, bureaucratic procedures, long delays in disbursement are employed to eliminate excessive credit demand. These factors need to be considered in determining the effective transaction cost of procuring credit.

Borrowers also incur transaction costs. Borrower transactions costs mainly involve various charges imposed by lenders beyond interest payments such as application fees, service fees, photographs, etc. The most important transaction cost is borrower's travel time and time spent in obtaining the loan. Loss of time from work is an important part of the transaction cost for most borrowers. The addition of costs such as the cost of transportation and inconveniences indicate that the efficient opportunity sets of borrowers would vary not only with the size of their portfolios, but also with the physical location and the opportunity cost of their time.

Table 5.1. Effective Transactions Costs

	- Collateral	
	- Compensating Depository Balance	
Conditions	- Financial Accounts	Borrower's Cost
	- Business proposals/Plans	
	- Company Registration	
	- Information Gathering	
Search Costs	- Screening Fees	Lender's Cost
	- Service Fees	
Transacting Costs	- Travel/Contact Time	
	- Photos	Borrower's Cost
	- Time Spent in Obtaining Loan	

Table 5.1 splits both the lenders and borrowers cost onto those that go towards meeting conditional requirement and those that are part of the credit search. In the current study, transacting costs and search costs were considered and measured. These include service fees, travel and telephones fees, photos, and time spent in obtaining the loan and administrative fees. These were calculated for each firm, which was sampled. Finally, these transactions costs, from borrowers view point are classified into two categories: (a) explicit costs-costs that include

expenditure on travel, bribes and gratitude, forced purchases of other lender services and products, and other expenses, (b) implicit or opportunity costs - costs of time spent, applying for and obtaining the loan (Zia Ahmed, 1989). It was noticed that due to the NABARD's SHG Bank Linkage Programme, the borrowers are able to reduce their transaction costs by 85 per cent, compared to the cost incurred in getting loan from formal credit. This is mainly due to the elimination of cumbersome documentation procedures and time spent and costs incurred on repeated visits to banks etc. (Nanda, 1994).

5.3. Effective Cost of Borrowing

The effective cost of borrowing includes financial costs as well as non-financial costs incurred by the borrower. Financial Costs are costs that are incurred during the loan repayment period. These include the interest cost of loans. Non-financial costs are costs that are incurred prior to and at the time of obtaining the loan. These include the transaction costs. The decision of an individual, whether to borrow from a particular source, depends on both financial and non-financial costs. Therefore, the cost of borrowing includes the interest costs as well as non interest costs incurred by the borrowers in connection with the loans (Adams Dale and Nehman, 1979).

In the theory, two explanations are offered for the limited participation of the poor in the formal credit sources with regard to transaction costs. One explanation focuses on lender's costs and the other on borrower's costs. A model developed on lender's costs shows how concessional interest rates on loans discourage formal lenders from lending to the poor, especially when lenders incur relatively high TCL in rural areas. Another model on borrower's costs shows that excessive TCB from formal institutions due to high borrower's transaction costs, discourage many borrowers from using formal sources of credit (Adams Dale and Nehman, 1979). Ladman added to this aspect, by developing a model to show that TCB result chiefly from the rationing mechanism employed by formal lenders, who face high TCL but are unable to cover these costs due to limitations set by the financial authorities, in the form of fixed and concessional lending rates (Ladman, 1984).

An extension of this model shows that with controlled interest rates lenders engage in implicit price setting that involves differential treatment of loan application, disbursement, monitoring and supervision. This implicit price setting procedure enables the lenders to exclude or ration unwanted clients. The activities involved in the screening mechanism led to increased transaction costs for both the lenders and the borrowers. The spread between the TCB and the explicit interest costs, reflects the value of the implicit charges. Based on this, a TCB can be defined as the trade-off between the controlled (explicit) interest rates and transaction costs, arising from the rationing activities of the lenders. Another development in the estimation of the cost of borrowing function is consideration of the net value of the incremental funds received by the borrower. An important feature of the TCL is that they are invariably incurred prior to and at the time of obtaining the loan. Therefore, it will be appropriate to consider the net loan received than the actual amount borrowed. That means, additional funds borrowed should be arrived at only after discounting the total transaction costs from the total loan amount. Hence, the relevant measure is the Effective Cost of Borrowing.

The effective cost is the annualised incremental payment, measured as a percentage of the actual additional funds borrowed. Ahmed estimated the effective cost of borrowing of the rural loans in Bangladesh and found that effective cost of borrowing of the formal loans is higher than that of informal loans for the small borrowers, whereas the effective cost of borrowing of the formal loans is lower than the informal loans for the large borrowers (Zia Ahmed, 1989).

5.3.1. The Model

In a regime of fixed, concessional lending rates, the share of the transaction cost in total borrowing costs, has been found to be very high in the formal market (Shahjahan, 1968; Alam Mohammed Ferdous, 1981). Borrowers' costs of credit (BC) include not only nominal interest cost (NI) but also borrower transaction cost (TC). Admas and Nahman (1979) defined the borrower's price of credit in terms of real net costs of the loan, by including the changes in purchasing power (DP) over the loan period as:

$$BC = NI + TC - DP \qquad \dots (1)$$

An important feature of borrowers' transaction cost is that they are invariably incurred prior to and at the time of obtaining the loan. Therefore, instead of a simple linear addition to the interest cost of funds, these transaction costs should be discounted from the loan amount to get the net value of the incremental funds received by the borrower. The difference between the total repayment that is due at maturity and the net addition of fund from the loan proceeds, will give a more accurate measure of the total absolute cost of borrowing, a given amount of net useable funds. This incremental payment expressed as a percentage of net loan received, can be defined as the annualized effective cost of the loan. This effective rate of interest (E) per unit of time can be calculated as:

$$E = (1+r)\ \sqrt[n]{L/(L-TC)} - 1 \qquad \ldots(2)$$

Where r is the explicit interest rate, n is the loan term in years *.

For borrowers with a positive transaction cost, the effective rate of interest will, therefore, be higher than the explicit interest rate of the loan. Differentiating equation 2 partially with respect to TC gives:

$$\partial E / \partial TC = [(1+r)/n]\ \sqrt[n]{L/(L-TC)^{n+1}} > 0 \qquad \ldots(3)$$

Which implies that borrowers incurring high transaction costs of borrowing will bear high effective cost of interest on their loans.

5.4. Empirical Results

5.4.1 Transactions Costs

The present study has estimated the transaction cost of borrowing for sample households from different sources and a comparative analysis is carried out to observe the differences in the transaction cost of borrowing of the tribal loans.

An analysis of the average transaction csots of the borrowing and its components from different sources by the sample households is presented in the table 5.2 and Fig. 5.1A and B. It could be observed from the table that in both the households, the Transaction Costs of Borrowing (TCB) from formal sources of credit is higher than the TCB from informal sources. This supports the general hypothesis that the borrowers' transaction costs are higher for the loans from formal sources than for the loans from informal sources. The transaction costs include travel and miscellaneous and opportunity costs. The transaction costs considerably lower in Micro credit. The reduction in transaction costs in group lending is mainly due to the reduction in the opportunity costs. Therefore, it can be concluded that through group–lending the TCB can reduce considerably.

5.4.2. Relation between Loan Amount and Transactions Costs

An examination of the transaction costs incurred against the amount of loan obtained will provide a better understanding of the implications of transaction costs from the borrowers' view point. Table 5.3 presents the percentage of transaction costs to the amount of the loan, for different ranges. It can be observed from the table that the transaction cost as a percentage of the amount of loan, decreased with the increase in the

---

* If the interest rate is defined as the nominal interest rate, the E is the nominal effective rate. This can be converted into real terms by calculating the real interest rate on the loan rr = (r-P) /(1+p), and using it in place of r in the equation (2) to get real effective rate, where P is the yearly inflation rate.

quantum of loan for all sources of credit. It ranged from five per cent to 0.28 per cent of formal loans in NMFB households and from 4.25 per cent to 0.17 per cent in OMFB households. It also ranged from five per cent to 0.20 per cent of informal loans in NMFB households and from 3.87 per cent to 0.08 per cent in OMFB households. In case of micro credit, in both the households it ranged from around three per cent to around 0.1 per cent. Upto the loan amount of Rs. 3000, the percentage of transaction costs to the loan amount is higher for formal credit than for informal credit. For the loan amount above Rs. 3000, the percentage of transaction costs is more or less similar for both formal and informal loans in both the households. The transation costs are lower for micro credit loans in both the households. Hence, it can be concluded that by minimizing the gourp maintenance costs, the effect of TCB can be reduced to a great extent for the small borrowers.

5.4.3. Effective Costs

The present study estimates the nominal effective cost of borrowing of the micro, formal and informal loans in relation to the amount of transaction cost and the amount of the loan obtained.

Average Effective Cost of borrowing by the amount of transaction costs is presented in Table 5.4. It can be inferred from the table that the effective cost of borrowing decreased as the amount of transaction costs increased for all sources, in both the households. Table 5.5 presents the nominal annualized effective cost of loans from different size of the loan amount. It can be observed from the table that the effective cost is higher for small loans than for larger loans, for all sources in both the households. It ranged from 39 to 35 per cent for formal credit in NMFB households and from 43 per cent to 30 per cent in OMFB households. It also ranged from 78 per cent to 40 per cent for informal credit in NMFB households and from 50 per cent to 12 per cent in OMFB households. In the case of micro credit, it ranged from 49 per cent to 47 per cent in NMFB households and from 40 per cent to 30 per cent in OMFB households. It is revealed that for all loans the effective cost is higher for informal credit than for formal credit in both the households. This may be due to the differences in the rates of interest changed by the formal and informal lenders.

5.4.4. Means and Standard Deviations of Transaction Costs and Effective Costs of borrowing

It has been discussed in the preceding analysis that there are differences in the transaction costs and effective costs of the loans borrowed from different sources. Here an attempt is made to observe the significance of these differences among different sources of credit of the NMFB and the OMFB households by using the Z-test. Table 5.6 presents the same means and standard deviations of the transaction costs and effective costs for different sources of credit. Table 5.7 presents the results of the Z-test, comparing the transaction costs and effective costs of the loans borrowed, for both the households. The Z test used is as follows:

$$z = \sqrt{\frac{\overline{X_1}-\overline{X_2}}{\frac{\sigma_1^2}{n_1}+\frac{\sigma_2^2}{n_2}}}$$

Where

$\overline{X_1}$ = Mean of the Transaction Costs/Mean of the Effective Cost of borrowing of the first category.

$\overline{X_2}$ = Mean of the transaction costs/Mean of the Effective Cost of borrowing of the second category.

σ_1^2 = Variance of the transaction costs/Variance of the Effective Cost of Borrowing of the first category.

σ_2^2 = Variance of the transaction costs/Variance of the Effective Costs of borrowing of the second category.

n_1 = Number of observations of first category.

n_2 = Number of observations of second category.

Test procedure is summarized below:

1. Nuall Hypothesis (H_0) = There is no difference between the means of the two Categories i.e $X_1 = X_2$
   Alternative Hypothesis: $X_1 \neq X_1$.
2. Level of significance: $\alpha = 0.05$
3. Criterion Reject the null hypothesis if $Z < -1.96$ or $Z > 1.96$.

It is hypothesized that there is no difference in the

1. Average transaction costs of the Micro credit loans and formal loans of the NMFB households.
2. Average effective cost of borrowing of the micro credit loans and formal of the NMFB households.
3. Average transaction costs of borrowing Micro credit loans and informal loans of the NMFB households.
4. Average effective costs of borrowing of Micro credit loans and informal loans of the NMFB households.

5. Average transaction costs of borrowing of formal loans and informal loans of the NMFB households.
6. Average effective cost of borrowing of formal and Informal; loans of the NMFB households.
7. Average transaction costs of the Micro credit loans and formal loans of the OMFB households.
8. Average effective cost of borrowing of the micro credit loans and formal of the OMFB households.
9. Average transaction costs of borrowing Micro credit loans and informal loans of the OMFB households.
10. Average effective costs of borrowing of Micro credit loans and Informal loans of the OMFB households.
11. Average transaction costs of borrowing of formal loans and informal loans of the OMFB households.
12. Average effective cost of borrowing of formal and Informal loans of the OMFB households.

It could be observed from the table 5.7 that all the calculated Z values are greater than the critical value of Z for the OMFB households as well as for the NMFB households. Hence, it could be concluded that there are significant differences in the average transaction costs and average effective costs of borrowing between micro credit and formal credit, micro credit and informal credit and between formal and informal credit in both the households.

5.5. Summary

Transaction costs are broadly referred to as the cost involoved in exchange. Transaction costs occur both from the lenders side as well as from the borrowers' side. All the lenders side, transaction costs involves costs of information gathering, loan administration, enforcement, etc. Borrowers' transactions costs mainly involve various charges imposed by lenders beyond interest payment such as application fees, service fees, photographs, etc. The effective cost of borrowing includes financial costs as well as non-financial costs incurred by the borrowers. The financial costs are costs that are incurred during the loan repayment period. These include the interest costs on loans. Nonfinancial costs are costs that are incurred prior to and at the time of obtaining of the loan.These include the transaction costs.

In both NMFB and OMFB households, the transaction cost of borrowing (TCB) from formal sources of credit is higher than from informal sources. The transaction costs are considerably lower in micro credit. The reduction in transaction costs in group lending is mainly due to the reduction in the opportinuty costs. It can conclude that through group lending the TCB can reduce considerably. The effective cost is higher for small loans than for larger loans, for all sources in both the households. The effective cost is also high for micro credit in the study area.

The major policy conclusion that evolved from the study is that the effective cost of borrowing for the non-preferred borrowers of the formal sector is being lowered by the new financial innovation of group lending. If this new innovation could aim at further reducing the transaction costs by minimizing the group formation costs, maintenance costs etc., it will serve the poor more effectively. This can be achieved by making suitable changes in the micro finance lending.

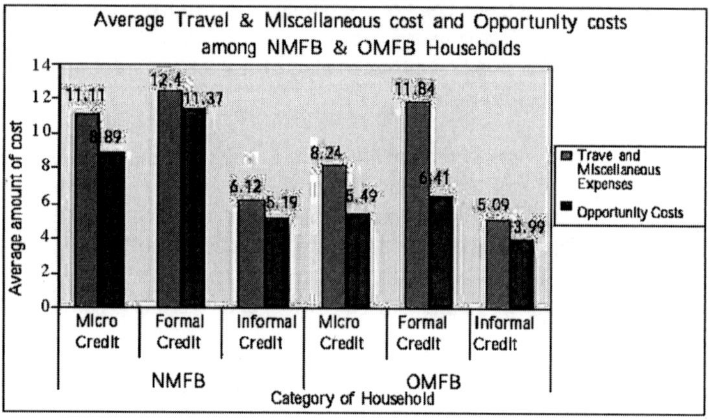

Fig. 5.1A

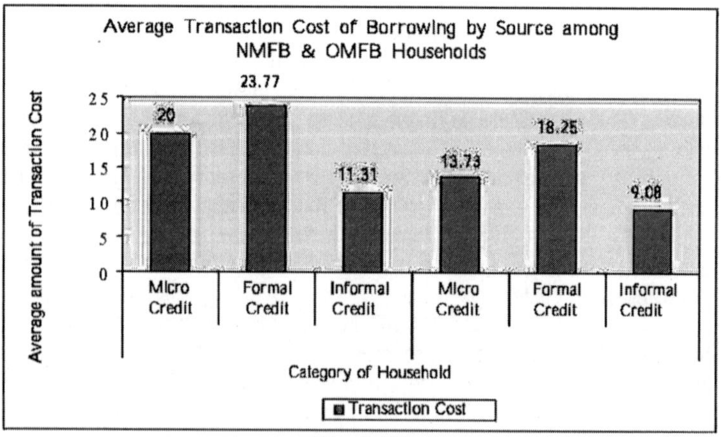

Fig. 5.1B

Table 5.2. Average Transaction Costs of the Borrowing by Source

Item	*NMFB*			*OMFB*		
	Micro Credit	*Formal Credit*	*Informal Credit*	*Micro Credit*	*Formal Credit*	*Informal Credit*
(A) Travel and Miscellaneous Expenses	11.11	12.40	6.12	8.24	11.84	5.09
(B) Opportunity Costs	8.89	11.37	5.19	5.49	6.41	3.99
Transactions Costs (A+B)	20.0	23.77	11.31	13.73	18.25	9.08

Table 5.3. Percentage of Transaction Cost to Loan Amount

	NMFB			OMFB		
Loan Size	*Micro Credit*	*Formal Credit*	*Informal Credit*	*Micro Credit*	*Formal Credit*	*Informal Credit*
Below 1000	3.05	5.05	4.95	2.83	4.25	3.87
1000-3000	2.16	4.26	3.12	1.41	3.07	2.16
3000-5000	1.00	2.26	3.0	0.60	1.96	1.43
5000-10000	0.66	1.15	1.98	0.35	0.85	0.69
10000-25000	0.32	0.48	0.66	0.16	0.29	0.17
Above 25000	0.12	0.28	0.20	0.06	0.17	0.08

Table 5.4. Average Effective Cost of Borrowing by Amount of Transaction Cost

Amount of Transaction Cost	NMFB			OMFB		
	Micro Credit	*Formal Credit*	*Informal Credit*	*Micro Credit*	*Formal Credit*	*Informal Credit*
0-100	7.20	6.56	9.85	6.73	5.54	8.27
100-200	8.98	5.37	8.20	7.23	4.83	7.22
200-500	6.67	3.92	7.51	5.62	2.94	6.76
Above 500	5.68	2.61	6.62	4.86	1.86	5.22

Table 5.5. Average Effective Cost of Borrowing by Loan Size

Loan Size in Rs.	*NMFB*			*OMFB*		
	Micro Credit	*Formal Credit*	*Informal Credit*	*Micro Credit*	*Formal Credit*	*Informal Credit*
Upto 1000	49.28	35.92	78.34	40.00	39.26	30.05
1000-3000	47.74	38.95	42.08	39.72	36.12	30.00
3000-5000	48.52	36.64	40.24	30.00	43.02	40.57
5000-10000	47.30	34.72	55.40	30.48	40.00	40.23
10000 above	47.65	36.26	45.12	31.36	30.00	12.01

Table 5.6. Means and Standard Deviations of the Transaction Cost, and Effective Cost of Borrowing

Item	NMFB			OMFB		
	Micro Credit (n = 301)	*Formal Credit (n = 14)*	*Informal Credit (n = 83)*	*Micro Credit (n = 334)*	*Formal Credit (n = 18)*	*Informal Credit (n = 81)*
Transaction Cost						
Mean	20.00	23.77	11.31	13.73	18.25	9.08
Standard Deviation	18.97	22.12	24.27	12.28	19.55	10.42
Effective Cost						
Mean	19.89	21.00	13.12	27.79	29.72	34.07
Standard Deviation	13.82	7.45	15.69	12.28	19.55	10.42

Table 5.7. Difference between Means – Hypothesis Testing

Item	NMFB			OMFB		
	Micro Credit Vs Formal Credit	*Micro Credit Vs Informal Credit*	*Formal Credit Vs Informal Credit*	*Micro Credit Vs Formal Credit*	*Micro Credit Vs Informal Credit*	*Formal Credit Vs Informal Credit*
Transaction Cost	1.51 (Reject H_0)	4.94 (Reject H_0)	2.58 (Reject H_0)	2.01 (Reject H_0)	5.30 (Reject H_0)	2.75 (Reject H_0)
Effective Cost	1.39 (Reject H_0)	5.37 (Reject H_0)	3.31 (Reject H_0)	1.31 (Reject H_0)	6.16 (Reject H_0)	1.89 (Reject H_0)

References

1. Alam, Mohammed Ferdous (1981) *"Cost of Credit from institutional sources in Bangladesh"*, Journal of Agricultural Economics, Vol. 4, No. 2, pp. 51-60.
2. Adams Dale W., and C.I Nehman (1979): *"Borrowing costs and the demand for rural credit"*, Journal for Development Studies, Vol. 15, No. 2, pp. 165-176.
3. Bhatt N and Tang S Y (1998) *"Group based micro finance and economic development"* In Handbook of Economic Development, ed. Liou, T. Marcel Dekeer, New York.
4. Herath, G (1994) *"Rural Credit Markets and Institutional Reform: Developing Countries: Potential and Problems."* Savings and Development, Quarterly review No. 2, Vol. XVII, 169-191.
5. Hoff K and J E Stiglitz (1990) *"Introduction : Imperfect information and rural credit markets – puzzles, policy perspectives."* The World Bank Economic Review. Vol. 4, No. 3, pp. 235-250.
6. Liedholm,C (1985) *"Small scale enterprise credit schemes: administrative costs and the role of inventory norms."* Working paper No. 25 Department of Agricultural Economics, Michigan State University.
7. Lin J Y and J Negent (1995) *"Institutions and Economic Development:"* Handbook of Development Economics. Vol. 3, Chap. XX.
8. Ladman J R (1984): *"Loan transaction costs, credit rationing and market structure: The case of Bolivia"*, in D.W. Admas D.H Graham and J D Von Pischke ed., Undermining Rural Development with Cheap Credit, Wesview Press, Inc., Boulder.
9. Mckinnon R (1973) *"Money and Capital in Economic Development,* (Washington D.C).
10. Nabli M K and J A Nudent (1989) *"The New Institutional Economics and its Applicability to Development."* World Development. Vol.17, No. 9, pp.1333-47.
11. Nanda Y C (1994): *"Significance of Establishing Linkage of SHGs with Banks"*, Paper presented at a Seminar on linkages of SHGs with FIS on 17-18 September. 94 at DHAKA, BANGLADESH, National Bank News Review, Vol. 1, No.4, October- December, p. 26.
12. North, D C (1992) *"Transaction cost, Institutional and Economic Performance."* ICEG Occasional Papers No. 30. International Centre for Economic Growth.
13. Olomola, A.S (1999) *"Determinants of Smallholders' Transaction Cost of Procuring Non- Bank Loans in Nigeria."* Savings and Development. Quarterly Review No.1, Vol. XXIII, 95-108.

14. Roman, L (1994) "*Transactions Costs and Transition: The Case of Vietnamese Banking Sector.*" Savings and Development. Quarterly Review, No. 3, Vol. XVIII.
15. Saito, K., and D. Villaneuva (1981) "*Transactions Cost of credit to the Small Scale Sector in the Philippines.*" Economic Development and Cultural Change. Vol. 29, 631-40.
16. Shahjahan M (1968): "*Agricultural Finance in East Pakistan*", The Asiatic Press, Dhaka, Bangladesh.
17. Stiglitiz (1981) "*Credit Rationing in Markets with Imperfect Information*". American Economic Review. Vol. 71, No. 3, 393-410.
18. Zia U. Ahmed (1989): "*Effective Costs of Rural Loans in Bangladesh*", World Development, Vol. 17, No.3, pp. 357-363.

6

Micro Finance Repayment Performance In India

6.1. Introduction

The best level of repayment performance is a percent (100 per cent) repayment rate on time. If the maximum repayment rate the Micro Finance Institutions (MFI) can reach, given its lending methodology, is lower than the targeted 100 per cent, the MFI will use second level strategy to increase its repayment performance. Such strategy includes the allocation of larger loans to borrowers with lower default probability and attempts to reduce the delay in repayment. The MFI will develop incentive mechanisms so as to meet these objectives (Marie Godquin, 2004). The main factors influencing repayment are related to either the information asymmetries or to the low performance of institutions such as justice or education.

Information asymmetries generate problems of adverse selection - i.e. allocation of loans to borrowers with undesirable characteristics such as high level of risk or inability to take advantage of the loan-as well as moral hazard-the borrower may behave in an undesirable way. Borrowers that have enough money to reimburse their loan might also default strategically. The cost of strategic default might indeed below if the lending institution has low collateral requirements and if the legal system gives little power to the MFI to enforce contracts. MFIs try to restrict the occurrence of those three types of situations in designing appropriate credit schemes. (Marie Godquin, 2004).

This Chapter has been divided into two sections. Section I presents the repayment performance of borrowers towards formal and micro credit and informal credit. In Section II, an attempt is made to study the factors influencing repayment performance of borrowers through regression analysis. In this chapter, we wish to contribute to the improvement of MFI repayment performance by examining their determinants with a particular emphasis on "microfinance innovations" such as the use of nonfinancial services, group lending, and dynamic incentives. In view of the involvement of formal agencies in lending to tribal poor households both under individual approach, and group approach, a study of the repayment performance of the OMFB and the NMFB households is considered useful. Towards this end, information has been collected from the sample households on the sources of repayment to formal, micro and informal agencies. These aspects are examined with reference to agency wise borrowing, purpose of borrowing, the rate of interest involved in borrowing etc.

SECTION –I

6.2. Repayment Performance of Respondents

6.2.1. Percentage of Repayments to Borrowings

Credit rationing and collateral requirement are the traditional means used by banks to cope with information asymmetries in the credit market (Stiglitz and Weiss, 1981) but both method leads to the exclusion of the poor borrowers. To explain the success of microfinance in providing credit to the poor, a large literature uses the principal/agent theory to demonstrate that microfinance contracts lending to joint-liable groups allow the lender to bypass moral hazard (Stigliz, 1990) and adverse selection (Ghatak, 1999) due to information asymmetries. It is also argued that joint-liable lending groups help enforce repayment as social interactions make strategic default more costly (Besley and Coates, 1995). Social ties (Besley and Coates, 1995) and group homogeneity (Besley and Coates, 1995, Stiglitz, 1990) are also indirectly linked to repayment performance as they can facilitate peer monitoring and peer pressure or an effective peer selection of group members.

In general the formal loan repayments are postponed in preference to the informal loans. This is attributable to the proximity between the lender and the borrower in respect of informal loans, compared to the formal loans. The proximity between the lender and the borrower was also noticed in respect of micro credit. In group-lending programmes, the functions of screening, monitoring and enforcement of repayment are to a large extent transferred from the formal lender to the borrowers – the group members themselves. To assess whether such functions as mentioned above apply to the repayments of formal, micro and informal loans by the sample households are examined and shown in Table 6.1.

It may be noticed from the table that the repayment performance of loans is low in all sources of borrowing. It may be further noticed that while the repayment of micro credit is accounted for around 35 per cent, the repayment of formal and informal credit is accounted for only around 25 per cent. The analysis of repayment of loans shows that the repayment of micro credit is slightly better compared to formal and informal credit. The analysis confirms that there is a marginal impact of micro credit in the repayment performance of borrowers.

6.2.2. Sources of Finance for Repayment

Usually the repayment of the loan is a problem for the poor because of their deficit budgets. The sources of repayment towards formal, micro and informal credit and their relative share for OMFB and NMFB are shown in table 6.2. Crop income and income from wage are the major sources of repayment of formal, micro, and informal credit in both the households.

6.2.3. Repayment of Loans by Purpose

Usually the repayment performance of the borrowers depends largely upon the purpose for which the loans are contracted. In general, the loans taken for productive purposes are repaid promptly because they generate income and thereby enhance the repaying capacity of the borrowers. While the loans taken for unproductive purposes do not generate any income and result in the debt burden. The repayment performance of the loans contracted from formal, micro and informal credit agencies has been examined with reference to the purposes of borrowing and is presented in Table 6.3.

The loans contracted from micro credit sources for all purposes is found to be better compared to formal and informal credit sources however it is marginal. But in the case of NMFB there is no observable difference in repayment performance towards different sources of finance. The above analysis confirms that micro credit has no impact in purpose wise repayment of loans by tribal households.

6.2.4. Repayment of Loans by Rate of Interest

In general it is assumed that loans carrying a higher rate of interest will be repaid in preference to those with lower rates of interest. It is examined here as to what extent, it will hold good in the case of tribal poor households and the details are shown in Table 6.4. It can be observed that in respect of micro credit among both the OMFB and NMFB, the repayment performance is slightly better for all ranges of interest rates. But in respect of formal and informal credit among both the households, there is no specific trend as such, to show that the repayment performance varies with the rate of interest.

SECTION – II

6.3. Determinants of Repayment of Loans

In the preceding section, an attempt is made to study the repayment performance of loans, sources of Repayment, the rate of interest at which are repayment of loans among tribal households in the study area. In this section, an attempt is made to examine the factors affecting repayment of loans by using multiple regression analysis. Regression methods may be used for time series data considering historical evidence or cross-section data representing the present technological relationships. The purpose of regression models is to quantify the degree of the effect of each of the variables under consideration, in explaining the variation in the dependent variable. Since our study is based on cross-section data, the regression analysis will help us to identify the significant factors that influence the dependent variable.

6.3.1. Specification of the Variables and Model

In this study, the total amount of repayment of tribal households is the relevant dependent variable. Accordingly, y is the total repayment of tribal households. Repayments of loans include all loans by the tribal households during the year under the study. The following explanatory variables are considered as the important determinants: Age, Head, Education, Work Participation, Occupation, Family Size, Assets, Income, Expenditure, Dependency Ratio, Food Expenditure, Non-Foo Expenditure.

By considering the above variables, the regression function adopted in this study is specified as below:

AGE = Age of the respondent
Head = Dummy variable, whether the respondent is head of household
Education = Number of Years of Education of respondent
Work participation = Dummy variable, whether the respondent is working
Occupation = Dummy variable, whether the respondent is employed
Family size = Family size of the house
Assets = Value of the Assets owned by the household
Income = Annual Income of the household

Expenditure = Expenditure of the household
Dependency ratio= Dependency ration of the household
Food expenditure= Food Expenditure of Household
Non-food Expenditure = Non-food Expenditure of the household.
Repayment = Repayment of loans taken (Dependent Variable)

Based on the above given variables, a multiple linear regression model is presented as follows:

$$Y=a+x_1b_1+x_2b_2+x_3b_3+x_4b_4+x_5b_5+x_6b_6+x_7b_7+x_8b_8 \quad \ldots\ldots\ldots\ldots$$

Age of the respondent is expected to have a positive relation in the repayment of loans. The older the individual more will be the repayment by the household.

Head is a dummy variable, and takes the value 1 for the individual who is the head of the household and 0 for other family members. Head of the household is expected to have more responsibility in the repayment of loans.

Education, years of schooling is expected to have a positive relation in repayment among both the households. It is expected that literacy improves the repayment capacity in the households.

Work Participation is a dummy variable and specifies the working status of the respondent. It takes the value 1 for workers and 0 for non-workers. It is expected to have a negative relation as worker will have a less repayment capacity of the respondent in both the households.

Occupation is a dummy variable and specifies the employment status of the respondent. It takes the value 1 for employee and 0 for non-employee. It is expected to have a positive relation as an employee will have more repayment capacity and vice versa.

Family Size, which represents number of family members living in the household. It has both positive and negative types of influence.

Assets represent the fixed property of the household. It is a quantitative variable, which takes the actual value of the assets holding by the household. It is expected to have a negative relation as more and more asset holdings reduce the repayment capacity of the household.

Income, If the household income is reduced, the repayment capacity is expected to decrease.

Dependency ratio, Food and Non-food expenditure is included in the model with the assumption that more the expenditure more the dependency ratio and less may be the repayment of loans by the poor households.

According to a regression equation presented earlier, we have computed the regression analysis. The results of this analysis are found satisfactory i.e. the coefficient of determination – R^2 which measures the proportion or percentage of the total variation in y explained by the regression model is significant. The existing explanatory variables are comparatively significant. Based on the above aspects, the annual per capita income of the household is considered as the variable, which determines the repayments of the tribal households. These variables are expected to have a positive and significant correlation with repayments of tribal households.

6.3.2. Results of Regression Analysis

The calculations, means, standard deviations and odds-ratio are presented in Appendix 6.1 for the OMFB households and in Appendix 6.2 for the NMFB households. To facilitate a comparison, regression results are presented in Table 6.5. It can be noted from the Table that the estimated regression coefficient of variable Work Participation has got a positive sign, as expected and is statistically significant. The repayment is higher in NMFB households than in OMFB households.

The results point out that it is the head of the household, HEAD, who participate more in repayment than the members of the household. In OMFB households repayment by the head of the household is 1.17 per cent where as in the case of NMFB households repayments by the head of the household is 0.10 per cent. This factor is statistically significant.

The variable year of schooling (EDU), has got a negative sign in OMFB households and positive sign in NMFB households. The hypothesis is that higher the education higher will be the repayment. This factor is statistically significant.

The variable Total Expenditure has got a positive sign in the case of NMFB and OMFB households. The hypothesis is that higher the expenditure lower will be the repayment. In NMFB households repayment is high which is 5.84 per cent and in OMFB households repayment is low which is 0.66 supporting the above hypothesis. This is significant at the 1 per cent level.

The Variable Non-food Expenditure is significant at 5 per cent level; Working Status is significant at 10 per cent level and Occupation is significant 1 per cent level. The other variables Age, Family Size, Assets and Income are statistically significant in determining the households' repayment.

Thus, the results reveal that the variable dependency ratio, food and non-food expenditure, work participation and occupation are the main factors affecting the repayment of loans by the tribal households. Hence, an increase in income may help in increasing the repayment performance of tribal households.

6.4. Summary

The repayment performance of loans is low in all sources of borrowing, however the repayment of micro credit is slightly better compared to formal and informal credit. Crop income and income from wage are the major source of repayment of formal, micro and informal credit. Regarding repayment of loans by purpose the loans contracted from micro credit sources for all purposes are found to be better compared to formal and informal credit sources but it is marginal. The repayment performance is slightly better for all ranges of interest rates in respect of micro credit but there is no specific trend as such to show that the repayment performance varies with the rates of the interest in respect of formal and informal credit. The regression results revealed that the variance dependent ratio, food and non-food expenditure, work participation and occupation are responsible in the repayment performance of tribal households. Therefore, efforts should be made by the governments to provide gainful employment opportunities, which will help in improving the repayment performance among tribal households.

Table 6.1. Repayment Performance of Borrowers

Category	*Amount Borrowed (Rs)*				*Amount Repaid (Rs)*				*Amount Outstanding (Rs)*			
	Micro credit	*Formal credit*	*Informal credit*	*All*	*Micro credit*	*Formal credit*	*Informal credit*	*All*	*Micro credit*	*Formal credit*	*Informal credit*	*All*
NMFB	(736124) 100.0	(158100) 100.0	(507866) 100.0	(1402090) 100.0	(173862) 23.61	(30200) 19.10	(98546) 19.40	(302608) 21.58	(562262) 76.39	(127900) 80.90	(409320) 80.60	(1099482) 78.42
OMFB	(1625857) 100.0	(264000) 100.0	(447700) 100.0	(2337557) 100.0	(654771) 40.27	(82980) 31.43	(168191) 37.56	(905942) 38.75	(971086) 59.73	(181020) 68.57	(279509) 62.43	(1431615) 61.24
ALL	(2361981) 100.0	(422100) 100.0	(955566) 100.0	(3739647) 100.0	(828633) 35.08	(113180) 26.81	(266737) 27.91	(1208550) 32.31	(1533348) 64.92	(308920) 73.19	(688829) 72.08	(2531097) 67.68

Note: Figures in brackets are Amount Borrowed, Repaid and Outstanding.

Table 6.2. Percentage Distribution of Repayment of Loans Borrowed from Different Agencies: Source-Wise

Source of Income for Repayment	NMFB				OMFB			
	Micro Credit	Formal Credit	Informal Credit	All	Micro Credit	Formal Credit	Informal Credit	All
Wage	16.65	-	4.05	10.88	25.66	15.03	18.68	23.39
Crop Income	69.41	56.95	83.76	72.84	40.30	42.78	71.59	46.34
Horticulture	3.73	33.11	7.10	7.76	1.18	13.85	5.70	3.18
Savings	4.65	-	1.01	3.0	12.77	28.32	0.03	11.83
Borrowed from the Institution	-	-	-	-	0.61	-	2.14	0.84
Borrowed from Private Sources	5.54	9.93	-	4.17	7.96	-	1.83	6.09
Others	-	-	4.05	1.32	10.69	-	-	7.72
Total	**100.0 (173862)**	**100.0 (30200)**	**100.0 (98546)**	**100.0 (302608)**	**100.0 (654771)**	**100.0 (82980)**	**100.0 (168191)**	**100.0 (905942)**

Note. Figures in brackets are Rupees.

Table 6.3. Repayment of Loans by Purpose of Borrowing

Purpose of Borrowing	NMFB Micro Credit Amount Borrowed	NMFB Micro Credit Amount Repaid	NMFB Formal Credit Amount Borrowed	NMFB Formal Credit Amount Repaid	NMFB Informal Credit Amount Borrowed	NMFB Informal Credit Amount Repaid	OMFB Micro Credit Amount Borrowed	OMFB Micro Credit Amount Repaid	OMFB Formal Credit Amount Borrowed	OMFB Formal Credit Amount Repaid	OMFB Informal Credit Amount Borrowed	OMFB Informal Credit Amount Repaid
Agrl. Investment	159424	45038 (28.25)	-	-	50600	22000 (43.47)	424082	159078 (37.51)	40000	0	68300	41420 (60.64)
Land Development	226387	26060 (11.51)	24100	0	10400	3100 (29.80)	352033	201146 (57.13)	18000	8880 (49.33)	59300	31240 (52.68)
Live Stock	154698	38094 (24.62)	36000	15200 (42.22)	117500	26000 (0.22)	304448	67780 (22.26)	-	-	-	-
Purchase of Asset	-	-	46000	13000 (28.26)	32000	1380 (4.31)	90000	38000 (42.22)	30000	12000 (40.0)	54500	19600 (35.96)
Health	4500	3500 (77.77)	-	-	77000	11000 (14.28)	67245	19025 (28.29)	50000	9500 (19.0)	39000	25760 (66.05)
Education	1000	0 (0.00)	-	-	1000	0	5850	737 (12.59)	-	-	-	-

(Contd.)

(Contd. Table 6.3)

Purpose of Borrowing	NMFB						OMFB					
	Micro Credit		Formal Credit		Informal Credit		Micro Credit		Formal Credit		Informal Credit	
	Amount Borrowed	Amount Repaid	Amount Borrowed	Amount Repaid	Amount Borrowed	Amount Repaid	Amount Borrowed	Amount Repaid	Amount Borrowed	Amount Repaid	Amount Borrowed	Amount Repaid
House Construction and Repair	-	-	15000	2000 (13.33)	-	-	35500	13000 (36.61)	10000	10000 (100.0)	10500	3300 (31.42)
Marriage and Cere monies	117150	18850 (16.09)	10000	0	47500	22800 (48.0)	108500	76000 (70.04)	110000	41100 (37.36)	177000	38900 (21.97)
Consumption	72965	42320 (58.00)	27000	0	34366	7266 (21.14)	238199	80005 (33.58)	6000	1500 (25.0)	39100	7971 (20.38)
Total	736124	173862 (23.61)	158100	30200 (19.10)	507866	98546 (19.40)	1625857	654771 (40.27)	264000	82980 (31.43)	447700	168191 (37.56)

Note: Figures in brackets are percentages.

Table 6.4. Repayment of Loans by Rate of Interest

Rate of Interest (%)	NMFB						OMFB					
	Micro Credit		*Formal Credit*		*Informal Credit*		*Micro Credit*		*Formal Credit*		*Informal Credit*	
	Amount Borrowed	*Amount Repaid*	*Amount Borrowed*	*Amount Repaid*	*Amount Borrowed*	*Amount Repaid*	*Amount Borrowed*	*Amount Repaid*	*Amount Borrowed*	*Amount Repaid*	*Amount Borrowed*	*Amount Repaid*
Less than 12	504079	122878 (24.37)	154000	30200 (19.61)	-	-	1513257	576171 (38.07)	264000	82980 (31.43)	-	-
12-24	232045	50984 (21.97)	4100	0	129266	34366 (26.58)	112600	78600 (69.80)	-	-	62600	9531 (15.22)
24 and above	-	-	-	-	378600	64180 (16.95)	-	-	-	-	385100	158660 (41.19)
Total	**736124**	**173862 (23.61)**	**158100**	**30200 (19.10)**	**507866**	**98546 (19.40)**	**1625857**	**654771 (40.27)**	**264000**	**82980 (31.43)**	**447700**	**168191 (37.56)**

Note: Figures in brackets are percentages.

Table 6.5. Estimated Co-efficient and Slopes of the Explanatory Variables of Repayment for the NMFB and OMFB Households – Multiple Regression

Item	*NMFB*		*OMFB*	
	Individual Borrowings	*Slope*	*Individual Borrowings*	*Slope*
Constant	-4022.3343	-0.7314	-1550.6807	-0.1541
Age	0.1230 (134.7344	1.5611	0.0951 (153.4264)	-0.1541
Head	0.0079 (341.6674)	0.1048	-0.0345 (-3305.4096)	1.1778
Education	0.0430 (654.4763)	0.5299	0.0621 (2285.5766)	-0.4408
Work Participation	-0.1943 (-5800.64)	-1.9680***	-0.0201 (-1922.6759)	0.8277
Occupation	0.3143 (3809.9273)	3.1543**	0.0392 (624.7135)	0.5332
Family Size	0.0996 (674.7690)	1.1065	-0.0492 (-483.0165)	-0.4358
Assets	-0.0725 (-0.0094)	-1.0072	-0.0165 (-0.0146)	-0.1991

(Contd.)

(Contd. Table 6.5)

Item	*NMFB*		*OMFB*	
	Individual Borrowings	*Slope*	*Individual Borrowings*	*Slope*
Income	-0.0916 (-0.0988)	-1.0760	-0.1524 (-0.1916)	-1.5119
Other Expenditure	0.6978 (0.3775)	5.8435*	0.0516 (0.0132)	0.6664
Dependent Ratio	0.0432 (344.0926)	0.5631	-0.0399 (-404.9141)	-0.5287
Food Expenditure	-0.0026 (-0.0084)	0.0304	0.2185 (0.5297)	1.9751***
Non-food Expenditure	-0.2832 (-0.3298)	-2.2884	0.5541 (0.4526)	5.8915**
No. of Observations	150		150	
R	0.590272773		0.60778135	
R^2	0.34842189		0.36939817	
$\bar{R}^2$	0.29134936		0.31416297	
F	(12.137) = 6.1049		(12.137) = 6.6877	
Error of Estimate	9883.6		14302.0	

* Significant at 0.01 level

** Significant at 0.05 level

*** Significant at 0.1 level

NMFB = New Micro Finance Borrowers

OMFB = Old Micro Finance Borrowers

References

1. Besley, T., and Coates, S. (1995): *"Group lending, repayment incentives and social Collateral"*, Journal of Development Economics, Vol.46, pp.1-18.
2. Ghatak, M. (1999): "Group lending, local information and peer selection". Journal of Development Economics, 60, 27-50.
3. Marie Godquin (2004): *"Microfinance Repayment Performance in Bangladesh: How to Improve the Allocation of Loans by MFIs"* World Development, Vol: 32, No. 11, p. 1909.
4. Stiglitz, J.E., and Weiss, A. (1981); *"Credit Rationing in markets with information"*. American Economic Review, 17(3), pp. 393-410.
5. Stiglitz, J.E.(1990): *"Peer Monitoring and credit markets"*. The World Bank Economic Review, Vol. 4((3), pp. 351-366.

7

Social Mobilisation for Empowerment and Poverty Reduction

7.1. Introduction

It is not income growth alone that has brought about poverty reduction through the trickle-down process there have been direct interventions too in a major way for poverty alleviation in India. Employment creation through investment in infrastructure development and pension schemes for the elderly is the recent initiatives. There has also been some shift in strategy from the individual approach to community-based approach and social mobilization for improving livelihood of the poor is gaining some momentum. This chapter has been organised into two sections. Section – I focus on Poverty in India and in Section – II, an attempt is made to outline the Concept, Strategies and Processes of Social Mobilization and Empowerment aimed at sustainable poverty alleviation.

SECTION – I

7.2. Poverty in India

7.2.1. Concept of Poverty

Several scholars attempted to provide estimates of poverty in the seventies (Minhas, 1970; Bardhan, 1970; Dandekar and Rath, 1971; Ahulwalia, 1978). Since then, the Planning Commission has been providing official estimates of poverty. It adopted the normative consumption baskets suggested for rural and urban areas by the Task Force on Poverty (1978).

The rural consumption basket contains 2400 kcal per day per person and urban consumption basket 2100 Kacl/day/person. State specific poverty lines were arrived at by valuing consumption baskets at state specific prices. Poverty lines were periodically updated for inflation. The procedure of arriving at the poverty line implies that the poverty line income at current prices would enable a household to acquire the normative basket, identified by the Task Force at current prices (Radhakrishna and Shovan Ray, 2005). However, in actual practice, the household at the poverty line may not acquire the normative consumption basket. For instance, in the recent period, the calorie intake of a household at the poverty line was less than the norm, due to changes in relative prices and consumer preferences.

7.2.2. Types of Poverty-Absolute and Relative

The concept of poverty has been defined mainly as a concept of nutritional deficiency and lack of minimum subsistence. At the conceptual level, a distinction is frequently drawn between the 'absolute' and 'relative' poverty. A household is considered as poor, in the absolute sense when it is unable to provide itself with the minimum subsistence, which is the nutritional standard. Relative poverty is defined as deprivation of income and wealth of a household in relation to that of the community. On this basis, a household is said to be poor when its income falls short of a certain proportion of the average income of the community. The concept of 'relative poverty' has limited applicability to low income countries like India since the problem here is the low level of subsistence. If this concept is used for estimating the levels of poverty, many households whose income does not provide minimum subsistence are likely to be considered as non-poor. Therefore, the concept of 'absolute poverty' is more relevant to the measurement of poverty in low-income countries like India.

7.2.3 Poverty Measurement

A number of researchers and organizations have used alternative ways of measuring poverty and many studies have considered income dimension of poverty. There are also differences among researchers as to how to adjust a given poverty line to the changes in the relative prices over different periods and across different regions. In this study, to know the level of living of the poorest of the poor households, the estimates of poverty are computed. These estimates are based on the primary household expenditure data, which are collected by researchers. In other words, using per capita household consumer expenditure as a measure of standard of living, the poverty analysis is carried out.

Accordingly, by using a weighted average of family size, per capita monthly total expenditure of each household, is computed. Therefore, for identifying the poor, one looks at the level of personal expenditure that enables the individual to satisfy the minimum consumption level. The proportion of the population not able to attain the specified level of expenditure is segregated as poor. Defining this level of expenditure, the poverty line is the first step in estimating poverty. However, instead of estimating poverty line for the purpose of our study, we updated the poverty line, which is adopted by the Expert Group of the planning Commission.

The Expert Group of planning Commission has estimated the poverty line for each state for the year 1973-74 and the subsequent years. Since the present study area is located in Andhra Pradesh, the poverty line estimated by the Expert Group for this State for the year 2004-05 is taken i.e., Rs. 292.95 per capita monthly total expenditure in rural Andhra Pradesh corresponded to an intake of 2400 kcal and it served as the cutoff line for dividing the poor from non-poor.

To measure the three different aspects of poverty, i.e. incidence, shortfall and severity of poverty among the sample households in the study area, three poverty measures were used. These are Head Count Ratio, Poverty Gap Ratio and Modified Sen's Index of Poverty. Each of these measures is separately discussed below:

(A) Head Count Ratio (HCR)

Head Count Ratio at the individual level is calculated by comparing households' per capita monthly expenditure with the updated poverty line. It can be written as:

$$HCR = \frac{q}{n}$$

Where
'q' is the number of poor,
'n' is the total population

This measure ignores how poor the poor are and, therefore, remains unchanged when the poor become poorer or move upward on the income ladder.

(B) Poverty Gap Ratio (PGR)

The total income needed to bring all the poor upto the poverty line is given by an average poverty gap (GAP) as:

$$GAP = (z-m) \times q$$

Where

'm' is mean per capita monthly expenditure of the poor,

'z' is the poverty line expressed in the monetary terms.

If the degree of misery suffered by an individual is proportional the expenditure shortfall of that individual from poverty line, then the sum total of these shortfalls may be considered as an adequate measure of poverty. Such a measure is called the Poverty Gap Ratio Index (PGR) and can be written as:

$$\text{PGR} = \frac{(z-m)}{Z}\ \text{HCR}$$

The measure PGR will provide adequate information about the intensity of poverty if and only if all the poor households are assumed to have exactly the same expenditure, which is less than the poverty line. In practice, the expenditure of the poor is unequally distributed and, therefore, PGR cannot be an adequate measure of poverty. It is an improvement over Head Count Ratio. Besides, it has an interpretation which makes it extremely attractive from a policy point of view. It indicates the poverty gap as a fraction of total expenditure needed to support everyone in the population at the poverty line. Thus, the transfer of resources required to eradicate poverty, completely could be assessed with this index. Although, perfect targeting of resources is not possible, this index provides at least a lower limit on the amount of transfer.

(C) Modified Sen's Index of Poverty (P)

As the Poverty Gap Ratio is insensitive to the redistribution of income among the poor is corrected by modifying Sen's Index (P) that assigns a specific rank order to individuals according to the extent of poverty. A higher rank to the person is far away from the poverty line is assumed by Sen, such that

$$\text{P} = \frac{\text{q}\left|(\text{z-m})(1\text{-Gp})\right|}{\text{z}\times\text{m}}$$

Where,

'GP' is the Ginni Coefficient of the distribution of expenditure and the poor among the other terms carry the same definitions.

So if the GP is zero, the modified Sen's index is reduced to the Sen's index as given earlier. We may note that the Sen's modified poverty index has taken into consideration, the expenditure inequality among the poor and is the product of head count and measure the proportion of the equally distributed expenditure of the poor from the poverty line. Its value lies between zero and unity. It assumes zero value when everyone's income is above the poverty line 'z' and becomes unity when every one has zero income. Both possibilities are unlikely to occur. This study works out and discusses all these indices.

7.2.4. Empirical Results

Table 7.1. Group-Wise Estimates of Poverty Measures

Groups of Households	*Head Count Ratio*	*Poverty Gap Ratio*	*Modified Sen's Index of Poverty*
NMFB	59.25	23.97	0.1856
OMFB	42.59	11.84	0.2431

Head Count Ratio

For the NMFB as whole, around 60 per cent of total households are found to be below the poverty line, while this picture is accounted for only 43 per cent in the case of OMFB. Based on the above fact it can be concluded that almost half of the households in both the groups are below the poverty line and the incidence of poverty is comparatively higher among NMFB households than OMFB households (Table 7.1.

The Poverty Gap Ratio

From the Table 7.1, the estimates of Sen's poverty gap ratio clearly indicate the poverty, as a fraction of total expenditure needed to support everyone in the population at the poverty line. Thus, the larger the estimate, the larger is the requirement of resources to guarantee the entire population an expenditure equivalent to the poverty line. Moreover, its smaller estimated value denotes lesser resource requirement to do the needful. The empirical results, when analysed, helped us in deriving the following inferences. The results of this poverty measure show that, the poverty gap ratio was found to be higher in the NMFB households.

Modified Sen's Index of Poverty

As said earlier, the Sen's modified poverty measure overcomes the limitation of his earlier measure, viz., poverty gap ratio. The latter measure suffers from the limitation of being an insensitive redistribution of income among the poor. The modified Sen's Index of Poverty overcomes this drawback by the use of a specific rank order weighing scale. Empirical values of the modified measure of poverty lie between zero and unity. It assumes zero value when every one's income is above the poverty line and becomes unity when everyone has zero income. Therefore, we may infer that the lower the value of this measure, the closer is the distribution of the poor to the poverty line and vice versa. The measure of Sen's Index of Poverty assumed value close to 0 in both NMFB and OMFB groups (0.1856 for the NMFB and 0.2431 for OMFB) (See Table 7.1). This indicates that the distribution of the poor is closer to the poverty line.

The empirical result shows that the incidence of poverty is high in both the households, i.e. 40 per cent in OMFB households and 60 percent in NMFB households. The poverty gap ratio is found to be higher in NMFB households. The modify Sen Index poverty indicates that the distribution of poor is closer to the poverty line in both the groups of households.

SECTION – II

7.3. Social Mobilisation for Empowerment and Poverty Reduction

7.3.1. Concept of Social Mobilisation

Social mobilization envisages education and organization of the poor for improved socioeconomic status through collective efforts. In this dynamic process, the poor will be empowered enough to come out of the dependency syndrome as well as poverty. As a means of empowerment, the Social Mobilization (SM) process involves continuous awareness campaigns among the poor by facilitators/social animators so that the poor can participate in the development process and thereby access the basic amenities and resources for socioeconomic betterment. It also provides a suitable framework for holism in development, first by catering to the needs and aspirations of the poor; and second, by seeking to engineer socioeconomic change on the basis of self-reliance (Radhakrishna and Shovon Roy, 2005).

Empowerment is a complex process by which the marginalized become aware of the power dynamics at work in the life context and develop skills and capacity for gaining some control over their lives without infringing upon the rights of others (Rowlands, 1997). In the development context, it is essentially a change of social relations, change in the attitudes of non-poor as well and emphasizes the need for re-negotiations in regard to access and control over resources.

A core methodology of SM was suggested for inclusion in the poverty policy frameworks of national and international agencies (Susil, Sirivardana, 2001). SM is a multi-stage process, which includes: (a) formation of poor into groups; entry point can be any social or Economic activity having immediate relevance to the poor; (b) awareness building; (c) capacitating the groups; (d) initiating social or economic activity for collective action and also provide social protection whenever necessary;

(e) capacity building and skill development to access new knowledge bases/ non- traditional spheres which may open up new powerful networks.

7.3.2. Strategies to Social Mobilization

The strategies to SM, range from 'Welfarist' to 'Development' to 'Empowerment'. A few development interventions emphasized on the 'access' dimension and creation of more opportunities to land, credit, education, and health services. Also, some institutional reforms like land reforms and reservations in government jobs and local self-governments for the socially disadvantaged have been introduced for facilitating active participation of the poor in key decisions and exercise of greater control over resources. However, a gradual shift in government strategies is evident from its changed stance and role that is, from 'provider of services' to 'facilitator of processes' initiated by the poor to break the vicious circle of poverty and dependency. Economic interventions, viz., employment as a means for enhancing people's capacity to participate and credit support have been the entry points largely opted by NGOs and GOs for social mobilization and poverty reduction during the 1980s and 1990s in India. 'Entrepreneurship development' and 'linking SHGs to financial institutions' have been the two most crucial events in their development strategy for sustainable poverty reduction.

7.3.3. Process of Social Mobilization for Empowerment

Strengthening of people's institutions like the Panchayat Raj Institutions (PRIs) Village Organizations (VOs) and Community Based Organisations (CBOs); enhancing the quality of governance through decentralization of development process, and earmarking larger allocations for social development have been the key elements of the strategy for achieving the Plan objective of growth with social justice. These institutions are expected to improve the quality of delivery of development goods and in the process make governments more responsive and responsible. Development of professional and managerial capabilities of VOs and CBOs has also been another significant measure in this regard. Revamping the delivery system and widening the social security net, among others, comprised the major government initiatives for improving the quality of life of the people as well as poverty reduction.

The Ninth Five Year Plan has made a qualitative shift in its approach from 'welfare' to 'empowerment' for ensuring the well-being of the disadvantaged. Economic independence and self-reliance through employment and income generating activities and group action have been the main planks. Therefore, it can be inferred that the ingredients essential for the social mobilization process for empowerment and poverty reduction, viz., creation of an enabling environment, building up the capacities of facilitating agencies, creation of opportunities for social and economic development and social protection measures, are well articulated in the Plan documents.

The SHG-Bank linkage approach has helped in tapping the latent potential of the poor in mobilizing their own savings, meeting their needs and managing their own affairs. Poverty alleviation through micro-credit is not mere provision of credit and services to the poor but helping the poor participate in the society's value added processes. The SHG-credit linkage has grown remarkably over time from 32,995 SHGs with a bank loan of Rs. 571 million during 1992-99 to 22,38,565 SHGs with a loan of Rs. 113,995 million by March 2006.

Therefore, financing SHGs had become a mainstream activity of the banking sector by 1996 and it emerged as one of the national priorities in 1999. The much desired 'partnership mode' of development with the participation of public and private sector banks (about 444) in SHG (micro) financing became a reality thereafter. Banks, GOs, NGOs and CBOs have been involved in social intimidation in forming and nurturing the SHGs. But the entrepreneurship development activities (of the SHGs and others) need to be qualitatively enriched so that poverty reduction will not be a transient phenomenon. In fact, this is one of the major challenges encountered by the voluntary sector also in their efforts to address poverty squarely.

The Swarnajayanti Gram Swaraozgar Yojana (SGSY) of the Government of India, launched in 1999, is a holistic programme covering all aspects of self-employment such as organization of the poor into SHGs, promotion of thrift and credit, training for management of group activities and skill acquisition and linking the SHGs with credit institutions. Under the SGSY, out of 8,13,290 SHGs 1,28,081 and 44,516 SHGs have passed the Grade – I and Grade – II performance tests conducted by banks by February 2002; and about 20,308 SHGs have taken up economic activities. The Government of India aims at formation of at least one SHG in each of the 1.4 million habitations in the country by 2004. Therefore, the capacities of the stakeholders' viz., bankers, functionaries in development departments, and PRIs, swarozgaris etc., need to be upgraded for effective implementation of SGSY.

The Janmabhoomi programme, launched in 1999 by the Andhra Pradesh government, introduces the concept of micro-level planning to sensitize the villagers about the scope and need for planning at the village level. This novel endeavor, which draws inspiration from the successful Saemaul Undong programme of South Korea, focuses on people-centered participatory development process. South Asia Poverty Alleviation Programme (SAPAP) of UNDP in Andhra Pradesh, aims at mobilizing and empowering the people for sustainable rural development and improved quality of life. The project points to the lesson that micro-credit intervention can reduce poverty and empower women if it is (a) accompanied by gender aware social mobilization, adequate capital formation, and transformative capacity building, and (b) combined with strategies to expand land rights, returns to wages and produce, and access to social security schemes for those outside the ambit of micro-credit

SEWA, Gujarat organizes workers to achieve their goals of full employment and self-reliance through the strategy of struggle and development. Its countrywide operations cover the states of Gujarat, MP, UP, Bihar, Kerala, and Delhi. The empowerment and poverty alleviation impact of full form SHARE's interventions at individual, collective and wider levels are summarized in Appendix 7.1. As can be seen, the project has enhanced women's control over their lives significantly, especially with respect to women's access to and control over resources, mobility, returns, to productive labour, self-confidence and esteem. They consequently have greater fallback position in the event of marital conflicts. Interestingly, they no longer view children as assets for future, but as sources of present expenditure leading to smaller families. Women are also yet to make political processes accountable to women. The empowerment impact has been higher amongst members who joined the groups a long time back over recent entrants.

Mysore Resettlement and Development Association MYRADA's strategy supported by NABARD went beyond banking with the poor towards banking with credit institutions which the poor have established and which they control. For these groups to be bankable, requires that the groups maintain records, which indicate the quality not only of their finance management but also of their institutional health. For example whether the level of participation of every member is increasingly effective, whether a few members are attempting to capture power, whether the boundaries of its activities are clearly defined, whether the groups have developed a culture of regular savings, repayment, and pattern of social behaviour that resolves conflicts, discourages conspicuous consumption and allows them to apply sanctions effectively and fairly to ensure behavior that sustains and enhances the quality of their performance and financial management. What is even more unique is MYRADA's gradual diversification of members' activities. They include: afforestation, watershed, wasteland management, livestock and dairying, and partnerships and networking.

Further, the past three decades have witnessed a steady increase in awareness of the need to empower women to increase social, economic and political equity and broader access to fundamental human rights, improvements in nutrition, basic health and education. Women's empowerment is not a one-way process, where some activities and experts can go and empower others. It is a multidimensional process which enables individuals and group to realize their full identity and powers in all spheres of life. Education would surely literate and equip women and take control of their lives (Sheetal Sharma, 2006).

The policy of the Government of India for employment and development of women, lays emphasis on removal of women's illiteracy and obstacles inhabiting their access to elementary education, women's participation in occasional, technical and professional education at different levels. As a consequence of the measures taken by the government, the literacy rate of women has gone up from 39.29 per cent in 1991 to 54.16 percent in 2001. Infact, the increase in female literacy (by 14.8 per cent) outpaced that for male literacy (11.7 per cent). The male female literacy gap has reduced from 24.84 per cent 1991 to 21.70 per cent in 2001 (See Table 7.2 and Fig. 7.1).

For various historic and socio-cultural reasons, women are a vulnerable section of our society and several macro indicators related to education, health, employment, economic participation, etc, point towards an adverse status. Women vis-à-vis men. Development and empowerment of women has been a priority in successive plans and several public expenditure programs are directed to this objective. However, outcomes of administrative intent are not often realized. Women face gender specific barriers to access of public services and expenditure.

7.3.4. Empirical Results

Social Empowerment

Size of the Family and Average Family Size

The family size affects the activities of each family. Majority of the households in NMFB (48 per cent) and in OMFB (63 per cent) are having a family size of four and below. The average size of the family is also low i.e. 4.05 in OMFB and 4.51 in NMFB households (Tables 3.15A & B). This implies that household have got awareness of the two child norm and about family planning techniques.

Educational Status

Education and Health has recongised as important components of human development. The proportion of illiterate heads are very high among NMFB (75 per cent) and OMFB (84 per cent) households. The proportion of illiterate members is also high in both the catagories i.e. 50 per cent in NMFB and 60 percent in OMFB (Tables 3.16 A & B). It implies that micro finance does't help much in increasing the educational status of the heads of households as well as other members in the family.

With regard to female literacy, the majority of the female members are illiterates in both the households, i.e. 55 per cent in NMFB and 62 per cent in OMFB (Table 7.3A). Even among female literates, two-thirds are having a literacy level up to 5th standard only (Table 7.3B). The analysis shows that micro finance doesn't help in improving the female literacy levels in the tribal households.

Economic Empowerment

Income

Usually income of the household indicates the economic status of the household. Around 50 per cent of the households are in the income range of below Rs. 20,000 per year indicating that the micro finance has marginal impact on the income levels of the sample tribal households (Table 3.20 A).

Savings

Generally savings supplements the family income of the household and improve their living standards. Around 75 per cent of the households are in the monthly savings range of less than 100 Rupees in both the households (Table 7.4). This implies that micro finance has no effect in improving the savings of the tribal households.

Utilisation of Additional Income Generated in the Family

In both the households around 40 per cent of the additional income generated in the family is utilized for health and educational purposes (Table 7.5, Figs. 7.2A and 7.2B). This shows that the role of micro finance has marginal impact on the income utilization of the households.

Decision Making

Our main concern is to examine women's empowerment and to identify the factors associated with variation in the empowerment. The wife appears to be the most important decision maker with the regard to their children schooling and husband appears to be the most important decision maker with regard to loans and purchase of household items in both the households (Table 7.6).

Nutritional Empowerment

Health and Nutritional Status

The national health statistics on Health show that the majority of the family members suffered with malnutrition resulting in health problems.

Around 30 per cent of the total family members are suffering with health problems in both the households.

The family members reporting dullness are high i.e., 12 per cent followed by growth failure, Odema, Fatigue in both the households (Table 7.7). The analysis shows that a child suffering with nutritional deficiency is more in NMFB households i.e. around 60 per cent than in OMFB households (53 per cent) (Table 7.8A). The majority of the adults are suffering with nutritional deficiency in both the households i.e. around 70 per cent (Table 7.8B).

Members Views–on Socio Economic and Nutritional Empowerment

The concept of micro finance was introduced with an opinion that it helps to empower people in social and economic aspects but the empirical study shows that both the households fared better in respect of children education, girl child education, discontinuation of child labour employment increase in bargaining power, increase in self confidence, increase in decision making and increase in credit worthiness but it doesn't help much in increasing the health status and nutritional development of the tribal households (Table 7.9).

7.4. Summary

The empirical result shows that the incidence of poverty is high in both the households i.e. 40 per cent in OMFB and 60 per cent in NMFB. The poverty gap ratio is found to be higher NMFB households. The modify sen's index poverty indicates that the distribution of poor is closer to the poverty line in both the households. With regard to empowerment micro finance has an effect on empowering people in certain aspects only. The average size of the family in both the households is lower, i.e., 4. Around 75 per cent of the households are in the monthly savings range of less than 100 rupees in both the households. The wife appears to be the most important decision maker with regard to their children's schooling and husband appears to be the most important decision maker with regard to loans and purchases of household items in the both the households. Around 30 per cent of total family members are suffering with health problems in both the households. The more the half of the female members are illiterates in both the households.To sum up, micro finance has an effect in respect of children's education, girl child education, discontinuation of child labour employment and increase in bargaining power, self confidence, decision making, credit worthiness but it does not help much in increasing the health status and nutritional development of the tribal households.

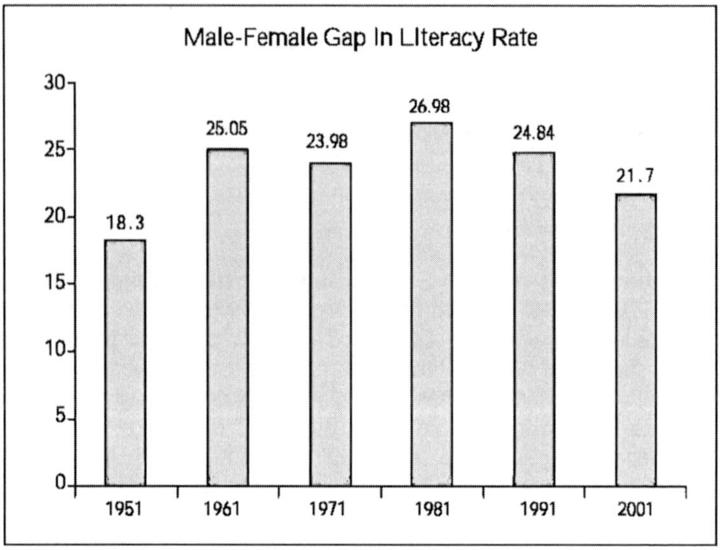

Fig. 7.1.

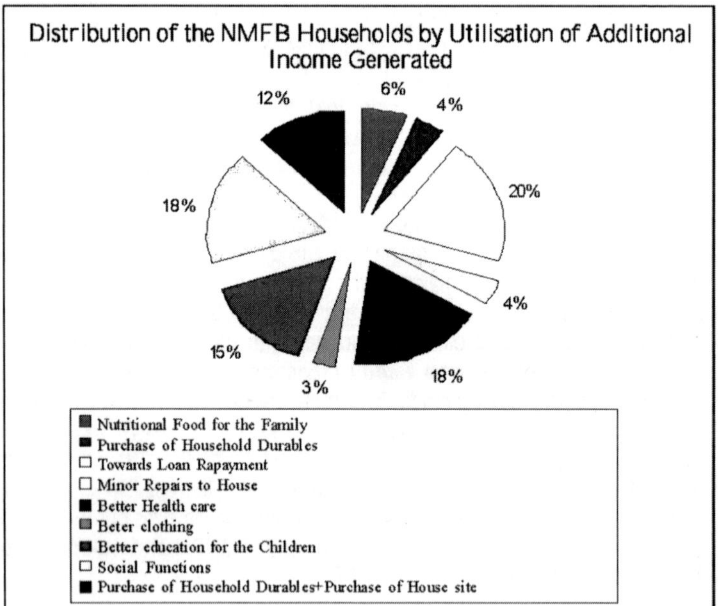

Fig. 7.2A.

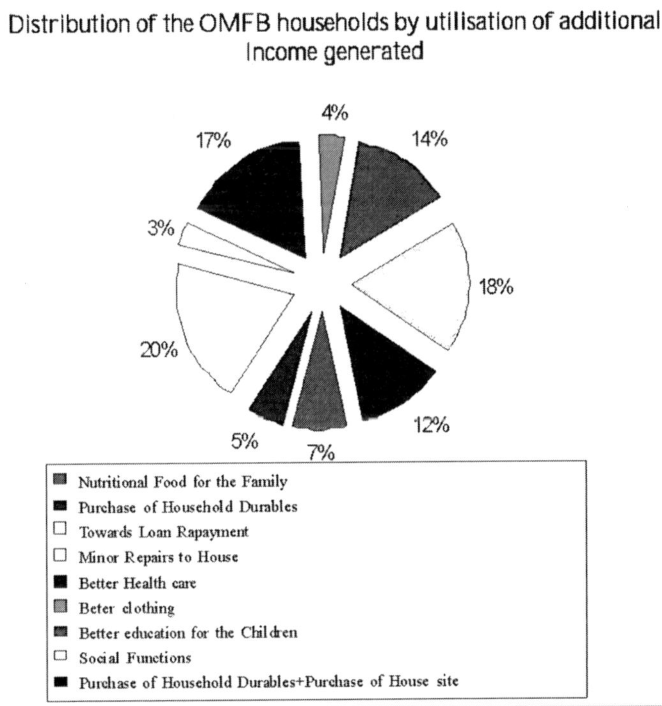

Fig. 7.2B.

Table 7.2. Literacy Rate in India

Census Year	*Persons*	*Males*	*Females*	*Male – Female Gap in Literacy Rate*
1951	18.33	27.16	8.86	18.30
1961	28.30	40.40	15.35	25.05
1971	34.45	45.96	21.97	23.98
1981	43.57	56.38	29.76	26.98
1991	52.21	64.13	39.29	24.84
2001	65.38	75.85	54.16	21.70

Table 7.3A. Female Literates in the Households

Literacy Status	*NMFB*	*OMFB*
Illiterates	55.17	61.66
Literates	44.82	38.33
Total	100.0	100.0
	(348)	(313)

Note: Figures in brackets are Female Literates.

Table 7.3B. Female Literacy Level

Literacy Level	*NMFB*	*OMFB*
Upto 5	64.10	79.16
6-10	23.07	16.66
11 and above	12.82	4.16
Total	100.0	100.0
	(156)	(120)

Note: Figures in brackets are Female Literacy.

Table 7.4. Distribution of Households by Monthly Savings

Monthly Savings (In Rupees)	*NMFB*	*OMFB*
Less than 50	24.6	18.0
50-100	52.0	56.6
100 and above	23.3	25.3
	100.0	100.0
Total	(150)	(150)

Figures in brackets are Households.

Table 7.5. Distribution of the Households by Utilization of Additional Income generated

Items	*NMFB*	*OMFB*
Nutritious food for the family	6.2	7.2
Purchase of household durables	4.1	5.0
Towards loan repayment	19.6	20.1
Minor repairs to house	4.0	3.0
Better health care	17.8	17.2
Better clothing	3.2	3.9
Better education for the children	14.9	13.5
Social functions	18.0	18.0
Purchase of household durables + purchase of house site	12.2	12.0
Total	100	100
	(150)	(150)

Figures in brackets are Households.

Table -7.6. Who takes Decisions In the Households

Decision making	*NMFB*				*OMFB*			
	Wife	*Husband*	*Both*	*Elderly people*	*Wife*	*Husband*	*Both*	*Elderly people*
Whether the boy should go to school	75 (50.0)	22 (14.66)	15 (10.0)	38 (25.33)	59 (39.3)	20 (13.3)	15 (10.0)	56 (37.3)
Whether the girl should go to school	66 (44.0)	17 (11.33)	18 (12.0)	49 (32.66)	70 (46.6)	24 (16.0)	26 (17.3)	30 (20.0)
Whether the female member should work	35 (23.3)	46 (30.6)	35 (23.3)	34 (22.6)	44 (29.3)	48 (32.0)	36 (24.0)	22 (14.6)
Loans	36 (24.0)	42 (28.0)	59 (39.3)	13 (8.66)	34 (22.6)	40 (26.6)	62 (41.3)	114 (76.0)
Purchase of Household items	44 (29.3)	27 (18.0)	53 (35.3)	26 (17.3)	46 (30.6)	25 (16.6)	49 (32.6)	30 (20.0)

Figures In brackets are percentages.

Table 7.7. Distribution of the Family Members Suffering with Health Problems

Nature of Health Problem	*NMFB*	*OMFB*
Oedema	6.05	3.45
Growth failure	9.45	5.09
Fatigue	5.90	4.60
Dullness	13.58	12.17
Improper eye sight	1.03	4.11
Nil	63.95	70.55
Total	100.0 (677)	100.0 (608)

Figures in brackets are Family Members.

Table 7.8A. Distribution of the Children Suffering with Nutritional Deficiency

Nutritional Deficiency	*NMFB*	*OMFB*
Anemia	24	27
B-complex Deficiency	19	26
Vitamin-A Deficiency	29	34
Nil	114	98
Total	100.0 (186)	100.0 (185)

Figures in brackets are Children.

Table 7.8B. Distribution of the Adults suffering with Nutritional Deficiency

Nutritional Deficiency	*NMFB*	*OMFB*
Anemia	31	35
B-complex deficiency	29	32
Vitamin-A deficiency	59	14.89
Nil	372	293
Total	100.0 (491)	100.0 (423)

Figures in brackets are Adults.

Table 7.9. Distribution of Member's Views on Social Empowerment and Economic Development

Items	*NMFB**	*OMFB**
Utilisation of Resources	22.0	82.0
Access to Information about Govt. programmes	17.33	18.0
Improvement in children's education	92.0	94.0
Improvement in girl child education	96.0	96.66
Improvement in sanitation	2.66	7.33
Discontinuation of child labour employment	88.66	97.33
Access to markets	18.0	70.0
Increase in bargaining power	40.66	78.66
Increase in self confidence	86.66	89.33
Increase in self employment potential	16.0	72.0
Improvement in marketing and communication skills	37.32	96.66
Improvement in decision making	75.33	86.66
Freedom from Money lender	57.33	66.0
Improvement in Nutritional status	42.66	45.33
Access to Public Participation	7.33	10.0
Improvement in credit worthiness	44.66	74.6
Improvement in productive skills	12.66	22.0
Mobility	24.66	78.66
Participation in the Developmental Programmes	4.66	10.66

Note* NMFB Households – 150; OMFB Households-150.

Source: Figures are in percentages.

References

1. Ahulwalia (1978): *"Rural Poverty and Agricultural Performance in India"*, Journal of Development Studies, 14 April, pp. 298-323.
2. Bardhan (1970): *"On the Minimum Level of Living and the Rural Poor"*, Indian Economic Review, 5(1), April, pp. 129-36.
3. Dandekar, and Rath (1971): *"Poverty in India"*, Indian School of Political Economy, Pune.
4. Minhas (1970): *"Rural Poverty, Land Redistribution, and Development Strategy: Facts and Policy"*, Indian Economic Review, 5(1), April, pp.98-128.
5. Radhakrishna R.and Shovan Ray (2005): *"Handbook of Poverty in India – Perspectives Policies, and Programmes"*, p.1.
6. Rowlands, J (1997): *"Questioning Empowerment: Working with Women in Honduras"*, Oxford, UK.

7. Susil, Sirivardana, (2001): *"The Core Methodology of Social mobilization in Women's Empowerment as a Transformative strategy for Poverty Eradication"*, SAPNA Regional Centre, New Delhi.

8. Sheetal Sharma (2006): *"Educated Women, Empower Women"* Yojana, October, pp. 52.

8

Conclusions and Policy Suggestions

India ranks second in tribal population in the world next only to Africa. India holds unique position in the concentration of tribal communities. There are about 532 Scheduled Tribes in India. They speak about 100 languages and 255 subsidiary languages. Topographically the tribal areas are generally inaccessible due to hilly terrains, deep forests and lack of communications. Nearly 80 per cent of the tribals live in rural areas and 93 per cent of them depend on agriculture and allied sectors. They are at different stages of culture and development, which vary from area to area in regard to the size of population, language and socioeconic organization. Tribal India depicts the persistence of a large number of problems. As the geographical configuration of tribal areas is mostly located in altitudes between 1000 to 3000ft. and the terrain is hilly with the consequent loss of fertility and soil erosion, agriculture as a source of their livelihood has been mostly unproductive. Due to prevalence of unemployment and underemployment, agriculture alone cannot sustain them throughout the year. So the tribals must rely on labour works and the forest produce which plays an important role in their daily life. Hence the tribal economy may rightly be called as "Agro forest based economy".

According to the 2001 Census the tribal population is estimated to be 84.3 million constituting 8.2 per cent of total population of India. It is estimated that the predominant tribal areas comprise about 15 per cent of the total geographical area of the country. Andhra Pradesh is one of the states having large tracts of hilly and agency areas and sizeable Scheduled Tribe population. The total Scheduled Tribe (ST) Population in 1951 was

7.66 lakhs which increased to 56.76 lakhs in 2001, an eight–fold increase, as a result the proportion in total population has increased from 2.46 per cent in 1951 to 6.59 per cent 2001, a three–fold increase.

One of the most serious problems faced by the tribals is indebtedness. Tribal debts are perpetuated by various devices and it is often reported that "a tribal is born in debt, live in debt and finally die in debt". Generally speaking, the tribals appear to accept indebtedness as a normal almost inescapable aspect of their existence. The tribals whose income is below the subsistence level and who indulged in costly religious and social practices have to necessarily depend on the traditional sources of finance, viz., moneylenders or traders. The trader-cum-moneylenders aggravate the tribal debts through unscrupulous methods. Indebtedness and exploitation grew faster in an atmosphere of ignorance prevailing in tribal communities.

In spite of the heavy dependence of the informal sector for credit on informal sources in India, there are also institutional sources of credit. The impressive growth of the banking sector, in India in the last four and half decades and introduction of different poverty alleviation programmes like IRDP, Jawahar Rojgar Yojana, increased access of credit to weaker sections. However, the emphasis throughout has been on achieving certain quantitative targets, leading to loan defaults and virtual erosion of repayment ethics. The end result was the disturbing growth in overdues which has not only hampered the recycling of scarce resources of banks but also affected the profitability and viability of the financial institutions.

Micro-Credit institutions evolved their own design features such as class, eligibility for membership in the group ranging from landless to minimum land holding; a prior entrepreneurial experience to no experience; monthly repayments to weekly repayments; individual lending to group-based lending; requirement of collateral to no collateral and group lending contracts to no group lending contracts. The group formation under micro-credit institutions is based on a growing institutional concept in terms of resources and management skills of the women members to reduce the gender inequality and to increase their confidence to get involved in issues and programmes in the public and private spheres. The success of group lending is attributed to various factors such as the ability of the group to mitigate asymmetric information problems in the credit markets through active screening of members; information advantage of the groups about the applicant's credit worthiness; social cohesion and heterogeneity of asset holdings; assortative matching of members; social ties between borrowing group members; group pressure to repay the loans; and peer monitoring through intra group insurance.

Micro finance revolution in recent times occupies a prime role on women's empowerment and poverty alleviation. Studies on micro finance indicate that adopting the method of group lending through SHGs could reduce the lending and supervision costs of public sector banks and raise repayment rates and systematically analysed the various aspects of micro-finance. While answering the various aspects of micro finance, the borrower's viewpoint is frequently missing. The access of the poor to formal credit through SHGs and its cost efficiency in reducing the transaction costs for the borrower's needs have to be analysed in order to understand the benefits of group lending for the poor. However, the existing studies are limited in number. More field studies are required to pass any judgment on the outcome of the Micro Finance Innovation.

Relevance of the Study

In India during the last five decades the strategy of increase in real per capita income had indicated increasing unemployment, poverty and income inequalities. The socio-economic position of the poorest of the poor had worsened. Indebtedness has been considered as one of the most vicious causes of the exploitation of tribals in the country. In fact, the tribal economy is essentially non-monetary with little cash surplus being generated. Once debt has been incurred, it is very difficult to repay by the poor tribals, even over generations due to exorbitant interest rates and lack of knowledge of repayment terms etc.

The laws passed by the Government to check the problem of usury were totally inadequate and largely ineffective. The institutional credit agencies, however, have come to play a significant role in providing development credit to tribal communities for their economic upliftment. In fact, the supply of adequate and timely credit through institutional credit agencies is considered as a sine-qua non for balanced development of the tribal economy. An attempt is made in the present study to assess the levels of employment, income and expenditure, poverty and indebtedness of the tribal households, in the light of Micro Credit Innovations.

Objectives

1. To bring together the available evidence on the magnitude of indebtedness among tribals, the purposes for which loans are contracted and sources of finance.
2. To review the credit policy for the poor and to assess the significance of Micro Finance.
3. To study the factors influencing borrowing and indebtedness among tribals.

4. To study the factors determining the access towards different sources of finance.
5. To assess the relative efficiency of alternative channels of credit in reducing transaction costs of loans.
6. To examine the effect of micro credit in enhancing loan repayment rates among borrowers.
7. To examine the Impact of micro credit on the socioeconomic empowerment and Nutritionaldevelopment of borrowers.
8. To suggest policy for further improvement of Micro Finance mechanisms.

Methodology

The methodology, used in the study, has been presented under three heads viz., sampling design, database, and techniques of analysis.

A multi- stage sampling technique is used in this study for the selection of units. Out of the nine districts of Andhra Pradesh which have more tribal concentration Srikakulam District is selected due to the fact that the district has drawn worldwide attention through the tribal participation in the political upheaval of 1969-71. The second stage of sampling is the selection of Mandal. Out of the 38 mandals in the Srikakulam District, Seetampeta Mandal was selected for the study which had the maximum coverage of tribal poor households and also maximum coverage of Self-Help Groups (SHGs) households. The third stage of sampling involves the selection of households. In all 300 households were selected for the study by using random sampling techniques. While 150 of these households are members of newly formed SHGs (NMFB), the remaining 150 households are members of old SHGs (OMFB). New Micro Finance Borrowers are borrowers whose membership in SHGs is less than two years from the data of the Survey and Old Micro Finance Borrowers are those whose membership in SHGs is five years from the data of survey. The reference period selected for the old SHGs is 2000-01 and for the new SHGs is 2003-04. These two groups of sample households have been chosen, keeping in view, that the old SHGs will fare better when compared to new SHGs in improving the living conditions of Tribal households in the study area.

In analysing the data, different statistical techniques are used apart from tabular analysis. Tabular analysis with averages and percentages are used to explain the general profile of the sample tribal households.

Poverty Measures

To examine the poverty levels, the Headcount Ratio (HCR) is used. Since all the sample households are poor, PGR and Sen's Index Poverty are used to measure shortfall and severity of poverty.

Probit Analysis

The participation of the individuals in borrowings is analysed with the help of Probit Model. The following equation is used for estimating the probability of participation in borrowing.

Prob (BORROW) = F (IC, HC)

Where Prob (BORROW) is the probability of an individual borrowing and IC is vector of Individual Characteristics and HC is a vector of Household Characteristics.

Individual Characteristics

SEX = Sex of the individual
AGE = Age of the individual (18 years of age and above)
REL = Dummy variable, whether the individual is relationship o the head of Household
EDU = Number of Years of Education of Individual
WP = Dummy variable, whether the individual is working participation.
IINC = Annual Earnings of the Individual

Household Characteristics

FINC = Annual family Income of the household
FEXP = Annual food expenditure of household
NPEXP = Annual non-food expenditure of household

Tobit Analysis

Tobit model is used to assess the determinants of access to different sources of credit. The amount borrowed from a particular source is determined by different factors, which will have influence on the amont demanded and borrowed. These factors are crucial in assessing the credit worthiness of the individual and other aspects, which limit his access to different sources of credit.

The following function is used for estimating the amount borrowed from different sources of credit.

AMT = f (SEX, AGE, REL, EDU, WP, IINC, FINC, FEXP, NFEXP)
SEX = Sex of the individual
AGE = Age of the individual (18 years of age and above)
REL = Dummy variable, whether the individual is relationship of the head of household
EDU = Number of Years of Education of the Individual
WP = Dummy variable, whether the individual is working status
IINC = Annual Earnings of the individual
FINC = Annual Income of the household family

FEXP = Annual food expenditure of household
NFEXP = Annual non-food expenditure of household.

Econometric Model

For estimating the effective cost of borrowing tribal loans from different sources, the following Econometric Model for calculating the effective rate of Interest, Is used.

$$E = (1+r)\, n\sqrt{L/(L-TC)-1}$$

Where

E = the effective rate of Interest
r = Nominal rate of interest
L = Amount of loan borrowed
TC = Amount of Transaction Costs
n = Loan duration in years

Regrsssion Analysis

To assess the factors responsible for repayment of debt, regression model is used. The amount of repayment from a particular source is determined by different factors. The following equation is used for estimating the probability of participation in repayment.

$$Y = a + x_1b_1 + x_2b_2 + x_3b_3 + x_4b_4 + x_5b_5 + x_6b_6 + x_7b_7 + x_8b_8 \ldots\ldots\ldots\ldots\ldots$$

AGE = Age of the respondent
Head = Dummy variable, whether the respondent is head of household
Education = Number of Years of Education of respondent
Work participation = Dummy variable, whether the respondent Is working or not

Occupation = Dummy variable, whether the respondent is employed
Family size = Family size of the house
Assets = Value of the Assets owned by the household
Income = Annual Income of the household
Expenditure = Expenditure of the household
Dependency ratio = Dependency ratlon of the household
Food expenditure = Food Expenditure of Household
Non-food Expenditure = Non-food Expenditure of the household.

Plan of the Study

The Study has been organised into eight chapters. The Introductory chapter highlights the tribal problems in general and Indebtedness in particular. This chapter also covers the objectives, methodology and Plan of the study. The Second chapter is organised into three sections. In the first section, an attempt is made to examine the credit policy for the poor and tribal development in India under five year plans. Second section attempts to examine the magnitude of indebtedness among tribals based on data from Debt and Investment Survey (NSSO 48th Round). The Genesis of the micro credit system and its progress in India is presented in the third section. The socioeconomic profile of the study area and sample respondents has been presented in the third chapter. The fourth chapter presents the factors influencing the participation of the tribals in borrowing as well as the determinants of their access to different sources of credit. The relative efficiency of alternative channels of credit with respect to the transaction costs of borrowing and its implications on the effective cost of borrowing for different sources of credit is presented in chapter-5. In the sixth chapter the repayment performance of sample tribal households in respect of borrowings from different sources is examined. The chapter seven explains the factors responsible for social mobilization and empowerment of tribal poor households in the study area. The major conclusions of the study are highlighted in the final and concluding chapter.

Major Findings of the Study

Credit Policy for the Poor and Genesis of Micro Credit System in India

The credit policy in the pre-independence period concentrated largely on the farming community and the problem of credit needs of the poor received only scant attention. In the first Three Five-year Plans, very little attention was paid to the credit needs of the poor. Because the planners believed in the theory of 'trickle down' effect and emphasis was laid on the over all development. From the Fourth Five-Year Plan onwards special agencies like SFDA and MFALDA were evolved to deal with the problems of the specific groups were evolved. In the banking sector also many changes have taken place and progressive shifts in lending policies in favour of poor and other weaker sections were undertaken. Some initiations were made to provide consumption loans to weaker sections and special target oriented programmes were designed to provide credit for the upliftment of the poor through promoting self employment.

The policy framework resulted in excessive target orientation in government-sponsored programmes. This resulted in high transaction costs and non-recovery problems to the formal credit institutions. All these weakened the strength of the financial institutions to serve the poor and further reduced their interest to transact such business. The failure of various programmes to address the root causes of the problem, brought home the need to confront poverty on a sustained basis. Policy makers and the NGOs recognized that both the human capital and the productive capacity of the poor need to be improved in order to reduce poverty. To address these needs, SHGs were introduced in 1992 following the example of Bangladesh Grameen Bank. To formalize the mechanism further, the RBI constituted a Working Group in November 1994 to review the functioning of the NGOs and the SHGs and make suitable recommendations for expanding their activities. Accepting the recommendations, the RBI advised the lending banks that the SHGs should be considered as an additional segment under priority sector advances and integrated them with the mainstream of credit operations. The Government of India bestowed national priority to the programme though its recognition in the Union Budget, 1999.

The progress of SHGs is very satisfactory in India. About 22,38,565 SHGs (cumulative) spread all over India, have been linked with banks by the end of March 2006. Model-wise analysis shows that upto March 2006, Model-II SHGs continued to have a major share of above 74 per cent of the total number of SHGs financed. Further, the spread of SHGs shows that the Southern Region occupied the first place in the Programme. Among the states of the Southern Region, Andhra Pradesh occupied the leading role. Agency-wise analysis shows that at the National level commercial banks are the major partners followed by the RRBs and the cooperatives' role is rather minimum in the programme.

The progress of SHGs is limited in term of spread, they certainly seem to hold a good potential in the field of credit for the poor. Precisely, based on such an assessment, the NABARD has an ambitious plan for expanding the SHGs all over the Country and promote them as instruments, which can supplement the institutional agencies in effectively reaching the poor. However, there are certain questions, need to be answered before one can think of the SHGs assuming the above role visualized for them.

Socio Economic Profile of the Sample Households

The socio-economic profile of the sample households shows that a majority of the heads of the households are in the age group of 18-39, for both the groups of households. The family size of the households is less than four members for both the groups of households. Regarding literacy levels of the heads of households, the proportion of literates is less in both OMFB and NMFB households. Similar picture was noticed among the family members of both the groups.

The high percentage of households are in the asset range of less than Rs.25000/- in the both the households. This shows that there is no impact of micro finance on the sample households. More than half of the total members in both the households are non-earners. Among the earners, the percentage in NMFB is higher than that in OMFB households. The dependency ratio is lower in NMFB households than in the OMFB households but it is marginal. In both the households around 50 per cent are in the income range of below Rs.20000 per year indicating that the micro finance has marginal impact on their income levels. The distribution income by source as indicated in Table 3.20B shows that in case of NMFB and OMFB households, income from agricultural labour is major one accounting for around 50 per cent followed by income from cultivation.

It was observed that the per capita expenditure (Recurring and Nonrecurring) for the OMFB households is greater, compared to the NMFB households. This may be due to the fact that the OMFB households are having access to the formal institutions since several years. In order to observe the income-consumption relationship, the Engle's Law is tested. It was observed that there is a decline in the share of expenditure on food items as income size increases. This decline is so sharp in the OMFB households compared to the NMFB households. This may be due to the fact that the OMFB households are having access to formal institutions since several years.

To sum up, in both the households the performance is not satisfactory in terms of literacy, value of assets, earning status and dependency ratio, occupational pattern, and income-consumption relationship. This may be due to lack of impact of micro finance among tribals.

Factors Determining Borrowing and Indebtedness

In general, the poor need credit for various requirements and raise credit from different sources. The above aspects were observed by analysing the structure of borrowings of tribal households. The analysis of borrowing between the NMFB and OMFB households reveal that the percentage of borrowing from informal sources of the NMFB households account for 36 per cent whereas it is 11 per cent in OMFB households. In both the households the formal credit accounts for more than half and in which micro credit constitutes around four-fifth of the total. This clearly indicates that group lending could be a good supplement for the formal credit system.

The agency wise analysis shows that rural banks play a vital role in providing formal credit and commercial banks play a major role in implementing the new innovative group lending approach. The purpose wise analysis shows that in both the households the percentage of formal and micro credit in productive purposes is high. The analysis of borrowing according to the rate of interest shows that formal and micro credit carries interest rates lower than informal credit. The analysis of borrowings by nature of security shows that by group security, the formal credit made available to the tribal poor without any physical collateral. Finally the above analysis conformed that micro credit supplements the informal sources of borrowings of the tribal poor households.

In order to enhance the tribal household's participation in micro credit programmes, the analysis was carried out to analyse the determinants of the participation in the borrowing of the individuals. While analysing the determinants the attention was shifted from the household level to the individual level. The participation of the individuals in borrowing is analysed with the help of Probit Model. The results of the Probit analysis indicated that factors like the position of the individual relationship of the family head (REL), the income of the individual (IINC) and sex of the individual (SEX) are significant. The probability of participation in borrowing by the head of the household is higher in OMFB than the NMFB. It is 0.002 percent in the OMFB households and only 1.123 percent in NMFB households. The parameter sex is positive in the NMFB and OMFB households, and it implies that the probability of female's participation in borrowing is higher by 0.095 percent than men in the OMFB and is higher by 10 per cent in the NMFB households. Regarding the variable IINC, the hypothesis is that higher the income lower will be the borrowing. In NMFB household the probability for borrowing is higher which is 0.42 per cent and in OMFB. To assess the level of borrowings from different sources of credit by the poor households, the Tobit model is used.

Transactions Costs of Loans

Transaction costs are broadly reffered to as the cost invoved in the exchange. Transaction costs occur both from the lenders' side as well as from the borrowers' side. Lenders' transaction costs involve costs of information gathering, loan administration, enforcement, etc. Borrowers' transactions costs mainly involve various charges imposed by lenders beyond interest payment such as application fees, service fees, photographs, etc. The effective cost of borrowing includes financial costs as well as non-financial costs incurred by the borrowers. The financial costs are costs that are incurred during the loan repayment period. These include the interest costs on loans. Nonfinacial costs are costs that were incurred prior to and at the time of obtaining of the loan. These include the transaction costs.

In both NMFB and OMFB households, the transaction cost of borrowing (TCB) from formal sources of credit is higher than from informal sources. The transactions costs are considerably lower in micro credit.

The reduction in transaction costs in group lending is mainly due to the reduction in the opportunity costs. It can conclude that through group lending the TCB can reduce considerably. The effective cost is higher for small loans than for larger loans, for all sources in both the households. The effective cost is also high for micro credit in the study area.

The major policy conclusion that evolved from the study is that the effective cost of borrowing for the non-preferred borrowers of the formal sector is being lowered by the new financial innovation of group lending. If this new innovation could aim at further reducing the transaction costs by minimizing the group formation costs, maintenance costs etc., it will serve the poor more effectively. This can be achieved by making suitable changes in the micro finance lending.

Repayment Performance of Tribal Debt

The repayment performance of loans is low in all sources of borrowing, however the repayment of micro credit is slightly better compared to formal and informal credit. Crop income and income from wage are the major source of repayment of formal, micro and informal credit. Regarding repayment of loans by purpose the loans contracted from micro credit sources for all purposes are found to be better compared to formal and informal credit sources but it is marginal. The repayment performance is slightly better for all ranges of interest rates in respect of micro credit but there is no specific trend as such to show that the repayment performance varies with the rates of the interest. The regression results revealed that the variance dependent ratio, food and non-food expenditure, work participation and occupation are responsible in effecting the repayment performance of tribal households. Therefore, efforts should be made by the governments to provide gainful employment opportunities, which will help in improving the repayment performance among tribal households.

Social Mobilisation, Empowerment and Poverty Reduction

The empirical results show that the incidence of poverty is high in both the households i.e. 40 per cent in OMFB and 60 per cent in NMFB. The poverty gap ratio is found to be higher in both the households. The modify Sen's index poverty indicates that the distribution of poor is closer to the poverty line in both the households. Micro finance has an effect on empowering people in certain aspects only. The average size of the family in both the households is lower i.e. 4. Around 75 per cent of the households are in the monthly savings range of less than 100 rupees in both the households. The wife appears to be the most important decision maker with regard to their children's schooling and husband appears to be the most important decision maker with regard to loans and purchases of household items in the both the households. Around 30 percent of total family members are suffering with health problems in both the households. More than the half of the female members are illiterates in both the households. Ultimately micro finance has helped the households in respect of children's education, girl child education, discontinuation of the child labour employment and increase in bargaining power, self confidence, decision making, credit worthiness but it does not help much in increasing the health status and nutritional development of the tribal households.

To sum up, the study has brought to the fore that the micro finance experiment has not helped the tribal poor in their employment pattern, income levels and borrowing pattern towards formal sources of finance. The effect of micro credit mechanisim led to a reduction in transaction costs of borrowing and benefited the lenders also by improving the loan repayment but it is marginal. Further, the SHG experiment has fared better in respect of socioeconomic empowerment and nutritional development but does not help much in reducing poverty and income inequality. However certain questions need to be answered before one can think of the SHG assuming the above role asulized for them.

1. There are limits to micro finance as a tool for poverty reduction. However effective the role of micro finance organizations in providing financial services to the poor, they cannot substitute for broader policies to promote pro-poor economic growth, equitable social development and democratic participation in collective forums of decision-making. In the absence of such policies, micro finance may at most provide a safety net for the poor rather than a ladder out of poverty.
2. Delivering micro credit to the poor and the poorest is primarily an NGO activity. They proved to be the best vehicles for the quick expansion of outreach of micro credit and they have matured in their management skills. But at the same time, they have started facing new problems because they are not part of the formal financial structure. The most critical problem faced by NGOs today is finding money to lend out to the poor. One solution that Bangladesh found to this problem is to create a national wholesale fund: Palli Karma Shahayak Foundation (PKSF). The government and the World Bank put their money into PKSF, which in turn made this money available to NGOs. The reason why NGOs in Bangladesh demonstrated a significant growth in recent years is because of the existence of this wholesale fund. Until the beginning of 2003, it had provided more than US$ 260 million to nearly 200 NGOs in Bangladesh to carry out micro credit programmes. Then, what is the best way of promoting SHG-NGO activity on a wider scale?

APPENDIX 1.1

Size and Growth Rate of Scheduled Tribe Population In Andhra Pradesh: 1951-2001.

Year	Schedule Tribe		percentage of ST Population	Andhra Pradesh	
	Size (in lakhs)	*Growth Rate*		*Size (in lakhs)*	*Growth Rate*
1951	7.66	-	2.46	311.15	-
1961	13.24	5.47	3.68	359.83	1.46
1971	16.58	2.24	3.81	435.03	2.92
1981	31.76	6.50	5.93	535.50	3.96
1991	41.99	2.79	6.31	665.08	3.59
2001	56.76	3.01	6.59	757.27	1.37

Source: Census of India Reports 1951 1961 1971 1981 1991 and 2001.

APPENDIX 1.2

Mandal Wise Population, Scheduled Tribe Population Census 2001

Sl. No.	Name of the Mandal	Population			Scheduled Tribe			Percentage of Col.10 over Col.3
		Persons	Male	Female	Persons	Male	Female	
1.	Veeraghatam	63882	31739	32143	4224	2056	2168	6.61
2.	Seethampeta	52282	26050	26232	45741	22647	23094	87.49
3.	Bhamini	41058	20265	20793	8178	4064	4114	19.92
4.	Kothuru	60876	30372	30504	7823	3913	3910	12.85
5..	Pathapatnam	59381	29369	29012	10603	5377	5226	18.16
6.	Meliaputti	50490	24947	25543	13435	6512	6923	26.61
7.	Palasa	87850	42978	44872	3208	1592	1616	3.65
8.	Mandasa	76402	37368	39034	10087	5257	4830	13.20
9.	Kanchili	59845	28930	30915	7597	3731	3866	12.69
10.	Ichapuram	76747	36043	40704	1304	617	687	1.70
11.	Kaviti	70945	33590	37355	6636	3107	3529	9.35
12.	Sompeta	74138	35481	38657	1063	541	522	1.43

(Contd.)

(Contd. Appendix 1.2)

Sl. No.	Name of the Mandal	Population			Scheduled Tribe			Percentage of Col.10 over Col.3
		Persons	Male	Female	Persons	Male	Female	
13.	Vajrapukothuru	69398	33380	36018	154	75	79	0.22
14.	Nandigam	53192	26348	26844	2842	1503	1339	5.34
15	Hiramandalam	46204	22954	23250	4382	2148	2234	9.48
16.	Palakonda	73592	36560	37032	2997	1622	1375	4.07
17.	Vangara	47879	24031	23848	1248	627	621	2.61
18.	Regidi	68422	34408	34014	578	292	286	0.84
19.	Lakshminarsupeta	27141	13611	13530	607	303	304	2024
20.	Saravakota	48793	24205	24588	6148	3107	3041	12.60
21.	Tekkali	70872	35011	35861	3596	1745	1851	5.07
22.	Santhabommali	64845	32198	32647	764	370	394	1.18
23.	Kotabommali	69906	35133	34773	1058	520	538	1.51
24.	Jalumuru	60200	29734	30466	391	187	204	0.65
25.	Sarubujjili	32630	16136	16494	801	418	383	2.45

(Contd.)

(Contd. Appendix 1.2)

Sl. No.	Name of the Mandal	Population			Scheduled Tribe			Percentage of Col.10 over Col.3
		Persons	Male	Female	Persons	Male	Female	
26.	Burja	41852	21113	20739	1288	638	650	3.08
27.	Santhakaviti	66893	33595	33298	132	58	74	0.20
28.	Rajam	81673	41265	40408	1041	530	511	1.27
29.	Ganguvarisigadam	55087	27860	27227	450	232	218	0.82
30.	Amadalavalasa	83945	42212	41733	226	113	113	0.27
31.	Narasannapeta	74284	36995	37289	242	115	127	0.33
32.	Polaki	65734	32880	32854	163	86	77	0.25
33.	Gara	75017	37373	37644	237	113	124	0.32
34.	Srikakulam	187132	93526	93606	772	431	341	0.41
35.	Ponduru	73175	37032	36143	271	145	126	0.37
36.	Laveru	67344	34071	33273	459	241	218	0.68
37.	Ranastalam	77436	39592	37844	131	70	61	0.17
38.	Etcherla	82051	41665	40386	372	181	191	0.45
	District Total	**2537593**	**1260020**	**1277573**	**151249**	**75284**	**75965**	**5.96**

APPENDIX 2.1
Plan-wise Tribal Development Polices and Programmes

Sl.No	*Plan Period*	*Tribal Development Programmes*
1.	1st Five Year Plan (1951-56)	Community Development Approach (Tribal Development Projects)
2.	2nd Five Year Plan (1956-61)	Special Multipurpose projects for Tribal people (Creation of TD Blocks)
3.	3rd Five Year Plan (1961-66)	Improvement of over the general CD approach (Improvement of TD Blocks)
4.	4th Five Year Plan (1969-74)	Administrative frame Programmeme implementation and protective measures [(Tribal Development Agencies (TDA)]
5.	5th Five Year Plan (1974-79)	Total and comprehensive view of the tribal problems and coordination of sectoral Programme (Tribal sub-plan and creation of AMPS)
6.	6th Five Year Plan (1980-85)	Integrated approach and large financial allocation (expansion plan of TSP)
7.	7th Five Year Plan (1985-90)	Mix-up of beneficiary oriented Programmeme and infrastructural development (Intensive Tribal Development)
8.	8th Five Year Plan (1992-97)	Plan considering the need of the people and participation (District/Regional Planning and Participation of voluntary organization)
9.	9th Five Year Plan (1997-2002)	Integrated development of the disadvantaged groups like scheduled castes through the programme like Rural Housing and Habit Development, National Social Assistance
10.	10th Five Year Plan (2002-07)	Focus on sustainable management of natural resources like water and land. Increase in forest cover and emphasize cross-sectoral synergies for special groups.

Source. Sundarapandian M., 'Tribal Development in India', Anmol Publication, New Delhi.

APPENDIX 2.2

Per Thousand Distribution of Households by Households Asset Holding for each Social Group

Rural

Social Group	*Size group of Outstanding Loan (Rs.)* Less than 5	5 -10	10 -20	20 -30	30 - 50	50 - 70	70 - 100	100 - 150	150-250	250 & Above	*All Classes*	*Distn. of HHS.*	*Av. Value of Assets per HH (Rs.)*	*No. of HHS. Reporting Cash Loan per 1000 HHS*	*AV. Amount of Cash Loan per HH (Rs.)*	*No. of Households* Estd. (00)	Sample
										INDIA							
Schedule Tribe	112	89	133	139	163	139	103	65	37	20	1000	110	52660	174	838	128429	5217
Schedule Caste/	111	129	183	123	163	91	83	56	34	25	1000	216	49189	259	1394	251286	6601
Neo-Buddhist Others	57	54	99	78	135	101	114	115	117	131	1000	674	134500	236	2246	783277	24578
All Households	75	74	121	94	144	103	106	97	91	96	1000	1000	107007	234	1906	1163947	36425

Note: Figures for the 'Group not record' category I.E. HHDS. Not reporting any social group are not shown separately.

APPENDIX 2.3

Number of Households Reporting Specified Items of Assets and Loan Outstanding as on 30.6.91 per Thousand Householdsand Corresponding Average Values (Rs.) Per Household Asset Holding and Social Group.

INDIA — SOCIAL GROUP: SCHEDULED TRIBE — RURAL

Household Asset Holding Group (Rs.000)	Type of Est.*	Items of Assets: Land	Building etc.	Live Stock and Poultry Birds	Agri. Machinery etc.	Non-Farm Business Equip.	All Trans Port Equipments	Durable Household Assets	Shares etc.	Deposits etc.	Loan Receivable: Cash	Loan Receivable: Kind	Total Assets	Cash Loan Payable	Number of Households: Estd. (00)	Number of Households: Sample
Less	P	478	593	258	542	46	56	897	1	25	.	1	906	93	14366	405
Than 5	A	453	813	189	43	9	31	592	-	42	-	-	2175	374		
	P	876	954	626	870	63	272	985	4	47	-	-	1000	121	11438	361
5-10	A	2873	2547	804	82	22	352	931	3	111	-	-	7725	289		
	P	948	973	710	908	40	178	1000	19	67	1	-	1000	139	17048	658
10-20	A	5673	5802	1415	128	23	120	1261	6	221	4	-	14652	374		
	P	984	980	774	895	61	249	993	12	89	1	-	1000	197	17788	650
20-30	A	11932	8177	2275	358	69	319	1777	1	139	2	-	25049	613		
	P	992	988	850	942	68	277	996	35	80	4	.	1000	225	20893	926
30-50	A	21065	11488	3626	332	137	276	2594	18	269	12	-	39817	970		
	P	827	840	752	817	44	474	996	35	239	3	1	1000	177	17912	698
50-70	A	26592	14867	4040	553	97	537	3554	63	7919	11	1	58235	717		
	P	1000	999	904	974	54	408	999	46	85	6	-	1000	192	13272	613

(Contd.)

(Contd. Appendix 2.3)

Household Asset Holding Group (Rs.000)	Type of Est.*	Items of Assets: Land	Building etc.	Live Stock and Poultry Birds	Agri. Machinery etc.	Non-Farm Business Equip.	All Trans Port Equipments	Durable Household Assets	Shares etc.	Deposits Etc.	Loan Receivable: Cash	Loan Receivable: Kind	Total Assets	Cash Loan Payable	Number of Households: Estd. (00)	Number of Households: Sample
70-100	A	50155	19827	5725	996	25	733	4216	9	405	20	-	82112	1223		
	P	1000	997	933	973	63	533	1000	74	148	3	7	1000	221		474
100-150	A	76983	29073	7915	1766	118	1168	5376	52	545	2	6	123004	1569	8389	
	P	1000	999	866	991	46	729	1000	133	284	22	1	1000	204		269
150-250	A	126959	31196	7148	3518	225	6113	8109	80	4512	26	-	187886	2367	4763	
	P	1000	999	980	977	72	733	1000	151	83	18	11	1000	188		163
250 & Above	A	313957	46096	13471	11910	301	5976	19204	256	1624	18	5	412819	3115	2559	
All Classes	P	896	920	735	870	54	318	985	33	105	3	1	989	174	128429	5217
	A	31025	12186	3391	796	76	713	2951	25	1489	8	1	52660	838		

APPENDIX 2.4

Number of Households Reporting Cash Loans Outstanding as on 30.6.91 Per Thousand Households and Per Thousand Distribution of Amount of Cash Loans Outstanding Over Credit Agency for each Social Group

INDIA RURAL

Credit Agency	*Social Group* *S.T* *P*	*S*	*S.C/Neo-buddhist* *P*	*S*	*Others* *P*	*S*	*All* *P*	*S*
Govt.	17	72	25	92	14	55	17	61
Co-op. Society/Bank	39	170	55	150	76	233	67	216
Commercial Bank Including RRB	64	378	91	346	73	333	75	337
Insurance	0	0	1	2	1	3	1	3
Provident Fund	0	0	2	11	3	7	2	7
Other Institutional Agencies	3	29	4	10	4	16	4	16
All Institutional Agenceies	120	649	171	611	158	646	156	640
Land Lord	6	38	19	85	9	31	11	40
Agriculturist Money Lender	16	75	31	80	21	68	23	71
Professional Money Lender	15	110	32	104	33	105	31	105
Traders	4	22	6	24	7	25	7	25
Doctors, Lawyers Etc.	-	-	1	3	1	2	1	2
Relatives and Friends	10	23	20	37	26	60	23	55
Others	16	70	12	33	10	26	11	30

(Contd.)

(Contd. Appendix 2.4)

Credit Agency	Social Group							
	S.T		S.C/Neo-buddhist		Others		All	
	P	S	P	S	P	S	P	S
All Non-Institutional Agencies	66	337	112	366	99	318	98	327
Unspecified Source	11	13	18	23	19	36	18	33
All Agencies	174	1000	259	1000	236	1000	234	1000
Estd. No. of H.HS. (00)	128430		251286		783277		1163948	
Amount (Rs.000)		10768370		35031377		176155977		222109887
No. of Sample Households Reporting	990		1890		6355		9239	

Note 1: P: Number of Households Reporting Cash Loan Outstanding as on 30.6.91 Per Thousand Households.

S: Per Thousand distribution of Amount of Cash Loans Outstanding as on 30.6.91.

Note 2: Figures in the 'Not Recorded' Category, I.E. HHDs. Not Reporting any Social Group, are not shown separately.

APPENDIX 2.5

Number of Households Reporting Cash Loans Outstanding as on 30.6.91 Per Thousand Households and per Thousand Distribution of Amount of Outstanding Cash Loans by Nature and Rate of Interest for each Social Group.

INDIA RURAL

Nature of Interest	*Rate of Interest*	*Social Group*							
		S.T		*S.C/Neo-buddhist*		*Others*		*All*	
		P	*S*	*P*	*S*	*P*	*S*	*P*	*S*
Interest Free	Nil	20	53	40	93	37	84	36	84
	Less Than 6	3	9	14	61	6	19	8	25
	6-10	3	14	6	23	6	23	6	22
Simple	10-15	42	244	66	233	72	265	67	259
	15-20	13	54	13	82	27	111	23	104
	20 and Above	40	247	70	245	58	197	58	207
	Unspecified	3	18	5	11	3	7	3	8
	All	97	588	158	654	154	622	148	625
	Less Than 6	1	2	3	9	1	2	1	3
Compound	6-10	1	2	2	7	1	5	1	6
	10-15	30	167	31	87	25	111	27	110
	15-20	3	11	6	19	10	61	8	52
	20 and Above	11	44	10	31	12	36	11	36
	Unspecified	2	47	1	4	1	3	1	5
	All	44	274	53	158	47	219	48	212

(Contd.)

(Contd. Appendix 2.5)

Nature of Interest	Rate of Interest	Social Group							
		S.T		S.C/Neo-buddhist		Others		All	
		P	S	P	S	P	S	P	S
Concessional	Less Than 6	2	8	3	7	1	2	2	3
	6-10	1	5	1	8	1	2	1	3
	10-15	10	48	13	39	7	27	8	29
	15-20	1	2	0	0	1	3	0	3
	20 and Above	0	0	0	2	0	1	0	1
	Unspecified	1	7	1	4	1	2	1	3
	All	15	70	18	59	11	37	13	42

(Contd.)

(Contd. Appendix 2.5)

Nature of Interest	Rate of Interest	Social Group							
		S.T		S.C/Neo-buddhist		Others		All	
		P	S	P	S	P	S	P	S
Not Specified	Un specified	12	15	23	36	19	38	19	37
	Nil	20	53	40	93	37	84	36	84
	Less Than 6	5	20	20	76	8	23	11	32
	6-10	5	21	10	38	8	31	8	31
Any	10-15	83	459	109	359	102	402	102	398
	15-20	17	67	19	101	37	175	31	158
	20 and Above	50	292	81	278	69	234	70	244
	Unspecified	18	88	29	55	24	50	24	53
	All	174	1000	259	1000	236	1000	234	1000
Estd. No of H.HS (00)/ Amount (Rs.000)		128430	10768370	251286	35031377	783277	176155977	1163948	222109887
No. of Sample Households Reporting Cash Loan Outstanding		990		1890		6355		9239	

Note 1: P: Number of Households Reporting Cash Loan Outstanding as on 30.6.91 Per Thousand Households.

S: Per Thousand distribution of Amount of Cash Loans Outstanding as on 30.6.91.

Note 2 : Figures for the 'Group Not Recorded' Category, I.E. HHDs. Not reporting any Social Group, are not shown separately.

APPENDIX 2.6

Number of Households Reporting Cash Loans Outstanding as on 30.6.91 Per Thousand Households and Per Thousand Distribution of Outstanding amount of cash loans over security of loan for each social group

INDIA — RURAL

Type of Security	*Social Group*							
	S.T		*S.C/Neo-Buddhis*		*Others*		*All*	
	P	*S*	*P*	*S*	*P*	*S*	*P*	*S*
Personal Security	110	555	177	598	143	446	147	476
Surety Security ETC.	16	76	22	86	22	82	22	83
Crop	11	33	7	20	7	22	7	22
First Charge on Immovable Property	10	47	14	48	18	93	16	83
Mortgage of Immovable Property	27	237	39	184	51	284	46	266
Bullion/Ornaments	1	1	10	19	10	17	9	16
Share of Companies ETC.			0	1	1	3	1	2
Agricultural Commodities	0	1	0	2	1	3	1	3
Other Movable Property	1	4	1	3	2	2	1	2

(Contd.)

(Contd. Appendix 2.6)

Type of Security	*Social Group*							
	S.T		*S.C/Neo-Buddhis*		*Others*		*All*	
	P	*S*	*P*	*S*	*P*	*S*	*P*	*S*
Other Type of Security	6	24	11	33	12	40	11	38
Unspecified	12	23	13	5	11	8	11	8
Total	174	1000	259	5	236	1000	234	1000
ESTD. No of HHs. (00)/Amount (Rs.000)	128430	10768370	251286	1000	783277	176155977	1163948	222109887
No. of Reporting Sample HHs.	990		1890	35031377	6355		9239	

Note 1. P: Number of Households Reporting Cash Loan Outstanding as on 30.6.91 Per Thousand Households.

S: Per Thousand distribution of Amount of Cash Loans Outstanding as on 30.6.91.

Note 2 : Figures for the 'Group Not Recorded' Category, I.E. HHDs. Not reporting any Social Group, are not shown separately.

APPENDIX 2.7

Number of Households Reporting Cash loans as on 30.6.91 Per thousand households and Per thousand Distribution of amount of cash loans Outstanding over purpose of loans for each Social Group.

INDIA RURAL

Purpose of Loan	*Social Group*							
	S.T		*S.C./Neo-Buddhist*		*Others*		*All*	
	P	*S*	*P*	*S*	*P*	*S*	*P*	*S*
In Farm Business								
Capital Expenditure	17	69	19	70	30	133	26	120
Current Expenditure Others	4	10	10	20	12	29	11	27
Others	23	147	20	48	30	105	27	98
In Non-Farm Business								
Capital Expenditure	7	28	12	33	10	64	10	58
Current Expenditure	7	37	7	21	6	18	7	20
Others	14	73	14	44	16	51	15	51

(Contd.)

(Contd. Appendix 2.7)

Purpose of Loan	Social Group							
	S.T		S.C./Neo-Buddhist		Others		All	
	P	S	P	S	P	S	P	S
In Household								
Capital Expenditure for Residential	6	76	17	72	13	63	13	65
Buildings	0	0	2	3	2	6	2	5
Current Expenditure	65	272	134	423	111	315	111	331
Others	57	288	72	266	48	217	54	228
Unspecified								
Any	174	1000	259	1000	236	1000	234	
Estd. No. of H.Hs. (00)	128430		251286		783277		1163948	
Amount (Rs.000)		10768370		35031377		176155977		222109887
No. of Reporting Sample Households	990		1890		6355		9239	

Note 1: P: Number of Households Reporting Cash Loan Outstanding as on 30.6.91 Per Thousand Households.

S: Per Thousand distribution of Amount of Cash Loans Outstanding as on 30.6.91.

Note 2: Figures for the 'Group Not Recorded' Category, I.E. HHDs. Not reporting any Social Group, are not show separately.

APPENDIX 2.8

SHG Bank Linkage–Model-wise Cumulative Position upto 31 March 2006

Sl No.	Region/State	Model-I		Model-II		Model-III		Total	
		No. of SHGs	Bank Loan	No. of SHGs	Bank Loan	No. of SHGs	Bank Loan	No. of SHGs	Bank Loan
(A) Northern Region									
1.	Haryana	613	30.50	4,254	285.51	-	-	4,867	316.01
2.	Himachal Pradesh	533	23.11	22,232	839.77	155	1.10	22,920	863.98
3.	Punjab	589	30.63	3,945	206.24	27	1.99	4,561	238.86
4.	Jammu & Kashmir	21	0.33	2,333	100.15	-	-	2,354	100.48
5.	New Delhi	-	-	224	18.58	-	-	224	18.58
6.	Rajastan	10,043	221.04	88.121	2,225.90	7	1.00	98.171	2,447.94
	Total	11.799	305.61	121.109	3.676.15	189	4.09	133,097	3,985.85
(B) North-Eastern Region									
7.	Assam	44.764	1,274.05	6.727	102.19	4,958	47.74	56,449	1,423.98
8.	Arunachal Pradesh	-	-	346	13.49	-	-	346	13.49
9.	Manipur	460	19.56	1,003	51.77	5	0.52	1,468	71.85

(Contd.)

(Contd. Appendix 2.8)

Sl. No.	Region/State	Model-I		Model-II		Model-III		Total	
		No. of SHGs	Bank Loan	No. of SHGs	Bank Loan	No. of SHGs	Bank Loan	No. of SHGs	Bank Loan
10.	Meghalaya	63	1.27	567	10.87	105	4.05	735	16.19
11.	Sikkim	95	0.92	32	0.94	-	-	127	1.86
12.	Nagaland	28	8.62	394	25.76	-	-	422	34.38
13.	Tripura	1,013	11.48	982	19.56	1	0.08	1996	31.12
14.	Mizoram	952	61.66	22	2.48	-	-	974	64.14
	Total	47,375	1,377.56	10,073	227.06	5,069	52.39	62,517	1,657.01
(C) Eastern Region									
15.	Bihar	918	12.77	45,032	1,034.25	271	5.17	46,221	1,052.19
16.	Jharkhand	742	20.57	27,863	1,020.73	2,214	73.30	30,819	1,114.60
17.	Orissa	67,227	1,796.87	93,232	2,598.48	20,437	359.30	180,896	4,754.65
18.	West Bengal	60,624	1,588.01	62,488	614.10	13,139	222.41	136,251	2,424.52
19.	A&N Island (UT)	10	1.49	154	6.74	-	-	164	8.23
	Total	129,521	3,419.71	228,769	5,274.30	36,061	660.18	394,351	9,354.19

(Contd.)

(Contd. Appendix 2.8)

Sl. No.	Region/State	Model-I		Model-II		Model-III		Total	
		No. of SHGs	Bank Loan	No. of SHGs	Bank Loan	No. of SHGs	Bank Loan	No. of SHGs	Bank Loan
(D) Central Region									
20.	Madhya Pradesh	17,184	477.80	39,307	1,173.83	634	15.23	57,125	1,666.86
21.	Chhattisgarh	4,137	29.67	27,154	308.14	-	-	31,291	337.81
22.	Uttar Pradesh	28,600	801.90	128,824	4,272.21	4,487	79.43	161,911	5,153.54
23.	Uttaranchal	2,842	94.03	14,746	797.83	-	-	17,588	891.86
	Total	52,763	1,403.40	210,031	6,552.01	5,121	94.66	267,915	8,050.07
(E) Western Region									
24.	Goa	187	18.13	436	37.06	1	0.02	624	55.21
25.	Gujarat	2,371	90.84	22,810	760.89	8,979	392.78	34,160	1,244.51
26.	Maharashtra	50,147	1,504.16	81,052	2,442.99	271	4.52	131,470	3,951.67
	Total	52,763	1,613.13	104,298	3,240.94	9,251	397.32	166,254	5,251.39
(F) Southern Region									
27.	Andhra Pradesh	2,263	85.86	577,016	42,817.14	7,959	552.18	587,238	43,455.18
28.	Karnataka	124,408	6,238.07	73,408	2,907.90	27,112	781.56	224,928	9,927.53
29.	Kerala	14,672	818.09	44,779	2,631.34	27,537	1,372.05	86,988	4,821.48

APPENDIX 2.9

SHG-Bank Linkage – Physical and Financial Progress of Commercial Banks upto 31 March 2006

Sl. No	Commercial Banks	No. of SHGs provided with bank loan during 1 April 2005 to 31 March 2006	Cumulative No. of SHgs provided with Bank loan upto 31 March 2006	Bank loan disbursed during 1 April 2005 to 31 March 2006	Cumulative bank loan disbursed upto 31 March 2006
1.	Allahabad Bank	4847	17,801	317.69	708.69
2.	Andhra Bank	11998	113,466	2800.93	8,429.00
3.	Bank of Baroda	10323	37,958	589.59	1547.15
4.	Bank of India	11032	40,633	684.02	1717.41
5.	Bank of Maharastra	3575	11,646	128.83	375.34
6.	Canara Bank	18455	58,914	1214.95	3081.42
7.	Corporation Bank	3124	12,964	259.54	644.64
8.	Central Bank of India	6347	25,796	470.92	1389.27
9.	Dena Bank	557	3,619	39.38	95.20
10.	Indian Bank	30632	96,460	3832.59	8,305.48
11.	Indian Overseas Bank	17254	70,962	1553.06	4,259.00
12.	Oriental Bank of Commerce	882	8,132	51.02	272.56
13.	Punjab & Sind Bank	295	1,075	21.09	55.76
14.	Punjab National Bank	16259	43,208	720.59	1804.41
15.	State Bank of India	142034	392,494	8878.92	20,470.33

(Contd.)

(Contd. Appendix 2.9)

Sl. No	Commercial Banks	No. of SHGs provided with bank loan during 1 April 2005 to 31 March 2006	Cumulative No. of SHgs provided with Bank loan upto 31 March 2006	Bank loan disbursed during 1 April 2005 to 31 March 2006	Cumulative bank loan disbursed upto 31 March 2006
16.	State Bank of Bikaner & Jaipur	7106	13,122	216.85	342.81
17.	State Bank of Hyderabad	8058	53,730	1182.41	3353.11
18.	State Bank of Indore	1258	4,778	93.03	197.87
19.	State Bank of Mysore	4908	10,131	515.53	807.11
20.	State Bank of Patiala	326	1,309	21.35	77.13
21.	State Bank of Saurashtra	80	1,423	5.87	22.14
22.	State Bank of Travancore	2560	8,719	258.12	520.80
23.	Syndicate Bank	8145	34,128	1091.79	2547.48
24.	Union Bank of India	5829	28,328	579.2	1749.80
25.	United Bank of India	5037	16,677	122.15	278.32
26.	UCO Bank	7313	20,248	352.28	736.27
27.	Vijaya Bank	3161	13,849	236.15	607.68
	Sub Total	331,395	1,141,570	26,237.85	64,396.78

(Contd.)

(Contd. Appendix 2.9)

Sl. No	Commercial Banks	No. of SHGs provided with bank loan during 1 April 2005 to 31 March 2006	Cumulative No. of SHgs provided with Bank loan upto 31 March 2006	Bank loan disbursed during 1 April 2005 to 31 March 2006	Cumulative bank loan disbursed upto 31 March 2006
PRIVATE SECTOR BANKS					
1.	Sangli Bank Ltd.	2	143	0.04	2.95
2.	Bank of Rajasthan Ltd.	746	2,588	13.93	35.77
3.	Dhanalaxmi Bank Ltd.	1201	5,592	114.29	251.42
4.	Global Trust Bank Ltd.	-	-	-	-
5.	Jammu & Kahmir Bank Ltd.	58	211	4.81	7.79
6.	Karnataka Bank Ltd.	620	1,791	35.45	73.77
7.	South Indian Bank Ltd.	643	2,155	53.19	112.68
8.	Tamilnad Mercantile Bank Ltd	4	344	0.1	15.67
9.	Vysya Bank Ltd.	1531	8,252	185.4	462.37
10.	Catholic Syrian Bank Ltd.	112	676	6.8	16.06

(Contd.)

(Contd. Appendix 2.9)

Sl. No	Commercial Banks	No. of SHGs provided with bank loan during 1 April 2005 to 31 March 2006	Cumulative No. of SHgs provided with Bank loan upto 31 March 2006	Bank loan disbursed during 1 April 2005 to 31 March 2006	Cumulative bank loan disbursed upto 31 March 2006
11.	Federal Bank Ltd.	1181	3,060	137.65	225.39
12.	Lord Krishna Bank Ltd.	39	106	4	10.02
13.	City Union Bank Ltd.	85	719	4.16	28.47
14.	Laxmi Vilas Bank Ltd.	0	450	0	10.36
15.	Karur Vysya Bank Ltd.	51	324	2.66	9.88
16.	ICICI Bank Ltd	6746	17,755	1470.42	4125.31
17.	Nainital Bank Ltd.	56	237	3.24	12.13
18.	The United Western Bank Ltd.	96	189	10.29	12.50
19.	Ratnakar Bank Ltd.	1	20	0.02	0.48
20.	UTI Bank Ltd.	-	328	0	20.00
21.	K.B.S Local Area Bank	0	663	0	28.49
	Sub Total	13,172	45,603	2,046.45	5,461.51
	Grand Total	344,567	1,188,040	28,284.30	69874

Source: Progress of SHG-Bank Linkage in India 2005-06, MICD, NABARD, New Delhi.

APPENDIX 2.10

SHG-Bank Linkage-Physical and Financial Progress of Participating Regional Rural Banks upto 31 March 2006

Sl. No.	*Name of the RRB*	*No. of SHGs provided with bank loan during 01 April 2005-31 March 2006*	*Cumulative no. of SHGs provided with bank loan upto 31 March 2006*	*Bank Loan disbursed during 1 April 2005 - 31 March 2006*	*Cumulative bank loan disbursed upto 31 March 2006*
Andhra Pradesh					
1.	Chaitanya Gr. Bank	829	5,537	134.51	460.46
2.	Godavari Gr. Bank	622	6,456	119.43	450.30
3.	Golconda Gr. Bank	223	2,672	85.93	184.24
4.	Kakatiya Gr. Bank	823	9,660	133.72	588.38
5.	Kanakadurga Gr. Bank	563	3,259	113.24	265.77
6.	Manjira Gr. Bank	1,382	11,750	348.46	848.83
7.	Nagarjuna Gr. Bank	4,925	27,879	532.78	1375.63
8.	Pinakini Gr. Bank	1,835	9,182	283.97	743.16
9.	Rayalaseema Gr. Bank	4,805	21,195	756.64	1566.17
10.	Sangameswara Gr. Bank	2,224	11,722	260.40	987.00
11.	Shri Satvahana Gr. Bank	1,641	9,048	119.63	400.65

(Contd.)

(Contd. Appendix 2.10)

Sl. No.	Name of the RRB	No. of SHGs provided with bank loan during 01 April 2005-31 March 2006	Cumulative no. of SHGs provided with bank loan upto 31 March 2006	Bank Loan disbursed during 1 April 2005 - 31 March 2006	Cumulative bank loan disbursed upto 31 March 2006
12.	Shri Venkateswara Gr. Bank	1,731	10,584	433.75	1203.72
13.	Sree Anantha Gr. Bank	1,907	9,841	243.26	622.70
14.	Sri Saraswathi Gr. Bank	1,094	11,618	210.06	687.08
15.	Sri Visakha Gr. Bank	4,132	35,875	1012.41	2782.31
16.	Srirama Gr. Bank	1,007	3,842	77.58	258.19
	Total	**29,743**	**190,120**	**4,865.77**	**13,424.59**

Source: Progress of SHG-Bank Linkage in India 2005-06, MICD, NABARD, New Delhi.

APPENDIX 2.11

SHG-Bank Linkage-Physical and Financial Progress of Participating Co-operative Banks upto 31 March 2006

Sl. No.	Name of the DCCB	No. of SHGs provided with bank loan during 1 April 2005 to 31 March 2006	Cumulative No. of SHGs provided with bank loan upto 31 March 2006	Bank Loan disbursed during 1 April 2005 to 31 March 2006	Cumulative bank loan disbursed upto 31 March 2006
Andhra Pradesh					
1.	Adilabad DCCB	0	227	0.00	6.23
2.	Anantapur DCCB	131	821	10.79	30.39
3.	Chittor DCCB	22	425	5.85	24.06
4.	Guntur DCCB	78	668	13.64	39.49
5.	East Godavari DCCB	134	264	5.38	7.55
6.	Krishna DCCB	512	3,914	66.77	198.71
7.	Nalgonda DCCB	507	1,007	13.50	38.09
8.	Nizamabad DCCB	544	4,466	25.96	173.01

(Contd.)

(Contd. Appendix 2.11)

Sl. No.	Name of the DCCB	No. of SHGs provided with bank loan during 1 April 2005 to 31 March 2006	Cumulative No. of SHGs provided with bank loan upto 31 March 2006	Bank Loan disbursed during 1 April 2005 to 31 March 2006	Cumulative bank loan disbursed upto 31 March 2006
9.	Prakasham DCCB	30	30	0.60	0.60
10.	Rangareddy DCCB	4	15	2.00	2.28
11.	Visakhpatnam DCCB	290	1,645	36.95	96.64
12.	Viziamgaram DCCB	4	28	1.35	3.84
13.	West Godavari DCCB	648	1,163	45.14	59.33
14.	Warangal DCCB	15	15	0.39	0.39
15.	Eluru DCCB	-	8	-	0.16
	Total	**2,919**	**14,696**	**228.32**	**680.77**

Source: Progress of SHG-Bank Linkage in India 2005-06, MICD, NABARD, New Delhi

APPENDIX 3.1
Srikakulam District Profile 2002-03

Sl. No.	Item	Unit	State	Srikakulam
1.	Area	000 sq. kms	275	5.8
2.	Population (As per 2001 Census)			
	(a) Total Population	No	76210007	2537593
	(b) Urban Population	No	20808940	278659
	(c) Urban Population as per cent to Total Population	%	27.30	10.98
	(d) Rural Population	No	55401067	2258934
	(e) Rural Population as per cent to Total Population	%	72.70	89.02
	(f) Population (0-6 years)	No	10171857	336093
	(g) No. of Households	No	16849857	593350
3.	Density of Population (per sq.km)	No	277	438

(Contd.)

(Contd. Appendix 3.1)

Sl. No	Item	Unit	State	Srikakulam
4.	Scheduled Caste Population	No	12339496	229609
5.	Scheduled Tribe Population	No	5024104	151249
6.	Literates			
	Male	No	23444788	731778
	Female	No	16489535	485881
	Total	No	39934323	1217659
7.	Literacy Rate			
	Male	%	70.3	67.2
	Female	No	50.4	43.7
	Total	No	60.5	55.3
8.	Classification of Workers			
	(A) Total Workers (i + ii)	No	34893859	1201816
	(i) Main Workers	No	29040873	870624
	(ii) Marginal Workers	No	5852986	331192
	(a) Cultivators (i + ii)	No	7859534	266702
	(b) Agriculture Labourers (i + ii)	No	13832152	557032
	(c) Household Industry (i + ii)	No	1642105	49540
	(d) Other Workers (i + ii)	No	11560068	328542
	(B) Nonworkers	No	41316148	1335777

(Contd.)

(Contd. Appendix 3.1)

Sl. No	Item	Unit	State	Srikakulam
9.	Revenue Divisions	No	81	3
10.	Towns	No	210	6
11.	Revenue Mandals	No	1127	38
12.	Mandal Parishads	No	1094	38
13.	Gram Panchayats as on 31.03.'01	No	21943	1112
14.	Revenue Villages	No	28124	1814
	(a) Inhabited Villages	No	26614	1715
	(b) Uninhabited Villages	No	1510	99
15.	Health			
	(a) Hospitals	No	379	16
	(b) Primary Health centres	No	1386	61
	(c) Hospital beds	No	34948	934
	(d) Dispensaries	No	263	9
	(e) Doctors (Regular+contract)	No	8617	202
16.	(a) Normal Rainfall	Mms	940	1162
	(b) Actual Rainfall	No	613	804

(Contd.)

(Contd. Appendix 3.1)

Sl. No.	Item	Unit	State	Srikakulam
17.	Gross Cropped Area	Hects.	11558629	350268
18.	Net Cropped Area	,,	9729388	268746
19.	(a) Gross Irrigated Area	,,	4536195	159413
	(b) Gross Area Irrigated as per cent to total cropped area	%	39.2	45.5
20.	Net Irrigated Area	Hects.	3613664	150433
21.	Area under Principal Crops			
	(a) Rice	Hects.	2822067	153780
	(b) Jowar	,,	623846	358
	(c) Bajra	,,	86979	3476
	(d) Maize	,,	525649	900
	(e) Red Gram	,,	431636	1523
	(f) Bengal Gram	,,	390150	-
	(g) Black Gram	,,	694431	28658
	(h) Green Gram	,,	473454	23120
	(i) Horse Gram	,,	81441	13692
	(j) Chillies	,,	223248	2167
	(k) Onions	,,	27128	1262
	(l) Ground nut	,,	1469624	33253
	(m) Castor	,,	231902	-

(Contd.)

(Contd. Appendix 3.1)

Sl. No	Item	Unit	State	Srikakulam
	(n) Sesamum	..	115135	4515
	(o) sunflower	..	416579	56
	(p) Cashewnut	..	150644	19080
	(q) Cotton	..	803274	1522
	(r) Tobbaco	..	116790	29
	(s) Sugarcane	..	232471	3150
	(t) Coconut	..	105291	13682
	(u) Turmeric	..	56822	229
	(v) Banana	..	39354	765
	(w) Mangoes	..	319587	8466
22.	Production			
	(a) Rice	Tonnes	7326786	269152
	(b) Jowar	..	607496	138
	(c) Bajra	..	57479	4508
	(d) Maize	..	1485742	3846
	(e) Red Gram	..	150365	533
	(f) Bengal Gram	..	381806	-
	(g) Black Gram (Mash)	..	376135	8591
	(h) Green Gram	..	117972	6059
	(i) Horse Gram	..	29099	5874

(Contd.)

(Contd. Appendix 3.1)

Sl. No.	Item	Unit	State	Srikakulam
	(j) Chillies	..	408813	4259
	(k) Onions	..	412607	11577
	(l) Ground nut	..	820654	25404
	(m) Castor	..	86818	-
	(n) Sesamum	..	18044	663
	(o) sunflower	..	276207	61
	(p) Cashewnut	..	19643	8414
	(q) Cotton	Bales	1085739	2704
	(r) Tobbaco	Tonnes	167673	65
	(s) Sugarcane (Gur)	..	1392117	18674
	(t) Coconut	Nos'in '000	1158626	112824
	(u) Turmeric	..	283541	1228
	(v) Banana	..	1027659	14829
23.	Livestock Population (1999 Census)	No	36010955	1219460
24.	Veterinary Hospitals	..	282	13

(Contd.)

APPENDIX 4.1
Intermediary Calculations of the Probit Model for NMFB Households

```
*-* Limdep *-* File
MODEL COMMAND:
PROBIT; LHS= BARROW; RHS=ONE, SEX, AGE, REL, EDU, WP, IINC, FINC, FEXP, NFEXP$
Dependent variable is binary, Y=0 or not equal 0
Ordinary least squares regression.   Dep. Variable =  BARROW
Observations         =  385      Weights        =  ONE
Mean of LHS          =  0.645345    Std. Dev of LHS          =  0.342562
Std Dev of           =  0.835468    Sum of squares           =  0.45682 3
residuals
R-squared            =  0.462345    Adjusted R-squared       –  0.212521
F[13,633]            =  0.543897    Prob value               =  0.563525
Log -likelihood      =  0.798445    Restr. (a=0)Log-l        =  0.415245
Amemiya Pr.          =  0.942213    Akaike info. Crit.       =  0.156325
Criter.

ANOVA
Source               Variation      Degrees of Freedom      Mean Square
Regression           0.265021              8.               0.562321
Residual             0.891253            148.               0.945213
Total                0.563403            150.               0.754632
N (0,1) used for significance levels.
```

(Contd.)

(Contd. Appendix 4.1)

Variable	Coefficient	Std. Error	t-ratio	Prob(t)ox	Mean of X	Std. Dev. of X
Constant	0.13219	0.03792	1.8422	0.11282		
SEX	0.76795	0.236306	0.13256	0.75648	0.4869	0.48967
AGE	0.62193	0.12774	-0.092	0.92643	34.374	12.031
REL	0.48801	0.31826	6.597	0.00000	0.38640	0.48730
EDU	0.34256	0.92433	-1.500	0.13366	6.10820	4.89681
WP	0.25463	0.60872	0.801	0.42340	0.51623	0.50012
IINC	0.21546	0.35232	2.451	0.01425	34621.51	2541.3
FINC	0.58973	0.39473	-0.842	0.39999	8645.35	7961.2
FEXP	0.56123	0.462501	16.631	0.00000	3956.42	2456.7
NFEXP	0.44523	0.370406	1.039	0.29887	4640.41	3254.1

(Contd.)

(Contd. Appendix 4.1)

```
Method = NEWTON: Maximum iterations = 25
Convergence criteria : Gradient    =    0.100000003
                       Function    =    0.100000003
                       Parameters  =    0.100000003
Starting values
      0.1175        0.35425       -0.2324        0.2415       -0.2524
      0.2541        0.11211       -0.3125        0.2563        0.4806
      0.2214        0.3214        -0.2541        0.22541

==> NEWTON Iterations
Iteration: 1Fn = 357.8573

Param
   0.118      -0.25401    -0.13003     0.355      -0.513      020.43301    0.107
  -0.75306     0.769       0.38506     0.22906     0.20401    -0.28506     0.87902
Gradnt
   114.        115.        0.37704     41.9        0.10504     71.3        41.6
   0.15707    -53.1        0.35907     0.32207     246.        0.14408     50.5
  Iteration  2Fn = 255.9978
Param
  -0.905      -0.188      -0.46403     0.933      -0.15101     0.169       0.303
  -0.21405     2.24        0.14205     0.65206     0.50001    -0.89406     0.15801
Gradnt
   10.5        11.4        253.       -4.05        142.        0.254       0.169
   0.25405    -10.4       -0.41306     0.32906     23.4        0.15207     5.70
  Iteration  3 Fn = 249.1208
```

(Contd.)

(Contd. Appendix 4.1)

Param						
-1.24	-0.398	0.68103	1.22	-0.20001	0.409	0.334
-0.26105	2.68	0.19505	0.10705	0.57201	-0.12705	0.11301
Gradnt						
2.35	2.28	60.1	-0.219	26.8	0.14001	0.104
0.12404	-1.05	-0.78004	0.63405	5.83	0.36106	1.27
Iteration	4Fn = 248.8752					
Param						
-1.31	-0.489	0.13202	1.27	-0.20801	0.502	0.339
-0.26805	2.75	0.20705	0.12005	0.57701	-0.13705	0.96102
Gradnt						
0.122	0.127	3.11	-0.26102	1.32	-0.10201	-0.70003
-65.1	-0.41401	384.	0.32604	0.311	0.18905	0.57101
Interation	5 Fn = 248.8745					
Param						
-1.32	-0.496	0.13602	1.27	-0.20901	0.509	0.339
-0.26805	2.75	0.20705	0.12105	0.57701	-0.13805	0.95202
Gradnt						
0.34605	0.43803	0.87502	-0.57005	0.38102	-0.79004	-0.31604
-0.620	-0.15603	-0.321	9.65	0.90503	54.5	0.13103
Iteration	6 Fn = 248.8745					
Param						
-1.32	-0.496	0.13602	1.27	-0.20901	0.509	0.339
-0.26805	2.75	0.20705	0.12105	0.57701	-0.13805	0.95202
Gradnt						
0.28309	0.32808	0.56407	0.19208	0.15107	0.52108	0.22408
-0.64704	-0.57708	-0.32303	-0.15904	0.69408	0.41204	-0.25508

(Contd.)

(Contd. Appendix 4.1)

** Gradient has converged.
** Function has converged.
** Bionomial Probit Model

Maximum Likelihood Estimates
Log – Likelihood .... -324.2542
Restricted (Slopes =0) Log - L, -345.2211
Chi – Squared (13) 256.3846
Significance Level 0.000000
N [0,1] used for significance levels.

Variable	Coefficient	Std.Error	t-ratio	Prob(t)ox	Mean of x	Std. Dev. of X
Constant	1.4379	0.13219	2.858	0.1123		
SEX	0.5261	0.76795	1.854	0.8545	0.4869	0.48967
AGE	0.2438	0.62193	0.854	0.1285	34.374	12.031
REL	1.4489	0.48801	5.656	0.0021	0.38640	0.48730
EDU	-0.1866	0.34256	1.391	0.1626	6.10820	4.89681
WP	0.6864	0.25463	1.963	0.2327	0.51623	0.50012
IINC	0.3955	0.21546	2.125	0.4252	34621.51	2541.3
FINC	0.2354	0.58973	1.125	0.1456	8645.35	7961.2
FEXP	2.6485	0.56123	9.127	0.0010	3956.42	2456.7
NFEXP	0.8145	0.44523	1.856	0.2185	4640.41	3254.1

APPENDIX 4.2

Intermediary Calculations of the Probit Model for OMFB Households

```
MODEL COMMAND: PROBIT
RHS = BARROW, SEX, AGE, REL, EDU, WP, IINC, FINC, FEXP, NFEXPS
Limited Dependent Variable Model - CENSORED      regression
Ordinary least squares regression.  Dep. Variable      = BARROW
Observations       = 356            Weights            = ONE
Mean of LHS        = 0.217609304    Std.Dev of LHS     = 0.427937504
Std Dev of residuals = 0.235707904  Sum of squares     = 0.336881910
R-squared          = 0.115816600    Adjusted R-squared = 0.184977700
F(12.318)          = 0.861553301    Prob value         = 0.688075312
Log-likelighood    = -0.369181604   Restr.(a=0)Log-l   = -0.373463104
Amemiya Pr.Criter  = 0.190479002    Akaike Info.Crit.  = 0.109630908
ANOVA
```

Source	Variation	Degrees of Freedom	Mean Square
Regression	0.86908509	12.	0.77507108
Residual	0.56741910	376.	0.23085608
Total	0.51422810	388.	0.28619308

(Contd.)

(Contd. Appendix 4.2)

N (0,1) used for significance levels.

Variable	Coefficient	Std. Error	t-ratio	Prob(t)ox	Mean of X	Std. Dev. of X
Constant	1816.5	1164.3	1.561	0.11862		
SEX	-1457.4	935.3	-1.558	0.11917	0.37789	0.48548
AGE	16.145	18.90	0.854	0.39291	34.841	9.8974
REL	-1329.1	766.4	-1.734	0.08287	0.40360	0.49125
EDU	-1.2233	39.28	-0.031	0.97515	5.2931	4.4665
WP	-463.25	628.5	-0.737	0.46110	0.49614	0.50063
IINC	-0.5235	0.205	-0.255	0.79893	8977.5	3964.0
FINC	499.68	677.7	0.737	0.46092	9452.5	5151.1
FEXP	0.7604	0.139	1.758	0.07875	50928.0	48634.0
NFEXP	0.2524	0.139	0.181	0.85623	23058.0	15341.0

(Contd.)

(Contd. Appendix 4.2)

Method = NEWTON:	Maximum iterations	=	25
Convergence criteria :	Gradient	=	01000000E - 03
	Function	=	0.1000000E - 03
	Parameters	=	0.100000003

Starting values

0.5687	-0.4475	0.4957	-0.4081	-0.3756
-0.3845	-0.16075	0.1534	0.2334	0.7749
0.4265	0.13046	-0.4790	0.3070	

= > NEWTON Iterations

Iteration 1 Fn = 2395.308

Param						
0.558	-0.447	0.49602	-0.408	-0.37603	-0.142	-0.16105
0.153	0.23305	0.77506	0.31001	0.13001	-0.47901	0.30703
Gradnt						
122.0	113.0	0.45404	112.0	728.0	113.0	0.22407
9.86	0.92707	0.28307	268.0	0.13808	62.0	0.46906

Iteration 2 Fn = 2297.519

Param						
0.51401	-1.07	0.57002	-0.672	-0.33502	-0.70101	-0.23805
0.339	0.33405	0.13005	0.45401	-0.11306	-0.50201	0.23103

(Contd.)

(Contd. Appendix 4.2)

Gradnt						
27.3	27.1	0.10304	26.3	165.0	26.3	0.52006
0.448	0 20607	0.63906	60.2	0.30007	14.0	-0.61705
Iteration	3 Fn = 2287.794					
Param						
-0.99801	-1.48	0.66602	-0.848	-0.47302	-0.67101	-0.17505
0.465	0.44005	0.13205	0.55801	-0.22606	-0.60701	0.23903
Gradnt						
6.59	6.58	250.0	6.34	39.8	6.34	0.12106
0.80901	0.49606	0.15106	14.6	0.72306	3.32	-0.11504
Iteration	4 Fn = 2286.814					
Param						
-0.167	-1.67	0.68002	-0.914	-0.53302	-0.76601	-0.48706
0.522	0.48605	0.13205	0.59301	-0.27306	-0.64201	0.23903
Gradnt						
0.983	0.981	37.6	0.935	5.83	0.935	0.16905
0.17101	0.80005	0.21605	2.21	0.11506	0.457	-2.15
Iteration	5 Fn - 2286.786					
Param						
-0.180	-1.71	0.68002	-0.926	-0.54402	-0.80501	-0.58307
0.534	0.49005	0.13205	0.59801	-0.28206	-0.64801	0.23903
Gradnt						
0.34701	0.34701	1.33	0.32901	0.203	0.32801	589.0
0.73003	0.29804	760.0	0.79001	0.42004	0.15501	-0.92002

(Contd.)

(Contd. Appendix 4.2)

Iteration	6 Fn = 2286.786					
Param						
-0.180	-1.71	0.68002	-0.927	-0.54502	-0.80701	-0.41107
0.535	0.49005	0.13205	0.59801	-0.28306	-0.64801	0.23903
Gradnt						
0.47604	0.47504	0.18302	0.45104	0.27703	0.45004	0.810
0.10505	4.14	1.05	0.10903	5.82	0.21104	-+0.50205

**Gradient has converged.
** Function has converged.
** B-vector has converged.
****
Limited Dependent Variable Model -CENSORED regression
Maximum Likelihood Estimates
Log-Likelihood .... - 2348.546
Threshold values for the model : Lower = 0.0000 Upper = + Infinity
N(0,1) used for significance levels.

(Contd.)

(Contd. Appendix 4.2)

Variable	Coefficient	Std. Error	t-ratio	Proh(t)ox	Mean of X	Std. Dev. of X
Constant	-0.2127	0.4259	-0.316	0.75205		
SEX	1.1640	0.3521	3.306	0.00095	0.4869	0.48967
AGE	0.8542	0.5202	0.347	0.72845	34.374	12.331
REL	1.8547	0.3638	4.329	0.00002	0.38640	0.48730
EDU	0.4502	0.2001	0.171	0.86410	6.10820	4.89681
WP	0.4252	0.6810	0.379	0.70482	0.51623	0.50012
IINC	0.6291	0.4242	1.736	0.08252	34621.51	2541.3
FINC	0.1852	0.8510	0.379	0.70482	8645.35	7961.2
FEXP	0.5624	0.3242	1.736	0.08252	3956.42	2456.7
NFEXP	0.2122	0.5610	0.379	0.70482	4640.41	3254.1

APPENDIX 4.3

Intermediary Calculations of the Tobit Model for NMFB Micro Credit Households

```
*-* Limdep *-*
MODEL COMMAND:
TOBIT; LHS= BARROW; RHS=ONE, SEX, AGE, REL, EDU, WP, IINC, FINC, FEXP, NFEXP
Dependent variable is binary, Y=1 or not equal 1
Ordinary least squares regression.   Dep. Variable   = BARROW
Observations        =  168            Weights        = ONE
Mean of LHS         =  1.534234       Std. Dev of LHS          =  1.231451
Std Dev of          =  1.724357       Sum of squares           =  1.34571 2
residuals
R-squared           =  1.351234       Adjusted R-squared       =  1.111411
F[12.522]           =  1.432786       Prob value               =  1.452414
Log -likelihood     =  1.576834       Restr. (a=1)Log-1        =  1.314134
Amemiya Pr.         =  1.831112       Akaike info. Crit.       =  1.145214
Criter.

ANOVA
Source        Variation      Degrees of Freedom      Mean Square
Regression    1.154111              7.               1.451211
Residual      1.781142            137.               1.834112
Total         1.452312            141.               1.643521
```

(Contd.)

(Contd. Appendix 4.3)

Variable	Coefficient	Std. Error	t-ratio	Prob(t)ox	Mean of X	Std. Dev. of X
Constant	1.12118	1.12681	1.7311	1.11171		
SEX	1.65684	1.125215	1.12145	1.64537	1.3758	1.37856
AGE	1.51182	1.11663	-1.181	1.81532	23.263	11.121
REL	1.37711	1.21715	5.486	1.12131	1.27531	1.37621
EDU	1.23145	1.81322	-1.411	1.12255	5.11711	3.78571
WP	1.14352	1.51761	1.711	1.31231	1.41512	1.41234
IINC	1.11435	1.24121	1.341	1.11314	23511.41	1431.2
FINC	1.47862	1.28362	-1.731	1.28888	7534.24	6851.1
FEXP	1.45112	1.351411	15.521	1.1234	2845.31	1345.6
NFEXP	1.33412	1.261315	1.128	1.18776	3531.31	2143.1

(Contd.)

(Contd. Appendix 4.3)

```
Method = NEWTON: Maximum iterations    =    14
Convergence criteria : Gradient        =    1.23412
                       Function        =    1.112546312
                       Parameters      =    1.11125432
Starting values
          1.1164        1.24314        -1.1213        1.1314        -1.1413
          1.1431        1.1231         -1.2114        1.1452        1.3715
          1.1113        1.2113         -1.1431        1.11431

=> NEWTON    Iterations
Iteration: 1Fn = 246.7462
Param
 1.117      -1.14311     -1.12112    1.244      -1.412      111.32211    1.116
-1.64215     1.658        1.27415    1.11815     1.11311    -1.17415     1.76811
Gradnt
 113.        114.         1.26613    31.8        1.11413     61.2        31.5
 1.14616    -42.1         1.24816    1.21116     135.        1.13317     41.4
 Iteration   1Fn = 144.8867
Param
-1.814      -1.177       -1.35312    1.822      -1.14111     1.158       1.212
-1.11314     1.13         1.13114    1.54115     1.41111    -1.78315     1.14711
Gradnt
 11.4        11.3         142.       -3.14       131.        1.143       1.158
 1.14314    -11.3        -1.31215    1.21815     12.3        1.14116     4.61
 Iteration   2 Fn= 138.1117
```

(Contd.)

(Contd. Appendix 4.3)

Param						
-1.13	-1.287	1.57112	1.11	-1.11111	1.318	1.223
-1.15114	1.57	1.18414	1.11614	1.46111	-1.11614	1.11211
Gradnt						
1.24	1.17	51.1	-1.118	15.7	1.13111	1.113
1.11313	-1.14	-1.67113	1.52314	4.72	1.25115	1.16
Iteration	3Fn = 137.7641					
Param						
-1.21	-1.378	1.12111	1.16	-1.11711	1.411	1.228
-1.15714	1.64	1.11614	1.11114	1.46611	-1.12614	1.85111
Gradnt						
1.111	1.116	2.11	-1.15111	1.21	-1.11111	-1.61112
-54.1	-1.31311	273.	1.21513	1.211	1.17814	1.46111
Interation	4 Fn = 137.7634					
Param						
-1.21	-1.385	1.12511	1.16	-1.11811	1.418	1.228
-1.15714	1.64	1.11614	1.11114	1.46611	-1.12714	1.84111
Gradnt						
1.23514	1.32712	1.76411	-1.46114	1.27111	-1.68113	-1.21513
-1.511	-1.14512	-1.211	8.54	1.81412	43.4	1.12112
Iteration	5 Fn = 137.7634					
Param						
-1.21	-1.385	1.12511	1.16	-1.11811	1.418	1.228
-1.15714	1.64	1.11614	1.11114	1.46611	-1.12714	1.84111
Gradnt						
-1.17218	1.21717	-1.45316	-1.18117	1.14116	-1.41117	-1.11317
-1.53613	-1.46617	-1.21212	-1.14813	1.58317	1.31113	-1.14417

(Contd.)

(Contd. Appendix 4.3)

** Gradient has converged.
** Function has converged.
** Bionomial Probit Model

Maximum Likelihood Estimates
Log - Likelihood .... -213.1431
Restricted (Slopes =1) Log - L. -234.2131
Chi - Squared (12) 223.4315
Significance Level 1.12213
N [1.1] used for significance levels.

Variable	Coefficient	Std.Error	t-ratio	Prob(t)ox	Mean of x	Std. Dev. of X
Constant	-1.2168	1.3218	-2.147	1.1112		
SEX	-1.3851	1.2135	-1.466	1.1134	1.3758	1.37856
AGE	1.1251	1.5553	1.113	1.7274	23.263	11.121
REL	1.1617	1.1431	4.115	1.1231	1.27531	1.37621
EDU	-1.1175	1.1411	-1.261	1.1615	5.11711	3.78571
WP	1.4175	1.1618	1.753	1.1516	1.41512	1.41415
IINC	1.2284	1.1661	1.815	1.1441	23511.41	1431.2
FINC	-1.1571	1.2588	-1.614	1.3575	7534.24	6851.1
FEXP	1.6413	1.1244	11.576	1.1213	2845.31	1345.6
NFEXP	1.1161	1.1431	1.235	1.1674	3531.31	2143.1

APPENDIX 4.4

Intermediary Calculations of the Tobit Model for NMFB Formal Credit Households

```
*-* Limdep *-*
MODEL COMMAND:
TOBIT: LHS= BARROW; RHS=ONE. SEX. AGE. REL. EDU. WP. IINC. FINC. FEXP. NFEXP$
Dependent variable is binary. Y=0 or not equal 0
Ordinary least squares regression.    Dep. Variable    = BARROW
Observations         = 143            Weights          = ONE
```

Mean of LHS	= 0.234234	Std. Dev of LHS	=	0.230420
Std Dev of residuals	= 0.424324	Sum of squares	=	0.34240 2
R-squared	= 0.320234	Adjusted R-squared	=	0.000400
F[02,222]	= 0.432453	Prob value	=	0.422404
Log -likelihood	= 0.243534	Restr. (a=0)Log-0	=	0.304034
Amemiya Pr. Criter.	= 0.530002	Akaike info. Crit.	=	0.042204

ANOVA

Source	Variation	Degrees of Freedom	Mean Square
Regression	0.024000	4.	0.420200
Residual	0.450042	034.	0.534002
Total	0.422302	040.	0.343220

(Contd.)

(Contd. Appendix 4.4)

N (0,0) used for significance levels.

Variable	Coefficient	Std. Error	t-ratio	Prob(t)ox	Mean of X	Std. Dev. of X
Constant	0.02005	0.02350	0.4300	0.00040		
SEX	0.32354	0.022202	0.02042	0.34234	0.3425	0.34523
AGE	0.20052	0.00333	-0.050	0.50232	23.233	00.020
REL	0.34400	0.20402	2.453	0.00000	0.24230	0.34320
EDU	0.23042	0.50322	-0.400	0.02222	2.00400	3.45240
WP	0.04322	0.20430	0.400	0.30230	0.40202	0.40000
IINC	0.00432	0.24020	0.340	0.00304	23200.40	0430.2
FINC	0.44532	0.25332	-0.430	0.25555	4234.24	3520.0
FEXP	0.42002	0.320400	02.220	0.00000	2542.30	0342.3
NFEXP	0.33402	0.230302	0.025	0.05443	3230.30	2043.0

Method = NEWTON: Maximum iterations = 04

Convergence criteria : Gradient = 0.000000002

Function = 0.000000002

Parameters = 0.000000002

Starting values

0.0034	0.24304	-0.0203	0.0304	-0.0403
0.0430	0.00000	-0.2004	0.0422	0.3402
0.0003	0.2003	-0.0430	0.00430	

(Contd.)

(Contd. Appendix 4.4)

```
= > NEWTON     Iterations
Iteration: 0Fn = 243.4432
Param

 0.004      -0.04300    -0.02002    0.244      -0.402     000.32200   0.003
-0.34202     0.325       0.24402    0.00502     0.00300   -0.04402     0.43500
Gradnt
 003.        004.        0.23303    30.5        0.00403    30.2        30.2
 0.04303    -42.0        0.24503    0.20003     032.       0.03304     40.4
Iteration   0Fn = 044.5534
Param
 0.504       0.044       0.32302    0.522      -0.04000    0.025       0.202
-0.00304     0.03        0.03004    0.24002     0.40000   -0.45302     0.04400
Gradnt
 00.4        00.3        042.       -3.04       030.       0.043       0.025
 0.04304    -00.3       -0.30202    0.20502     02.3       0.04003     4.30
Iteration   2 Fn= 035.0004
Param
-0.03       -0.254       0.24002    0.00       -0.00000    0.305       0.223
-0.02004     0.24        0.05404    0.00304     0.43000   -0.00304     0.00200
Gradnt
 0.24        0.04        20.0       -0.005      02.4       0.03000     0.003
 0.00303    -0.04       -0.34003    0.22304     4.42       0.22002     0.03
```

(Contd.)

(Contd. Appendix 4.4)

Iteration	3Fn = 034.4340					
Param						
-0.20	-0.345	0.02000	0.03	-0.00400	0.400	0.225
-0.02404	0.34	0.00304	0.00004	0.43300	-0.02304	0.52000
Gradnt						
0.000	0.003	2.00	-0.02000	0.20	-0.00000	-0.30002
-24.0	-0.30300	243.	0.20203	0.200	0.04504	0.43000
Interation	4 Fn = 034.4334					
Param						
-0.20	-0.352	0.02200	0.03	-0.00500	0.405	0.225
-0.02404	0.34	0.00304	0.00004	0.43300	-0.02404	0.54000
Gradnt						
0.23204	0.32402	0.43400	-0.43004	0.24000	-0.35003	-0.20203
-0.200	-0.04202	-0.200	5.24	0.50402	43.4	0.02002
Iteration	2 Fn = 034.4334					
Param						
-0.20	-0.352	0.02200	0.03	-0.00500	0.405	0.225
-0.02404	0.34	0.00304	0.00004	0.43300	-0.02404	0.54000
Gradnt						
-0.04205	0.20404	-0.42303	-0.05004	0.04003	-0.40004	-0.00304
-0.23303	-0.43304	-0.20202	-0.04503	0.25304	0.30003	-0.04404

(Contd.)

(Contd. Appendix 4.4)

** Gradient has converged.
** Function has converged.
** Bionomial Probit Model

Maximum Likelihood Estimates
Log - Likelihood .... -203.0430
Restricted (Slopes =0) Log – L, -234.0000
Chi – Squared (02) 223.4302
Significance Level 0.000000
N [0,0] used for significance levels.

Variable	Coefficient	Std. Error	t-ratio	Prob(t)ox	Mean of x	Std.Dev. of X
Constant	-0.2035	0.3205	-2.044	0.0002		
SEX	-0.3520	0.2032	-0.433	0.0034	0.3425	0.34523
AGE	0.0220	0.2223	0.003	0.4244	23.233	00.020
REL	0.0304	0.0430	4.002	0.0000	0.24230	0.34320
EDU	-0.0042	0.0400	-0.230	0.0302	2.00400	3.45240
WP	0.4042	0.0305	0.423	0.0203	0.40202	0.40000
IINC	0.2254	0.0330	0.502	0.0440	23200.40	0430.2
FINC	-0.0240	0.2255	-0.304	0.3242	4234.24	3520.0
FEXP	0.3403	0.0244	00.243	0.0000	2542.30	0342.3
NFEXP	0.0030	0.0430	0.232	0.0344	3230.30	2043.0

APPENDIX 4.5

Intermediary Calculations of the Tobit Model for NMFB Informal Credit Households

```
*-* Limdep *-*
MODEL COMMAND:
TOBIT: LHS= BARROW; RHS=ONE, SEX, AGE, REL, EDU, WP, IINC, FINC, FEXP, NFEXP
Dependent variable in binary, y =0 or y not equal 0
Ordinary least squares regression.            Dep. Variable      = BARROW
Observations             =  74                Weights            = ONE
Mean of LHS              =  0.402022000       Std.Dev of LHS     = 0.400634500
Std Dev of residuals     =  0.282662200       Sum of squares     = 0.377072302
R-squared                =  0.322825300       Adjusted R-squared= 0.276774500
F(22,227)                =  0.262234202       Prob value         = 0.333078224
Log-likelighood     = -0.242725702   Restr.(a=0)Log-l  = -0.230845602
Amemiya Pr.Criter=  0.200387202   Akaike Info.Crit.  =  0.248846500
ANOVA
```

Source	Variation	Degrees of Freedom	Mean Square
Regression	0. 32775	22.	0.25287
Residual	0. 7072	227.	0.37420
Total	0.8858	222.	0.35200

(Contd.)

(Contd. Appendix 4.5)

N (0,2) used for significance levels.

Variable	Coefficient	Std. Error	t-ratio	Prob(t)ox	Mean of X	Std. Dev. of X
Constant	0.2886	0.2207	2.506	0.00022		
SEX	-0.2277	0.6203	-2.224	0.00082	0.3758	0.37856
AGE	-0.5426	0.2734	-0.243	0.62222	23.263	22.022
REL	0.3635	0.8542	3.826	0.00000	0.27530	0.37620
EDU	0.2704	0.4262	0.042	0.84725	5.20720	3.78572
WP	0.5823	0.2235	0.042	0.84782	0.42522	0.40022
IINC	0.2222	0.6578	2.336	0.23670	23522.42	2432.2
FINC	0.2232	0.4752	2.280	0.02202	7534.24	6852.2
FEXP	0.4406	0.2002	2.642	0.00482	2845.32	2345.5
NFEXP	0.4200	0.7480	0.504	0.43382	3530.32	2243.2

Method = NEWTON: Maximum iterations = 24

Convergence criteria : Gradient = 0.200000002

Function = 0.200000002

Parameters = 0.200000002

Starting values

0.2886	-0.2277	-0.542602	0.3635	0.270402
0.582302	0.2222	0.223203	0.4406	0.420005
	-0.407204	0.284205	0.385502	-0.845802

(Contd.)

(Contd. Appendix 4.5)

= > **NEWTON Iterations**

Iteration	2Fn = 208.2482					
Param						
0.300	-0.228	-0.543E	-020.364	0.27202	0.58202	0.222
0.22303	0.442	0.42005	-0.4072	-040.28405	0.38602	-0.84602
Gradnt						
83.5	25.2	0.22303	-25.0	344.	-3.22	-5.24
-0.27205	-2.20	-0.73005	0.22806	0.52006	267.	76.5
Iteration	2Fn = 240.4854					
Param						
-0.254	-0.566	-0.28402	2.24	0.20402	-0.280	0.325
0.35203	2.85	0.27504	-0.22603	0.20204	-0.322E	-02-0.25202
Gradnt						
6.55	2.42	232.	-2.77	40.3	-2.06	-2.02
-0.42704	-0.347		0.20805	0.42005	22.4	20.6
Iteration	2Fn = 237.2334					
Param						
-0.232	-2.05	-0.25802	2.42	0.22202	-0.220	0.432
0.52203	2.55	0.23304	-0.28603	0.22804	-0.36002	-0.32802
Gradnt						
0.426	0.564	22.5	-0.232	5.53	-0.230	-0.243
-0.42003	-0.234	-0.27004	0.28404	0.34204	2.37	0.825

(Contd.)

(Contd. Appendix 4.5)

Iteration	3 Fn = 237.2333					
Param						
-0.224	-2.25	-0.24202	2.46	0.24202	-0.223	0.452
0.53203	2.23	0.24504	-0.20703	0.23204	-0.33302	-0.32702
Gradnt						
- 0.22202	0.20702	-0.842	-0.84702	0.275	-0.43602	-0.53202
-220.	-0.37002	-762.	-262.	-207.	-0.87702	-0.55302
Iteration	4 Fn = 237.2225					
Param						
-0.224	-2.25	-0.24002	2.46	0.24402	-0.222	0.452
0.53203	2.43	0.24604	-0.20703	0.23204	-0.33202	-0.32702
Gradnt						
- 0.25302	0.38203	-0.442	-0.27003	0.34502	-0.22203	-0.62704
-0.225	-0.25302	-24.2	-222.	-756.	-0.52202	-0.22502
Iteration	5 Fn = 237.2282					
Param						
-0.224	-2.25	-0.24002	2.46	0.244E	-02-0.222	0.452
0.53203	2.77	0.24604	-0.20703	0.23204	-0.33202	-0.32702
Gradnt						
- 0.46002	-0.63205	-0.284	-0.63205	-0.48304	-0.63205	-0.35208
- 0.25602	-0.46002	-22.2	-225.	-203.	-0.22502	-0.34302

(Contd.)

(Contd. Appendix 4.5)

Iteration	6Fn237.2270					
Param						
-0.224	-2.25	-0.24002	2.46	0.24402	-0.222	0.452
0.53203	3.28	0.24604	-0.20703	0.23204	-0.33202	-0.32702
Gradnt						
- 0.20002	-0.22205	-0.58202	-0.22305	-0.80605	-0.22205	-0.23820
- 0.30802	-0.20002	-3.25	-30.8	-206.	-0.65702	-0.25302
Iteration	7Fn=237.2265					
Param						
-0.224	-2.25	-0.24002	2.46	0.24402	-0.222	0.452
0.53203	3.36	0.24604	-0.20703	0.23204	-0.33202	0.32702
Gradnt						
- 0.60702	-0.28206	-0.23702	-0.28206	-0.24305	-0.28206	0.20322
- 0.58202	-0.60702	-2.42	-23.4	-27.2	-0.26302	-0.48302
Iteration	8Fn=237.2264					
Param						
-0.224	-2.25	-0.24002	2.46	0.24402	-0.222	0.452
0.53203	3.62	0.24604	-0.20703	0.23204	-0.33202	-0.32702
Gradnt						
- 0.24202	-0.24007	-0.77702	-0.24207	-0.27006	-0.24007	0.28522
- 0.22502	-0.24202	-0.432	-4.25	-22.5	-0.87302	-0.22402

(Contd.)

(Contd. Appendix 4.5)

Iteration 20 Fn = 237.2264

Param

-0.224	-2.25	-0.24002	2.46	0.24402	-0.222	0.452
0.53203	3.86	0.24604	-0.20703	0.23204	-0.33202	-0.32702

Gradnt

- 0.78803	-056508	-022002	-0.56608	-0.43207	-0.56508	0.62822
- 0.23303	-0.78803	-0.283	-2.74	-3.77	-0.24302	-0.67203

Function has converged.

****

Binomial Likelihood Estimates

Log - Likelihood	-225.2264
Restricted (Slopes = 0) Log-L.	-242.2275
Chi-Squared (22)	247.2678
Significance Level	0,0000000

(Contd.)

(Contd. Appendix 4.5)

N(0,2) used for significance levels.

Variable	Coefficient	Std. Error	t-ratio	Prob(t)ox	Mean of X	Std. Dev. of X
Constant	-0.22346	0.3248	-0.225	0.64204		
SEX	-2.2530	0.2422	-2.205	0.00084	0.3758	0.37856
AGE	-0.2400702	0.620202	-0.236	0.62734	23.263	22.022
REL	2.4636	0.2527	3.228	0.00002	0.27530	0.37620
EDU	0.2434802	0.206202	0.262	0.75320	5.20720	3.78572
WP	-0.22242	0.4520	-0.268	0.60372	0.42522	0.40022
IINC	0.45283	0.2232	2.625	0.07242	23522.42	2432.2
FINC	-0.22242	0.4520	-0.268	0.60372	7534.24	6852.2
FEXP	0.45283	0.2232	2.625	0.07242	2845.32	2345.6
NFEXP	-0.22242	0.4520	-0.268	0.60372	3530.32	2243.2

(Contd.)

APPENDIX 4.6
Intermediary Calculations of the Tobit Model for OMFB Micro Credit Households

MODEL COMMAND: TOBIT
RHS = BARROW, SEX, AGE, REL, EDU, WP, IINC, FINC, FEXP, NFEXP $
Limited Dependent Variable Model - CENSORED regression

Ordinary least squares regression.		Dep. Variable =	BARROW
Observations	= 128	Weights =	ONE
Mean of LHS	= 0.363133303	Std.Dev of LHS =	0.326131403
Std Dev of residuals	= 0.334306101	Sum of squares =	0.343403110
R-squared	= 0.326306101	Adjusted R-squared =	0.161333701
F(12,376)	= 0.2123360101	Prob value =	0.103074003
Log-likelighood	= -0.361416603	Restr.(a=0)Log-l =	-0.364427103
Amemiya Pr.Criter =	0.140371702	Akaike Info.Crit. =	0.1021237301

ANOVA

Source	Variation	Degrees of Freedom	Mean Square
Regression	0.14210	12.0	0.16701
Residual	0.34340	376.0	0.10301
Total	0.31331	311.0	0.10701

(Contd.)

(Contd. Appendix 4.6)

N (0,1) used for significance levels.

Variable	Coefficient	Std. Error	t-ratio	Prob(t)ox	Mean of X	Std. Dev. of X
Constant	-343.13	1311.0	-0.266	0.74033		
SEX	417.36	1216.0	0.112	0.31672	0.37714	0.31231
AGE	22.023	11.11	1.332	0.11242	33.131	4.1473
REL	-231.42	763.2	-0.326	0.73373	0.30360	0.34122
EDU	-31.112	34.04	-1.233	0.21761	2.2431	3.3662
WP	-172.23	626.0	-0.272	0.71321	0.34613	0.20063
IINC	-0.2272201	0.203301	-1.221	0.20132	1477.2	3463.0
FINC	-632.23	113.0	-0.277	0.26361	4322.2	2121.1
FEXP	0.1400702	0.331602	0.330	0.62463	20421.0	31633.0
NFEXP	0.1172001	0.131701	1.322	0.17631	23021.0	12331.0

Method = NEWTON: Maximum iterations = 22

Convergence criteria :	Gradient	=	0.1000000E - 03
	Function	=	0.1000000E - 03
	Parameters	=	0.100000003

Starting values

-0.1212	0.3037	0.7731	-0.7611	-0.1317
-0.2312	-0.7437	-0.1413	0.2162	0.2716
0.2202	-0.2311	0.2363	0.3016	

(Contd.)

(Contd. Appendix 4.6)

⇨ NEWTON Iterations
⇨

Iteration	1 Fn= 724.3713					
Param						
-0.122	0.302	0.77302	-0.76101	-0.13401	-0.23101	-0.74302
-0.141	0.21606	0.27402	0.22101	-0.23406	0.23601	0.30403
Gradnt						
264.0	13.2	0.42303	42.3	0.13603	122.0	0.20707
113.0	0.12601	0.60107	602.0	0.32301	117.0	0.11107
Iteration	2 Fn = 364.2213					
Param						
-1.06	0.113	-0.11003	0.121	-0.71402	-0.73101	0.16302
-0.127	0.22306	0.22302	0.27102	-0.17406	0.16101	0.10303
Gradnt						
63.1	20.2	0.22703	21.1	320.0	26.4	0.33706
33.2	0.24707	0.13107	132.0	0.77307	24.4	-0.24107
Iteration	3 Fn = 333.3471					
Param						
-1.24	0.44601	-0.21302	0.332	-0.70302	-0.17301	0.31002
-0.216	0.33706	0.14102	-0.13301	-0.33106	0.76202	0.14203
Gradnt						
10.1	1.26	377.0	1.31	21.2	2.71	0.34102
-0.301	0.24106	0.30602	-0.26201	-0.23306	0.12301	-0.13307

(Contd.)

(Contd. Appendix 4.6)

Iteration	3 Fn = 320.1442					
Param						
-1.33	0.136	-0.66202	0.362	-0.11202	-0.41101	0.30102
-0.301	0.24106	0.30602	-0.26201	-0.23306	0.12301	0.33703
Gradnt						
1.04	0.26701	36.2	0.31401	2.34	0.213	0.21103
1.06	0.21602	0.23302	2.61	0.13306	0.364	-0.22306
Iteration	2 Fn = 313.4642					
Param						
-1.31	0.111	-0.21102	0.363	-0.11601	-0.102	0.13302
-0.320	0.70106	0.32302	-0.21701	-0.24006	0.23301	0.23003
Gradnt						
0.42001	0.22201	3.71	0.22101	0.323	0.24001	427.0
0.36001	0.6113	0.33303	0.113	0.11202	0.31101	-0.16406
Iteration	6 Fn = 312.4124					
Param						
-1.30	0.210	-0.31402	0.323	-0.13701	-0.113	0.21706
-0.367	0.73406	0.21002	-0.17201	-0.24406	0.24701	0.63303
Gradnt						
0.30301	0.11401	1.33	0.11401	0.12301	0.17201	217.0
0.11201	0.20203	0.10303	0.62301	0.37403	0.11001	0.226402

(Contd.)

(Contd. Appendix 4.6)

Iteration	7 Fn = 312.1423					
Param						
-1.31	0.212	-0.30302	0.322	-0.13001	-0.116	0.36106
-0.364	0.73206	0.21102	-0.16101	-0.60006	0.30101	0.66303
Gradnt						
0.12103	0.23003	0.36301	0.22403	0.23002	0.34303	1.10
0.24103	26.2	27.3	0.17702	103.0	0.34403	-310.0
Iteration	1 Fn = 312.1423					
Param						
-1.31	0.212	-0.30302	0.322	-0.13101	-0.116	0.36606
-0.364	0.73206	0.21102	-0.16101	-0.60006	0.30101	0.66203
Gradnt						
0.37306	0.23406	0.16303	0.23406	0.10402	0.22306	0.36102
0.13106	0.22201	0.12301	0.74106	036701	0.22206	-0.213

(Contd.)

(Contd. Appendix 4.6)

**Gradient has converged.
** Function has converged.
** B-vector has converged.
****

Limited Dependent variable Model - CENSORED regression
Maximum Likelihood Estimates
Log- Likelihood .... -347.2361
Threshold values for the model : Lower = 0.0000 Upper = + Infinity
N (0,1) used for significance levels.

Variable	Coefficient	Std. Error	t-ratio	Prob(t)ox	Mean of X	Std. Dev. of X
Constant	-21137.	0.130202	-1.206	0.13214		
SEX	3237.2	0.104702	0.242	0.76742	0.37714	0.31231
AGE	-60.210	170.2	-0.326	0.72143	33.131	4.1473
REL	6743.7	6133.0	1.101	0.26101	0.30360	0.34122
EDU	-211.36	320.2	-0.603	0.23632	2.2431	3.3662
WP	-1732.1	6173.0	-0.212	0.77770	0.34613	0.20063
IINC	0.7003	0.1337	0.031	0.46131	1477.2	3463.0
FINC	-2222.3	0.1030	-0.234	0.21473	4322.2	2121.1
FEXP	0.1123	0.3616	0.303	0.76116	20421.0	31633.0
NFEXP	0.7707	0.1214	0.630	0.22230	23021.0	12331.0

APPENDIX 4.7

Intermediary Calculations of the Tobit Model for OMFB Formal Credit Households

```
MODEL COMMAND: TOBIT
RHS - BARROW, SEX, AGE, REL, EDU, WP, IINC, FINC, FEXP, NFEXP S
Limited Dependent Variable Model - CENSORED        regression
Ordinary least squares regression.    Dep. Variable      = BARROW
Observations              = 104       Weights            = ONE
Mean of LHS               = 0.161211101   Std.Dev of LHS     = 0.126212401
Std Dev of residuals      = 0.114106202   Sum of squares     = 0.141401220
R-squared                 = 0.126106202   Adjusted R-squared = 0.262111902
F(22,196)                 = 0.2221160202  Prob value         = 0.201094001
Log-[R1] likelihood              = -0.162426601   Restr.(a=0)Log-l  = 0.164429201
Amemiya Pr.Criter=  0.240192902   Akaike Info.Crit = 0.2022219102
```

ANOVA

Source	Variation	Degrees of Freedom	Mean Square
Regression	0.24220	22.0	0.26902
Residual	0.14140	196.0	0.20102
Total	0.12112	122.0	0.20902

(Contd.)

(Contd. Appendix 4.7)

N (0.2) used for significance levels.

Variable	Coefficient	Std. Error	t-ratio	Prob(t)ox	Mean of X	Std. Dev. of X
Constant	-141.21	2122.0	-0.266	0.94011		
SEX	429.16	2226.0	0.222	0.12692	0.19924	0.12212
AGE	22.021	22.22	2.112	0.22242	11.212	4.2491
REL	-212.42	961.2	-0.126	0.91191	0.10160	0.14222
EDU	-12.222	14.04	-2.211	0.22962	2.2412	1.1662
WP	-292.21	626.0	-0.292	0.92122	0.14621	0.20061
IINC	-0.2292202	0.201102	-2.222	0.20212	2499.2	1461.0
FINC	-612.21	221.0	-0.299	0.26162	4122.2	2222.2
FEXP	0.2400902	0.112602	0.110	0.62461	20422.0	12611.0
NFEXP	0.2292002	0.212902	2.122	0.29612	21022.0	22112.0

Method = NEWTON: Maximum iterations = 22

Convergence criteria : Gradient = 0.2000000E - 01 Function = 0.2000000E - 01

Parameters = 0.200000001

Starting values

-0.2222	0.1019	0.9912	-0.9622	-0.2129
-0.2122	-0.9419	-0.2421	0.2262	0.2926
0.2202	-0.2122	0.2161	0.1026	

(Contd.)

(Contd. Appendix 4.7)

= > NEWTON Iterations

Iteration	2 Fn = 924.1921					
Param						
-0.222	0.102	0.99102	-0.96202	-0.21402	-0.21202	-0.94102
-0.242	0.22606	0.29402	0.22202	-0.21406	0.21602	0.10401
Gradient						
264.0	21.2	0.42101	42.1	0.21601	222.0	0.20909
221.0	0.22602	0.60209	602.0	0.12102	229.0	0.22209
Iteration	2 Fn = 164.2221					
Param						
-2.06	0.221	-0.22001	0.222	-0.92402	-0.91202	0.26102
-0.229	0.22106	0.22102	0.29202	-0.29406	0.26202	0.20101
Gradient						
61.2	20.2	0.22901	22.2	120.0	26.4	0.11906
11.2	0.24909	0.21209	212.0	0.99109	24.4	-0.24209
Iteration	1 Fn = 111.1492					
Param						
-2.24	0.44602	-0.22102	0.112	-0.90102	-0.29102	0.12002
-0.226	0.11906	0.24202	-0.21102	-0.11206	0.96202	0.24201
Gradient						
20.2	2.26	199.0	2.12	22.2	2.92	0.14202
-0.102	0.24206	0.10602	-0.26202	-0.21106	0.22102	-0.21109

(Contd.)

(Contd. Appendix 4.7)

Iteration	1 Fn = 120.2442					
Param						
-2.11	0.216	-0.66202	0.162	-0.22202	-0.42202	0.10202
-0.102	0.24206	0.10602	-0.26202	-0.21106	0.22102	0.11901
Gradient						
2.04	0.26902	16.2	0.12402	2.14	0.221	0.22201
2.06	0.22602	0.21102	2.62	0.21106	0.164	-0.22106
Iteration	2 Fn = 121.4642					
Param						
-2.12	0.222	-0.22202	0.161	-0.22602	-0.202	0.21102
-0.120	0.90206	0.12102	-0.22902	-0.24006	0.21102	0.21001
Gradient						
0.42002	0.22202	1.92	0.22202	0.121	0.24002	429.0
0.16002	0.6221	0.11101	0.221	0.22202	0.12202	-0.26406
Iteration	6 Fn = 122.4224					
Param						
-2.10	0.220	-0.12402	0.121	-0.21902	-0.221	0.22906
-0.169	0.91406	0.22002	-0.29202	-0.24406	0.24902	0.61101
Gradient						
0.10102	0.22402	2.11	0.22402	0.22102	0.29202	229.0
0.22202	0.20201	0.20101	0.62102	0.19401	0.22002	0.226402

(Contd.)

(Contd. Appendix 4.7)

Iteration	9 Fn = 122.2421					
Param						
-2.12	0.222	-0.10102	0.122	-0.21002	-0.226	0.16206
-0.164	0.91206	0.22202	-0.26202	-0.60006	0.10202	0.66101
Gradient						
0.22201	0.21001	0.16102	0.22401	0.21002	0.14101	2.20
0.24201	26.2	29.1	0.29902	201.0	0.14401	-120.0
Iteration	2 Fn = 122.2421					
Param						
-2.12	0.222	-0.10102	0.122	-0.21202	-0.226	0.16606
-0.164	0.91206	0.22202	-0.26202	-0.60006	0.10202	0.66201
Gradient						
0.19106	0.21406	0.26101	0.21406	0.20402	0.22106	0.16202
0.21206	0.22202	0.22102	0.94206	016902	0.22206	-0.221

(Contd.)

(Contd. Appendix 4.7)

**Gradient has converged.
** Function has converged.
** B-vector has converged.
****

Limited Dependent variable Model – CENSORED regression
Maximum Likelihood Estimates
Log- Likelihood .... -149.2162
Threshold values for the model : Lower = 0.0000 Upper = + Infinity
N (0,2) used for significance levels.

Variable	Coefficient	Std. Error	t-ratio	Prob(t)ox	Mean of X	Std. Dev. of X
Constant	-22219.	0.210202	-2.206	0.21224		
SEX	1219.2	0.204902	0.242	0.96942	0.19924	0.12212
AGE	-60.220	290.2	-0.126	0.92241	11.212	4.2491
REL	6941.9	6211.0	2.202	0.26202	0.10160	0.14222
EDU	-222.16	120.2	-0.601	0.21612	2.2412	1.1662
WP	-2912.2	6291.0	-0.222	0.99990	0.14621	0.20061
IINC	0.9001	0.2119	0.012	0.46212	2499.2	1461.0
FINC	-2222.1	0.2010	-0.214	0.22491	4122.2	2222.2
FEXP	0.2221	0.1626	0.101	0.96226	20422.0	12611.0
NFEXP	0.9909	0.2224	0.610	0.22210	21022.0	22112.0

(Contd.)

APPENDIX 4.8

Intermediary Calculations of the Tobit Model for OMFB Informal Households

```
MODEL COMMAND: TOBIT
RHS = BARROW, SEX, AGE, REL, EDU, WP, IINC, FINC, FEXP, NFEXP 5
Limited Dependent Variable Model - CENSORED      regression
Ordinary least squares regression.       Dep. Variable      = BARROW
Observations            = 124            Weights            = ONE
Mean of LHS             = 0.115607204    Std.Dev of LHS     = 0.415725304
Std Dev of residuals    = 0.123505704    Sum of squares     = 0.226881710
R-squared               = 0.113816600    Adjusted R-squared = 0.184755500
F(11,218)               = 0.861332201    Prob value         = 0.688053211
Log-likelighood    = -0.267181604   Restr.(a=0)Log-l  = -0.252462104
Amemiya Pr.Criter=  0.170457001   Akaike Info.Crit.  =  0.107620708
```

ANOVA

Source	Variation	Degrees of Freedom	Mean Square
Regression	0.86708307	11.	0.55305108
Residual	0.36541710	256.	0.12083608
Total	0.31411810	288.	0.18617208

(Contd.)

(Contd. Appendix 4.8)

N (0.1) used for significance levels.

Variable	Coefficient	Std. Error	t-ratio	Prob(t)ox	Mean of X	Std. Dev. of X
Constant	1816.3	1164.2	1.361	0.11861		
SEX	-1435.4	723.2	-1.338	0.11715	0.25587	0.48348
AGE	16.143	18.70	0.834	0.27171	24.841	7.8754
REL	-1217.1	566.4	-1.524	0.08185	0.40260	0.47113
EDU	-1.1122	27.18	-0.021	0.75313	3.1721	4.4663
WP	-462.13	618.3	-0.525	0.46110	0.47614	0.30062
IINC	-0.3123	0.103	-0.133	0.57872	8755.3	2764.0
FINC	477.68	655.5	0.525	0.46071	7431.3	3131.1
FEXP	0.5604	0.127	1.538	0.05853	30718.0	48624.0
NFEXP	0.1314	0.127	0.181	0.83612	12038.0	13241.0

Method = NEWTON: Maximum iterations = 13
Convergence criteria: Gradient = 01000000E - 02
Function = 0.1000000E - 02
Parameters = 0.100000002
Starting values

0.3685	-0.4453	0.4735	-0.4081	-0.2536
-0.2843	-0.16053	0.1324	0.1224	0.5547
0.4163	0.12046	-0.4570	0.2050	

(Contd.)

(Contd. Appendix 4.8)

```
= > NEWTON Iterations

Iteration   1 Fn = 1273.208
Param
 0.338      -0.445      0.47601     -0.408      -0.25602    -0.141      -0.16103
 0.132      0.12203     0.55306     0.21001     0.12001     -0.45701    0.20502

Gradient
 111.0      112.0       0.43404     111.0       518.0       112.0       0.11405
 7.86       0.71505     0.18205     168.0       0.12808     61.0        0.46706
Iteration   1 Fn = 1175.317
Param
0.31401     -1.05       0.35001     -0.651      -0.22301    -0.50101    -0.12803
 0.227      0.22403     0.12003     0.43401     -0.11206    -0.30101    0.12102

Gradient
 15.2       15.1        0.10204     16.2        163.0       16.2        0.31006
 0.448      0.10605     0.62706     60.1        0.20005     14.0        -0.61503
```

(Contd.)

(Contd. Appendix 4.8)

Iteration	2 Fn = 1185.574					
Param						
- 0.77801	-1.48	0.66601	-0.848	-0.45201	-0.65101	-0.15303
0.463	0.44003	0.12103	0.33801	-0.11606	-0.60501	0.12702
Gradient						
6.37	6.38	130.0	6.24	27.8	6.24	0.11106
0.80701	0.47606	0.13106	14.6	0.51206	2.21	-0.11304
Iteration	4 Fn = 1186.814					
Param						
-0.165	-1.65	0.68001	-0.714	-0.32201	-0.56601	-0.48506
0.311	0.48603	0.12103	0.37201	-0.15206	-0.64101	0.12702
Gradient						
0.782	0.781	25.6	0.723	3.82	0.723	0.16703
0.15101	0.80003	0.11603	1.11	0.11306	0.435	-1.13

(Contd.)

(Contd. Appendix 4.8)

Iteration	3 Fn = 1186.586					
Param						
-0.180	-1.51	0.68001	-0.716	-0.34401	-0.80301	-0.38205
0.324	0.47003	0.12103	0.37801	-0.18106	-0.64801	0.12702
Gradient						
0.24501	0.24501	1.22	0.21701	0.102	0.21801	387.0
0.52002	0.17804	560.0	0.57001	0.41004	0.13301	-0.71001
Iteration	6 Fn= 1186.586					
Param						
-0.180	-1.51	0.68001	-0.715	-0.34301	-0.80501	-0.41105
0.323	0.47003	0.12103	0.37801	-0.18206	-0.64801	0.12702
Gradfient						
0.45604	0.45304	0.18201	0.43104	0.15502	0.43004	0.810
0.10303	4.14	1.03	0.10702	3.81	0.11104	-+0.30103

(Contd.)

(Contd. Appendix 4.8)

**Gradient has converged.
** Function has converged.
** B-vector has converged.

****
Limited Dependent Variable Model –CENSORED regression
Maximum Likelihood Estimates
Log-Likelihood .... - 1248.346
Threshold values for the model : Lower = 0.0000 Upper = + Infinity
N(0,1) used for significance levels.

Variable	Coefficient	Std. Error	t-ratio	Prob(t)ox	Mean of X	Std. Dev. of X
Constant	-532.31	1517.0	-0.426	0.66174		
SEX	-5131.7	1324.0	-4.662	0.00000	0.25587	0.48348
AGE	18.402	20.24	0.726	0.24714	24.841	7.8754
REL	-2852.0	1111.0	-2.176	0.00140	0.40260	0.47113
EDU	-11.562	61.41	-0.263	0.51325	3.1721	4.4663
WP	-225.10	774.6	-0.227	0.52435	0.47614	0.30062
IINC	-0.1516802	0.470101	-0.004	0.77511	8755.3	2764.0
FINC	1123.1	734.1	1.242	0.01713	7431.3	3131.1
FEXP	0.1047501	0.668001	2.067	0.00113	30718.0	48624.0
NFEXP	0.3325401	0.171401	0.187	0.55117	12038.0	13241.0

(Contd.)

APPENDIX 6.1

Regression Summary for Dependent Variable: REPAY MENT(NMFB)
R= .59027273 R^2= .34842189 Adjusted R^2= .29134936
F(12,137)=6.1049 p<.00000 Std.Error of estimate: 9883.6

	BETA	St. Err. of BETA	B	St. Err. of B	T(137)	p-level
Intercept			-4022.3343	5499.6615	-0.7314	0.4658
AGE	0.1230	0.0788	134.7344	86.3098	1.5611	0.1208
HEAD	0.0079	0.0756	341.6674	3260.6650	0.1048	0.9167
EDU	0.0430	0.0811	654.4763	1234.9946	0.5299	0.5970
WORKER	-0.1943	0.0987	-5800.6400	2947.3690	-1.9681	0.0511
OCCUPATI	0.3143	0.0996	3809.9273	1207.8461	3.1543	0.0020
F SIZE	0.0996	0.0900	674.7690	609.8066	1.1065	0.2704
ASSETS	-0.0725	0.0720	-0.0094	0.0093	-1.0072	0.3156
INCOME	-0.0916	0.0851	-0.0988	0.0918	-1.0760	0.2838
EXPENDIT	0.6978	0.1194	0.3775	0.0646	5.8435	0.0000
DEPRATIO	0.0432	0.0768	344.0926	611.0506	0.5631	0.5743
FOOD EXP	-0.0026	0.0840	-0.0084	0.2760	-0.0304	0.9758
NFOODEXP	-0.2832	0.1237	-0.3298	0.1441	-2.2884	0.0236

APPENDIX 6.2

Regression Summary for Dependent Variable: REPAYMENT (OMFB)
R= .60778135 R^2= .36939817 Adjusted R^2= .31416297
F(12,137)=6.6877 p<.00000 Std.Error of estimate: 14302.

	BETA	St. Err. of BETA	B	St. Err. of B	T(137)	p-level
Intercept			-1550.6807	10059.7925	-0.1541	0.8777
AGE	0.0951	0.0807	153.4264	130.2634	1.1778	0.2409
HEAD	-0.0345	0.0782	-3305.4096	7497.9152	-0.4408	0.6600
EDU	0.0621	0.0750	2285.5766	2761.4886	0.8277	0.4093
WORKER	-0.0201	0.0726	-1922.6759	6958.8609	-0.2763	0.7827
OCCUPATI	0.0392	0.0736	624.7135	1171.6600	0.5332	0.5948
F_SIZE	-0.0494	0.1134	-483.0165	1108.2490	-0.4358	0.6636
ASSETS	-0.0165	0.0830	-0.0146	0.0731	-0.1991	0.8424
INCOME	-0.1524	0.1008	-0.1916	0.1267	-1.5119	0.1329
EXPENDIT	0.0516	0.0774	0.0132	0.0198	0.6664	0.5062
DEPRATIO	-0.0399	0.0754	-404.9141	765.7958	-0.5287	0.5978
FOOD_EXP	0.2185	0.1106	0.5297	0.2682	1.9751	0.0503
NFOODEXP	0.5541	0.0940	0.4526	0.0768	5.8915	0.0000

APPENDIX 7.1
Empowerment and Poverty Alleviation Impact of SHARE's Interventions

	Achievements	Areas that Need Strengthening
Individual Level	***Awareness:*** -Greater self confidence and worth -Greater interest to seek information -Greater investment in girl child education	***Awareness:*** -Son preference continues -A few members vote as per husband's decisions
	Resources: -Greater control over their assets, earnings and income -Husbands consult them more than before on decisions on resources	***Resources:*** -Personal expenditure trend to be small in amount
	Work and mobility -Improved access to gas stoves and fans, reducing drudgery -Increased independent expenditure on themselves -Low wage workers to owner managers with diversification -Men have started helping in women's productive work	***Work and mobility*** -Increase in workload, but women are yet to complain -Men yet to share domestic work -The Danger that men's assistance productive work, coulc be at the cost of women's control over the activities.

(Contd.)

(Contd. Appendix 7.1)

	Achievements	*Areas that Need Strengthening*
	-Improved mobility, and ability to stay over for meetings	-Children's work loan increased during out of school hours -Women yet to start riding bicycles, mopeds and vehicles -Coming home late for meetings is accepted, but not for other reasons
	Body and reproduction	***Body and reproduction***
	-Reduced domestic violence and violence at work place	-Domestic violence persists
	-Universal access of women to contraception	-Responsibility for contraception primarily on women, and only follows after giving birth to a male child -Gap between desired & actual fertility
Collective Level	***Community:***	
	-Village communities have started to recognize women's groups Government/ bank	Government/bank linkage
	-Groups place demands of government and in some cases have succeeded in mobilizing porgrammes	-Government and banks yet to recognize SML for linkage and benefits

(Contd.)

(Contd. Appendix 7.1)

	Achievements	*Areas That Need Strengthening*
		-Systematic attention to linking groups with banks and government wings like ICDS, PDS, water supply, sanitation
	Political participation	***Political Participation***
	-More genuine women candidates contesting gram Panchayat elections	-Limited participation of groups in gram sabhas
		-Women yet to emerge as vote banks, wooing takes place on caste lines
Wider Level	***Markets***	Not all poverty groups have been reached.
	-Decline in money lender interest rates	
	-Diversification of rural economy	
	-Growth of service sector	
	-Poverty profile changing as more WHH are benefiting from SML	

Source: 1. Rajivan A.K (2002) 'SHARE' Micro-finance (SML) Interventions', In the Report of the Workshop on 'Social Mobilisation, Credit and Women's Empowerment', ASA, New Delhi, 10-11 January.

2. Rao, Hanumantha, K. and Durgaprasad, P. (2002), Social Mobilisation, Participation and Empowerment For Poverty Alleviation, working paper, NIRD, Hyderabad.

Bibliography

Adams Dale W. and G.I. Nehman (1979), *"Borrowing costs and the demand for rural credit"*, Journal of Development Studies, Vol. 15, No. 2, pp.165-176.

Ahulwalia (1978), *"Rural Poverty and Agricultural Performance in India"*, Journal of Development Studies, 14 April, pp. 298-323.

Aiyappan, A. (1948), *"Report on the Socioeconomic Conditions of the Aboriginal Tribes of the Province of Madras"*, Govt. of Madras.

Alam, Mohammed Ferdous (1981), *"Cost of Credit from Institutional Sources in Bangladesh"*, Journal of Agricultural Economics, Vol. 4, No. 2, pp. 51-60.

Aloysius P and Fernandez (2007), *"A Microfinance Institution with a Difference"* Economic and Political Weekly, March 31.

Bardhan (1970), *"On the Minimum Level of Living and the Rural Poor"*, Indian Economic Review, 5(1), April, pp. 129-36.

Bernett Lynn and Pamela Hunte (1996), "Ownership and Sustainability: Lessons on Group-Mike Goldberg Based Financial Services from Five NGOs in South Asia", World Bank, Washington D.C.

Besley, T., and Coates, S. (1995), *"Group Lending, Repayment Incentives Collateral"*, Journal of Development Economics, Vol. 46, pp. 1-18.

Bhagat L.N. (1983), "Factors determining adoption of new Agricultural practices in Tribal Areas – A quantitative Analysis", Agricultural situation in India, June.

Bhatt N. and S.Y. (1998), *"Group based Micro Finance and Economic* Tang *development"* In Handbook of Economic Development, ed. Liou, T. Marcel Dekeer, New York.

Bhange N.P. (1993), *"Tribal Commissions and Committees in India"*, Himalaya Publishing House, New Delhi.

Chandramoli (1969), *"A New deal for Tribals of Andhra Pradesh"*, ST Cooperative finance and Development Corporation, Visakhapatnam.

Chatopadhya K.P. (1953), *"Tribal Education"*, Man in India, A Quarterly Anthropology Journal.

Chaudhuri Budhadeb (1992), "Socio-Economic and Ecological Development", Inter India Publications, New Delhi.

Damodar N. Gujarati (2000), *Basic Econometrics*, McGraw – Hill International edition, p. 614.

Dandekar, and Rath (1971), *"Poverty in India"*, Indian School of Political Economy, Pune.

Das P.K., Guglani, P.L., (1980), "Credit Needs of Tribal Farms of *Singhbhum District Bihar"*, - Financing Agriculture, Oct.-Dec., p. 22.

Dersing Market (1990), *"Support for Micro Enterprises: Lessons for Sub-Saharan Africa"*: World Bank Technical Paper 122, Washington, D.C.

Devendra Thakur, DN (1995), *"Tribal Development and Planning"* (Tribal Life in India-9), Deep and Deep Publications, New Delhi.

Elwin Varrier (1965), *"Bondo Highlander"*, Oxford University Press, Bombay.

Eric Hanushek and John Jackson (1997), *Statistical Methods for Scientists*, Academic Press, New York, p. 189.

Fernandez A.P. (1994), "The Myrad Experience: Alternate Management Systems for Savings and Credit of the Rural Poor", Bangalore, MYRADA.

Floro and Yotopoulos (1991), "Informal Credit Markets and the New Institutional Economics: The Case of Philippine Agriculture", Westview Press, Boulder, Colorado, U.S.A.

Frances Sinha (2005), *"Access, Use and Contribution of Micro Finance in India-Finding from a National Study"*, Economic and Political Weekly, April 23.

Ghatak, M. (1999), "Group Lending, Local Information and Peer Selection". Journal of Development Economics, 60, 27-50.

Ghatak and Guinnone (1999), "The Economics of Lending with Joint Liability: *Theory and Practice"*, Journal of Development Economics, Vol. 60, No.1, October.

Gopala Rao N. (1978), *"Land Alienation–A Menace to Tribal Economy"*, Tribe, Vol. X, No.4.

Government of India (1931), *The Indian Central Banking Enquiry Committee*, Central Publication Branch, Culcutta, pp. 81-84.

Government of India (1953), First Five-Year Plan 1951-56, Planning Commission, New Delhi, p. 96.

________________ (1974), Draft Fifth Five Year Plan 1974-79, Planning Commission, New Delhi, pp. 88-89.

________________ (1976), *Report of the National Commission on Agricultural*, Ministry of Agriculture and Irrigation, New Delhi.

________________ (1976), *Report of the Expert Committee on Consumption Credit*, Department of Revenue and Banking (Chairman: B. Sivaraman), New Delhi.

Haimondorf Furer (1941) *"Seasonal Nomadism and Economics of the Chenchu of Hyderabad"*, Journal of Royal Asiatic Society of Bengal Vol.7.

Herath, G. (1994) *"Rural Credit Markets and Institutional Reform: Developing Countries: Potential and Problems."* Savings and Development, Quarterly review No. 2, Vol. XVII, pp. 169-191.

Heredia Rudolfc *"Tribal Education in India"*, New Frontiers in Education Vol. XXII, No. 9, 1992.

Hoff K. and J.E. Stiglitz (1990) *"Introduction : Imperfect information and rural credit markets – puzzles, policy perspectives."* The World Bank Economic Review. Vol. 4, No. 3, pp. 235-250.

Hoff K and J E Stiglitz (1990) *"Introduction: Imperfect Information and rural credit markets–puzzles, policy perspectives."* The World Bank Economic Review. Vol. 4, No. 3, pp. 235-250.

Hossain Mahabub (1988) *"Credit for Alleviation of Rural Poverty: The Grameen Bank in Bangladesh"*, IFPRI Research Report 65 International Food Policy Research Institute, Washington, D.C.

Humpl M. and G. Feder (1990) *"The Role of Groups and Credit Co-operatives in Rural Lending"*, The World bank Research Observer, Vol. 5, No. 2, July.

Hulme David and Paul Mosley (1996) *Finance against Poverty*, New York, Routledge Publishing.

Jagadish Capor (2001) Address at the Asia Pacific Region Micro Credit Summit Meeting of Councils at New Delhi, on February 3.

Jagannath Pathy (1981) *"Class Structure in Rural Orissa"*, Sociological Bulletin, Vol. 30, No. 2.

Jain H.C. and Das N. (1981) "A Study into Aspects of Farm Credit Provided by SBI to Tribal Farmers of Jagadalpur Block of Bastar Dist.", Financing Agriculture, Jan-Mar, pp.16-20.

Jena A.C. (1986) "Forms of Exploitation in Tribal Areas and Their consequences-Some Observations in Keonjhar Dist. of Orissa", - Man and Life, Vol.12, No. 3-4, July-December, pp.173-179.

Jayaraman B. (2001) *"Micro-Finance: Retrospect and Prospect"* Occasional Paper-20, NABARD, Mumbai.

Karmakar, K.G. (1998) "Rural Credit and Self-Help Groups: Micro Finance *Needs and Concepts in India"*, Sage Publications, New Delhi.

Khandker R. Shahidur (1998) *"Fighting Poverty with Micro Credit (Experience in Bangladesh)"*, Oxford University Press, Inc., p. 145.

Khan F.H. (1977) *"Consumption Credit: Cooperatives in New Perspective"*, Cooperative News Digest, Vol. 28, p. 92, June.

Khandker S.R., B. Khality and Z. Khan *"Grammeen Bank:Performance and Sustainability"*, (1995 World Bank Discussion Paper 306, The World Bank, Washington, D.C., U.S.A.

Khare P.K. *"Social Change of Indian Tribes"*, Deep and Deep Publications, New Delhi.

Kotari K.L. (1985) *"Tribal Social Change in India"* Himamsu Publications, Delhi.

Ladman J.R. (1984) *"Loan Transaction Costs, Credit Rationing and Market Structure: The case of Bolivia"*, in D.W. Admas D.H. Graham and J. D. Von Pischke ed., Underminlng Rural Development with Cheap Credit, Wesview Press, Inc., Boulder.

Liedholm, C. (1985) *"Small Scale Enterprise Credit Schemes: Administrative Costs and the Role of Inventory Norms."* Working paper No. 25 Department of Agricultural Economics, Michigan State University.

Lin J. Y. and J Negent (1995) *"Institutions and Economic Development."* Handbook of Development Economics. Vol. 3, Chap. XX.

Linga Murty N., Siva Ramakrishna Rao C. (1982) *" Debt Bondage in Tribal Areas – An Empirical Observation"*, Paper submitted to the National Seminar on "Political Economy of Tribal Development", held in Warangal during April.

Madheswaran S. and Dharmadhikary (2001), "Empowering Rural Women through Self- help Amita groups; Lessons from Maharashtra Rural Credit Project", Indian Journal of Agricultural Economics, Vol. 56, July-September 2001. p. 441.

Madhura Swaminathan (2007), *"The Micro Credit Alternative?"*, Economic and Political Weekly, March 31.

Mahilingam S. (1989), *"Tribal groups and Market Development in India"*, Journal of Rural Development, NIRD, Hyderabad, Vol. 8 (3).

Makhan Sha (1982) *"Readings in Tribal Culture"*, Inter – India Publications, New Delhi.

Manfred Zeller (1994), "Determinants of Credit Rationing: A study of Informal Lenders and Formal Credit Groups in Madagascar", World Development, Vol. 22, No.12, pp. 1895-1907.

Marie Godquin (2004), "Microfinance Repayment Performance in Bangladesh: How to Improve the Allocation of Loans by MFIs" World Development, Vol. 32, No. 11, p. 1909.

Maurya R.D. (1985), "Education for Tribals in A.P., Problems and Prospects", Kurukshetra, Vol. 33, No. 4.

Mc Donald Joh F., and A. Mofflitt (1980) *"The Uses of Tobit Analysis"*, the Review of Robert Economics and Statistics, 62(2): 318-21.

Mckinnon R. (1973) *"Money and Capital in Economic Development"*. (Washington D.C.).

Michael Chu (1995) *"Building Bridges: Financing Small and Medium Enterprises"*, Economic Reform Today, No. 3, p. 9.

Mishra R.K. (1974) *"Some Problems of Developmental Administration of Tribal Area in India"*, in *"Perspectives on Tribal Development and Administration"*, - Proceedings of the Workshop held at NICD, Hyderabad, 18-20, April, pp. 93-94.

Mohan Rao K. (1993), *"Socio-Cultural Profile of Tribes of Andhra Pradesh"*, Hyderabad.

Morduch Jonathan (1999), *"The Micro finance Promise"*, Journal of Economics Literature, Vol. 37, No. 4.

—————— (1999), *"Tribal Development in Andhra Pradesh – Problems, Performance and Prospects"*, Book lines Corporation, Hyderabad.

Minhas (1970) "Rural Poverty, Land Redistribution, and Development Strategy: *Facts and Policy"*, Indian Economic Review, 5(1), April, P.98-128.

Murty D.K. (1972), *"The Tribal Situation in South India"*, in Suresh Singh (ED), Tribal situation In India pp. 213-27, 1972.

NABARD (1995), *Report of the working group on Non-Governmental Organisations and Self-Help Groups*, Mumbai.

—————— (2006) *NABARD and Micro Finance 2005-2006*, Mumbai, p.3.

Nabli M.K. and (1989) "The New Institutional Economics and its J A Nudent Applicability to Development." World Development. Vol.17, No. 9, pp. 1333-47.

Nair T.S. (2000), "Rural Financial Intermediation and Commercial Banks:Review of Recent Trends", Economic and Political Weekly, January 29, pp. 300-301.

Nanda Y.C. (1994) *"Significance of Establishing Linkage of SHGs with Banks"*, Paper presented at a Seminar on linkages of SHGs with FIS on 17-18 September 1994 in DHAKA, BANGLADESH, National Bank News Review, Vol. 1, No. 4, October-December, p. 26.

Narayana Prasad (1990) *"Bonded Agricultural Labourers and Their* Sharma *Working Conditions"*, - Kurukshetras, November, pp.18-20.

National Sample Survey Organisation (1998), *Debt and Investment Survey*, 48 the round.

Nayar, D.P. (1974) *"Education for Tribals"*, - Kurukshetra, 1st October, pp. 38-39.

Nayer D.P. " Education for Tribals", Kurukshetra, Vol. 23 No. 4, pp. 35-40, 1974.

North, D.C. (1992) *"Transaction cost, Institutional and Economic Performance."* ICEG Occasional Papers No. 30. International Centre for Economic Growth.

Obroi R.C., Moorti T.V and Sharma RK (1989) *"Agricultural Development on Tribal Farms"*, Indian Journal of Regional Science, Vol. XXI, No. 2.

Olomola, A.S (1999) *"Determinants of Smallholders' Transaction Cost of Procuring Non-Bank Loans in Nigeria."* Savings and Development. Quarterly Review No.1, Vol. XXIII, 95-108.

Pallavi Chavan and R. Ramakumar (2002) " Micro credit and Rural Poverty-An Analysis of Empirical Evidence" Economic and Political Weekly, March 9. pp. 958.

Paxton et all, (2000), "Modeling Group Loan Repayment Behaviour: New *Insights from Burkiner Faso"*, Economic Development and Cultural Change, Vol. 48, No.3, April, pp. 639-655.

Pradeep Kumar Bose (1981) *Stratification among Tribals of Gujarat"*, Economic and Political Weekly, Vol. 26, No. 6.

Prasada Rao D.L. (1970) *"The Jatapus – A Scheduled Tribe in Andhra Pradesh"*, Unpublished Ph.D. thesis, A.U., Waltair.

———————— (1971-72) *"Shahukars and Tribal Society"*, Tribe Vol.III Nos. 3 & 4.

Pratap and Bose (1975) *"A Study of Andhra Pradesh Scheduled Tribes"*, Tribal Cultural Research and Training Institute, Hyderabad.

Priya Basu, Pradeep Srivastava (2005) " Exploring Possibilities: Microfinance and Rural Credit Access for the Poor in India", Economic and Political Weekly, April 23.

Puhazhendi V. (1995) *"Transaction Costs of Lending to the Rural Poor: Non-Governmental Organisations and Self- Help Groups of the Poor a Intermediary For Banks in India"*, The Foundation for Development Cooperation, Brisbane, Australia.

Puhazhendhi V. and Satyasai (2000) *"Micro Credit for the Rural People: An Impact* KJ *Evaluation"*, Study Report, National Bank for Agriculture and Rural Development, Mumbai.

Puhazhendi V. (2000) *"Evaluation Study of Self-Help Groups in Tamil Nadu"* National Bank for Agricultural and Rural Development, Mumbai.

Quraishi M.A. (1974) " *Tribal Development in the Fifth Plan"*, - Kurukshetra, 1st October, pp.13-15.

Radhakrishna R. and Shovan Ray (2005) "Handbook of Poverty in India –Perspectives, Policies, and Programmes", p. 1.

Rajaram Dasgupta (2005) "Micro Finance in India Empirical Evidence, *Alternative Models and Policy Imperatives"*, Economic and Political Weekly, March, 19.

Rowlands, J (1997) *"Questioning Empowerment: Working with Women in Honduras"*, Oxford, UK.

Ramaiah, P. (1981) *"Tribal Economy of India"*, Light and Life Publishers, Tilak Street, Paharganj, New Delhi.

Ramakrishna R.2001 *"Credit Needs of the Rural Poor and the Role of SHGs"*, Indian Journal of Agricultural Economics Conference No. July-Sep, Vol. 56, No. 3, pp. 459-460.

——————— 2003 *"Micro Credit for Rural Poor through SHGs"*, Cooperative Perspective (Journal of Cooperative Management) Oct-Dec, Vol. 38, No. 3, pp. 48-59.

——————— 2004 *" Empowering Rural Women through Self-Help Groups"*, Indira Devi M. (Ed), Strategies for Sustainability of Self Help Groups, Andhra University Press and Publications, Visakhapatnam, 2004, pp. 163-170.

Raghaviah V.C.T *"Tribal Revolts"*, Andhra Rashtriya Adimajati Sevak Sangh, Nellore, 1962.

Raghava Rao D.V. (1971) *"Marketing of Produce and Indebtedness among Tribals"*, A report on the study of Visakhapatnam District, AER Center, A.U., Waltair.

——————— (1975) *"Konda Dora's – A Study in Socio-Cultural Change"*, unpublished Ph.D. Thesis, A.U., Waltair.

Rai B.K. (1979), *"Man and Forest in Chota Nagpur"*, unpublished Ph.D. Thesis, Renchi University.

Rajasekhar D. (1994), *"Savings and Credit Systems of Poor as a Strategy of Economic Development: Some N.G.D.O. Experiences in India"*, Bangalore: NOVIB and HIVDS.

Ramaiah P. (1981) *"Tribal Economy of India"*, Life and Light Publications, New Delhi.

——————— (1988), *"The economic problems of Konda Reddies"*, Life and Light Publications, New Delhi.

Rama Rao V. (1988), *"Tribal Education and the role of the Teacher"*, Man and Life, Vol.14, Nos. 1 and 2.

Ratniah E.V. (1977) *"Structural Constraints in Tribal Education"*, Sterling Publishers, New Delhi.

Rama Mani V.S., "Tribal Economy-problems and prospects", Ph.D. Thesis, Andhra University, Waltair, 1988.

Reserve Bank of India (1955) *All India Rural Credit Survey 1951-52*, Bombay.

Reserve Bank of India (1960) *Report Regarding the Possibility of Introducing.*

Land and Agricultural Banks Into the Madras Presidency (1985), (Chairman: Nicholson), Bombay, p. 465.

———————————— (1992) *'All India Debt and Investment Survey',* Reserve Bank of India, Mumbai.

Rajaram Dasgupta (2001) *"An Informal Journey through Self-Help Groups",* Indian Journal of Agricultural Economics, July-September, Vol. 56, No. 3, p. 377.

Roman, L. (1994) *"Transactions Costs and Transition: The Case of Vietnamese Banking Sector."* Savings and Development. Quarterly Review, No. 3, Vol. XVIII.

Sebastoam Titus A.P. (2001) " Impact of Micro Credit Programmes of NGOs on Rural Women", IASSI Quarterly Vol. 20, No.2, p.136.

Sampti Gupta and Goutam Gupta (2005) *"Micro Credit far Income Generation: The role of ROSCA,* Economic and Political Weekly, April, 2.

Saito, K., and D. Villaneuva (1981) *"Transactions Cost of Credit to Scale Sector in the Philippines."* Economic Development and Cultural Change. Vol. 29, 631-40.

Satish P. (2005) *"Mainstreaming of Indian Micro Finance",* Economic and Political Weekly, April 23, pp. 1731-1739.

Shahjahan M. (1968) *" Agricultural Finance In East Pakistan"*, The Asiatic Press, Dhaka, Bangladesh.

Sheetal Sharma (2006) *"Educated Women, Empower Women"* Yojana, October, p. 52

Sexena R.P. (1964) *"Tribal Economy In Central India",* Calcutta, K.L. Mukhopadya.

Shylendra, H.S. (2006) *"Micro Finance Institutions in Andhra Pradesh: Crisis and Diagnosis",* Economic and Political Weekly, May 20.

Shah B. (1990) *"Research on Tribal Education",* Perspectives in Education, Vol. 6, No. 3.

Shah Vimal (1967) *"Tribal Economy In Gujarat",* Paper published in 'Tribal' Vol. IV, No. 2.

Shahidur R. Khandker (1998) *"Fighting Poverty with Micro Credit (Experience in Bangladesh)",* Oxford University Press, Inc., p. 122.

Shahidur R. Khandker (1998) *"Determinants of Repayment Performance in Credit Groups: The Role of Programme Design, Intra-group Risk Pooling and Social Cohesion",* Economic Development and Cultural Change, Vol. 46, No.3, April, pp. 599-620.

Sharma B.K. (1980), *"Tribal Employment and Linkages",* ICSSR Research Abstracts, Quarterly, Vol.XX, No. 1 and 2 pp. 73-82.

Siva Ramaiah C. (1991), *"Tribal Development Programmes in Adilabad District",* Inter India Publications, New Delhi.

Srivastava LRN, *"Education and Tribal Development"*, Journal of Rural Development, NIRD, Hyderabad.

Sinha, U.P. (1985), *"Demographic Profile of Tribal Population in India"* in *"Demography of Tribal Development"*, Inter India Publications, New Delhi.

Stiglitz (1981), *"Credit Rationing in Markets with Imperfect Information"*. American Economic Review. Vol. 71, No.3, 393-410.

Stiglitz–Joseph E. and Anren Wesis (1981), "Credit Rationing in Markets with *Imperfect Information"*, American Economic Review, 71(3): 393-410-1983.

Stiglitz–Joseph E. and Anren Wesis (1973) "Incentive Effects of Termination: Applications to the credit and Labour Markets", American Economic Review 73(5): pp. 912-27.

Subba Reddy N. (1977) *"Crisis of Confidence among Tribal People and the Naxalite Movement in Srikakulam District"*, Human Organization 36.

Sujatha K. (1988) *"Tribal Education in India"*, Perspectives in Education, No.4, Vol. 4.

Susil, Sirivardana, (2001) *"The Core Methodology of Social Mobilization in Women's Empowerment as a Transformative Strategy for Poverty Eradication"*, SAPNA Regional Centre, New Delhi.

Syam Prasad Rao C., (1993) "Changing Tribal Scena Prospects and Retrospect-A case study of North Coastal Andhra Pradesh", Unpublished Ph.D. Thesis, Andhra University.

United Nations (1986) *"Savings for Development"*: Report on the Third International Symposium on the Mobilisation of Personal Savings In Developing Countries, New York.

Vasimalai M.P. Narender K. (2007) *"Micro Finance for Poverty Reduction: The Kalanjam Way"*, Economic and Political Weekly, March 31.

Varma R.C. (1990) *"Indian Tribes through the Ages"*, Publications Division, Ministry of Information and Broadcasting, Govt. of India.

Vidyarhi L.P. (1963) *"The Maler – A Case Study in Nature Man – Spirit Complex of a Hill Tribe in Bihar"*, Book Land, Calcutta.

Wenner M.W. (1995) *"Group Credit: A Means to Improve Information Transfer and Loan Repayment Performance"*, Journal of Development Studies, Vol. 32, No. 2, December.

Wydick Bruce (1999) *"Can Social Cohesion be Harnessed to Repair Mrket Failures? Evidence from Group Lending in Guatemala"*, The Economic Journal, Vol. 109, No. 457.

World Bank (1997) *"Introducing Savings In Micro Credit Institutions: When and How?"* CGAP Focus Note, Consultative Group to Assist the Poorest of the Poor, Washington, D.C., U.S.A.

World Bank (1996) *"Bangladesh : Poverty Alleviation Micro Finance Project"* staff Appraisal Report South Asia Region, Country Department–I, Private sector development and Finance Division, Washington.

William H. Greene (2000) *Econometric Analysis,* Prentice–Hall, International Inc., p. 815.

Yaron Jacob (1992) *"Assessing Development Finance Institutions".* World Bank Discussion Paper 174, Washington D.C., p. 12.

Zeller (1995) *"Determinants of Credit Rationing: A Study of Informal Lenders and Formal Credit Groups in Madagascar"*, World Development, Vol. 22, No. 12, pp. 1885-1909.

Zia U. Ahmed (1989) *"Effective Costs of Rural Loans in Bangladesh"*, World Development, Vol. 17, No. 3, pp. 357-363.

Index